Blitzkrieg and the Russian art of war

Manchester University Press

RUSSIAN STRATEGY AND POWER

To buy or to find out more about the books currently available in this series, please go to: https://manchesteruniversitypress.co.uk/series/russian-strategy-and-power/

Blitzkrieg and the Russian art of war

Andrew Monaghan

MANCHESTER UNIVERSITY PRESS

Published by Manchester University Press
Oxford Road, Manchester, M13 9PL

www.manchesteruniversitypress.co.uk

British Library Cataloguing-in-Publication Data
A catalogue record for this book is available from the British Library

ISBN   978 1 5261 6451 3   hardback
ISBN   978 1 5261 6452 0   paperback

First published 2025

The publisher has no responsibility for the persistence or accuracy of URLs for any external or third-party internet websites referred to in this book, and does not guarantee that any content on such websites is, or will remain, accurate or appropriate.

EU authorised representative for GPSR:
Easy Access System Europe, Mustamäe tee 50, 10621 Tallinn, Estonia
gpsr.requests@easproject.com

Typeset
by New Best-set Typesetters Ltd

Contents

Because we never learned enough about him, the enemy rarely did what we expected him to do.

Marc Bloch

By its very methods, strategy is merely a systematic contemplation of war history.

Alexander Svechin

It's frightening, Misha, what they write about us in the West. They don't understand us, neither our temperament, nor the path we have chosen, and at present less than ever.

Boris Feldman to Mikhail Tukhachevsky

This baffled us. We could not see why you took such steps.

Colonel General Adrian Danilevich

It is high time to understand Russia with the mind.

Igor Guberman

Preface: what is at stake

This book examines Russia's 'way in war'. It explores recent Russian strategic history, reflecting on what 'war' means to Moscow, and how the Russian leadership has sought to shape strategy and use its military power over the last century, in order to interpret current developments and look to the future. In so doing, I look at persistent themes in Russian war fighting to explore continuity and change in Moscow's doctrine and strategy; in other words: how the Russian state and armed forces understand the evolving science and art of war in theory and practice.

The book offers a pocket history, framing the main thinkers and themes, priorities and problems of the Russian 'way in war' to offer some structure and context for thinking about how the Russian armed forces will evolve through the remainder of the 2020s. What are the 'ingredients' for which Euro-Atlantic officials and observers should be looking to interpret the Russian 'way in war'? What are the key strategic and military questions and dilemmas for the Russian leadership? What do 'victory' and 'defeat' look like? If we can distinguish a 'way in war' at the state level, what does this mean for how the Russian armed forces view the evolving 'art of war'?

Preface

In the West, many talk of Russia's renewed assault on Ukraine in 2022 – often described as a 'blitzkrieg' – as a turning point in international affairs. Accustomed over a generation to seeing war through the lenses of counter-terrorism and counter-insurgency, characterised by precision strikes and limited combat far from home, and in terms of war's 'hybridity' emphasising 'non-kinetic' force, the shock was such that many consider Moscow's assault to mark a challenge equivalent to the world wars of the twentieth century. For some, therefore, the situation echoes the late 1930s, and the start of a new 'pre-war' era.[1]

Indeed, the very *scale* of the fighting in Ukraine since early 2022 has surprised and shocked Western policy makers and public alike. The attack has resulted in an industrial war between two of the largest armed forces in Europe, a clash of steel and firepower, with all the attendant death, destruction and socio-economic dislocation. On the front lines, the grinding nature of the fighting echoes the wars of the twentieth century: extensive trench networks, dense minefields and thousands of wrecked military vehicles litter Ukraine's countryside. Artillery fires thousands, often tens of thousands of shells daily, inflicting appalling loss of life and limb, and condemning many to psychological trauma. The war is felt behind the lines, too, with critical infrastructure damaged or destroyed; the socio-economic effects of blockades and sanctions are felt at home and in global energy and grain markets. Millions have become refugees; Russia stands accused of grave war crimes.[2]

For their part, senior Russian politicians, officers and observers appear to offer an ambiguous – not to say confused and confusing – perspective. On one hand, they describe the campaign as a 'special war operation' (*spetsalnaya voennaya operatsiya*, SVO), a more limited effort. But on the other, they also suggest that Russia faces a 'Fatherland War'-type, existential struggle. The combat may (currently) be between Ukraine and Russia, but as Russian officials see it, the contest with (and challenge to Russia posed by) the Euro-Atlantic community is often described in global, even epochal terms. References to the Great Fatherland War, as the Eastern Front in World War II is known in Russia, permeate speeches and documents. Indeed, Putin even indicated that the Russian assault was intended to pre-empt a repeat of Operation Barbarossa, launched by Nazi Germany against the Soviet Union in 1941.[3]

So, a great deal is at stake. As the United Kingdom's then Chief of General Staff (CGS) Patrick Sanders noted in 2022, it would be 'dangerous to assume that Ukraine is a limited conflict'.[4] Moreover, if the actual combat has remained between Russia and Ukraine, and very largely on the territories of these two states, each side receives considerable support that lends a wider regional, even global aspect to the war that extends well beyond the Euro-Atlantic region to Iran, India, North Korea and China.

The high stakes involved are clear, particularly in the potential for the war to escalate. Moments of potential crisis, such as when missiles have fallen on the territory of a North Atlantic Treaty Organisation (NATO) member state causing casualties, illustrate the inherent tensions and widespread concerns that NATO could be drawn into the war. This remains a central question as the Euro-Atlantic community debates the implications of providing Kyiv with more powerful and longer-range weaponry, and whether Moscow's threatened responses are real or a bluff: whether Putin might resort to deploying nuclear weapons features repeatedly in the headlines.

Furthermore, if there is widespread consensus that the war between Russia and Ukraine will be a long one, the Euro-Atlantic community is preparing for a sustained Russian challenge to European security as a whole, even a possible wider war. Sanders, for instance, suggested that even if Russia's conventional military capacity is reduced, 'respite' will be temporary and the threat will become 'more acute': 'in most scenarios, Russia will be an even greater threat to European security after Ukraine than it was before'.[5] Not only is this an existential challenge for Ukraine, but the Euro-Atlantic community's relationship with Russia, already long dissonant and competitive, is now one of strategic contest, explicitly spoken of in adversarial terms. If some refer to a 'new Cold War', others talk of the dangers of World War III, or a new epoch of wars. Scenarios have begun to envisage what a war with Russia might look like, even when it might erupt.[6]

So, Russia poses both an acute and a longer-term challenge: accurately framing this is essential to shaping effective policy. This may appear so obvious as to hardly need saying. Indeed, for many, today's Russia is obviously a revanchist, imperialist expansionist power, willing to use extensive and blunt, brute military force to achieve its goals. The main question is where Moscow will attack next.

Yet some care is warranted: post-Cold War Western analysis of Russian power has yielded only mixed results, either in terms of foreseeing the outbreak and evolution of wars, or what might oblige Moscow to desist or agree to terms. When Moscow annexed Crimea, for instance, it was such a surprise that a senior NATO official called it 'the most amazing information blitzkrieg ever seen'.[7]

Throughout the 2010s, officials and observers persistently misinterpreted Russian theory and practice through a blend of wishful thinking, soundbites and buzzwords. A handful of honourable exceptions apart, analysis of Russian capabilities was often divorced from analysis of Moscow's intent, in turn becoming separated from Russian war history and culture, and from Russian doctrine and strategy. Attention focused on the new forms of war supposedly being invented by the Russian military to counter and avoid Western conventional superiority, and suggested that Moscow's definition and understanding of war had changed such that it was shaping a new art of war. Comment and analysis – and much policy – focused primarily on Russia's attempts to develop a 'hybrid' approach to war, even how its military no longer prioritised firepower or battle. A narrative of 'little green men' and 'ambiguity' took hold in the wake of Russia's annexation of Crimea in 2014, and continued even as Moscow built up its armed forces around Ukraine in 2021 and early 2022.[8]

Consequently, much of the discussion about Russian war strategy and military power began from the wrong premises, conflating grand strategy and military strategy, and so posed the wrong questions. The result was not just a lack of clarity about what causes Moscow to go to war, but even confusion over what 'war' means to Moscow. Essential features were missed, and outsized roles allocated to particular individuals and organisations, with others unnoticed or discounted. The practicalities of life in the Russian armed forces were ignored, from the capacity of the defence industry to conscription and conditions of service, such as health, military discipline and the culture of command. Likewise, critical aspects of how the armed forces worked were overlooked: if the air force and navy barely featured in analysis, the practicalities of how and why Moscow rehearsed its mobilisation and sought to reform its military logistics remained arcane.

Preface

To be sure, this changed once the renewed assault began: attention shifted to the battlefield and Moscow's blunt use of firepower. Officials and observers began to shine the spotlight on tactical failures and shortcomings in interoperability, the chain of command and leadership, and logistics. A sense emerged, therefore, that unwarranted hyperbole about the Russian security and defence challenge during the 2010s had turned into seeing Moscow's armed forces as impotent. One senior Western officer said that 'whereas before the assault we may have seen them as 10 feet tall, we now run the risk of seeing them as 3 feet tall'.[9] As planners and observers watch for change in Russian approaches and new theories of victory, and estimate how Russia's forces will be regenerated, there is a risk that the wrong lessons will be drawn about the Russian 'art of war' and what this actually means.

Certainly, we have a great deal of information, from satellite imagery to social media: some fine investigative journalism and open source analysis offers granular detail on a range of specific questions pertaining to how Moscow has waged this campaign. Yet many of the same analytical problems remain. Half-truths, more general imprecisions and specific inaccuracies about Moscow's approach to war are already being laundered – with plenty of speculation – into mainstream analysis as fact; the emergence of a new range of buzzwords and half-digested references to individual Russian theorists is only a matter of time. These are evident in the discussions about even vitally important questions such as whether Moscow is actually already 'at war', whether the economy is 'mobilised' – even what 'mobilisation' means – and the likelihood of whether Moscow will resort to nuclear weapons. Consequently, estimating what the Russian state and military leadership is doing and what it intends to do – and will be able to do – too often becomes a matter of surmise and conjecture, a high-stakes version of blind man's bluff.

Given the structural contest between Moscow and the Euro-Atlantic community, and concerns about miscalculation and escalation, we cannot afford to jump to the wrong conclusions about Russia's way in war again. The adages about knowing one's adversary and establishing the kind of war on which one is embarking, not mistaking it for nor trying to turn it into something alien to its nature, may be well-worn, but they remain essential guidelines.

Introduction: war returns to Europe

In September 2022 President Vladimir Putin ordered a 'partial' mobilisation of 300,000 men, and then, a month later, he moved Russia on to a graded war footing.[1] This was the first time that Moscow had initiated a mobilisation since 1941, when the Soviet Union faced the onslaught of Operation Barbarossa. This time it was to sustain the belaboured 'special war operation' that Moscow had itself initiated six months previously, but which, even in its early stages, had not gone to plan.[2]

In renewing its assault on Ukraine, Moscow's initial offensive in February was characterised by what many Western observers called a 'blitzkrieg'-type assault on multiple axes. The offensive seized swathes of territory, but failed to deliver the knockout blow. A combination of Ukrainian resistance, Western assistance to Kyiv and a range of practical Russian problems in waging their offensive caused the assaults to stall. Russian forces withdrew from the Kyiv and Zhitomir regions that April. The spring and summer of 2022 saw the most large-scale and high-intensity combat in Europe for decades. Indeed, Ukraine began to counter-attack in the directions of Kharkiv and Kherson, forcing further Russian withdrawals, and by the autumn Moscow had needed the extra capacity provided by the mobilisation simply to stabilise the front lines.

The draft and subsequent move to a war footing underlined that Moscow had suffered a series of expensive setbacks, and seemed to confirm a shift in the character of the Russian approach from attempted manoeuvre warfare to more attritional operations. Both sides dug networks of trenches and fired many thousands of artillery rounds daily. From autumn 2022 to spring 2023 the lines barely moved; the city of Bakhmut fell to Russian forces after months of assaults. Offensives by both Ukraine and Russia through the summer and autumn of 2023 offered very limited territorial gains at an appalling cost in life and limb. Indeed, by late 2023, if much of the discussion in the Euro-Atlantic community was about whether or not the war was a stalemate, there was more consensus that the war would be a long one and what advantages or disadvantages this might pose for both sides.

Moscow's shift to a war footing in autumn 2022 also reflected a raised level of state effort and the Russian leadership's commitment to pursuing its aims. Putin reiterated on several occasions his intent to press on with the campaign.[3] In practical terms, the leadership set up a Government Coordination Council to oversee the supply of the operation and shifted the defence industry into a higher gear; then, in January 2023, it established an armed forces high command to oversee the campaign. Various other measures were introduced through 2023 and into 2024, including an active recruitment campaign, modernising the mobilisation procedure and increasing defence spending.

If 'special war operation' remained the official term, senior Russian officials also began more explicitly to use other language and symbols recalling the 'Fatherland'-type wars against Napoleon and Hitler, suggesting that Russia was now embroiled in a similar situation. Dmitry Medvedev, head of the United Russia party and a senior figure in the national Security Council, stated that the war was about Russia's 'survival'. Sergei Kirienko, First Deputy Head of the Presidential Administration, emphasised that Russia would win if the war became a 'people's war'.[4] And in early 2024 presidential spokesman Dmitry Peskov stated that, while *de jure* the campaign against Ukraine remained an 'SVO', since the West 'increasingly and more directly enhances its involvement in the conflict' it had 'turned into a war for us'.[5]

At the same time, Moscow accused the 'collective West' of waging a proxy war against Russia; Putin used the term 'economic blitzkrieg' to describe the sanctions the Euro-Atlantic community imposed on Russia.[6] But he (and others, including then Defence Minister Sergei Shoigu and Chief of the General Staff Valeriy Gerasimov) became ever more explicit about what they saw as Western support for Ukraine being part of a broader effort to defeat Russia, even to break it up. Putin stated, for example, that 'it is well known that the military potential and capabilities of almost all major NATO countries are being widely used against Russia', even that they were 'waging war' against Russia, to 'break apart and destroy our country'.[7]

In this context, and with heavy fighting ongoing in Ukraine, in December 2022 and January 2023 Shoigu presented a series of recommendations for the further development of the Russian armed forces to 2026 and beyond. Rhetorically, these emphasised a sense of continuity of trends under consideration or work since the early 2010s, but in practice they are a turn to greater scale. He made clear the intent to increase substantially the size of the Russian armed forces by altering conscription legislation, establishing more divisions and strengthening the forces in the north-west of the country by (re-)creating Moscow and Leningrad military districts as two joint-force strategic territorial units.[8] Putin formalised this in February 2024.[9]

So, how do we interpret Russia's approach to war and the nature and character of the challenge that the Euro-Atlantic community faces today and in the future? As noted, the stakes are high: the multi-layered challenge to Euro-Atlantic security is serious. But how should we construe this evolving challenge? What is 'war' to the Russians, anyway – and is it really different to an 'SVO'? How does the Russian political and military leadership think that wars are won or lost? What are the central debates and concepts in war thinking and strategy – and what causes change? How does the current fighting in Ukraine fit into the longer-term context of how Moscow wages war? Importantly, what does this all mean for the rest of the 2020s, and how the Euro-Atlantic community should plan deterrence and defence?

The Russian art of war?

For much of the post-Cold War era, Russia has not been a primary focus for Western militaries, which instead have campaigned in Iraq and Afghanistan, thinking in terms of counter-terrorist or counter-insurgency operations. When Russia did begin to feature, especially after Moscow's annexation of Crimea in 2014, the picture became confused. On the one hand, the Russian challenge was seen to be one from the past: the so-called return to the Cold War framework, with Moscow – or more usually, Putin – trying to rebuild the Soviet Union. At the same time, on the other, Western capitals and militaries themselves thought in 'post-Iraq' war conceptual terms, such as 'hybrid' challenges and grey zone or 'liminal' warfare. If Moscow was seen to be trying to rebuild the USSR, therefore, it was considered to be using modern methods to do so. Especially following its annexation of Crimea, Moscow's approach was described as ambiguous and asymmetric, avoiding direct battle, withdrawing when met with strength, and relying on evasion, deception and psychology to attack Western cohesion. This is very much how observers in earlier times had characterised an 'Eastern' way of war.[10] This meant that analysis began from the wrong premises, and served to bake an aura of mystique or exoticism into analysis, often garnished with terms such as 'reflexive control' and *maskirovka*, but rarely delving into problems in theory or practice.

As the debate about Great Power competition took shape in the second half of the 2010s, Russia was grouped together with China, Iran, North Korea and jihadist threats, again in contrast to 'Western ways of war'.[11] Since February 2022 this view of Russia as 'the (Eastern) Other' has taken other forms, but it remains clear: discussion of Russia's (authoritarian/imperial) army of serfs fighting Ukraine's (democratic) army of free men echoes not only recent wars,[12] but the classical Greco-Persian wars.

At first glance, this appears reasonable. Russia *is* the Euro-Atlantic community's adversary. The Russian leadership explicitly emphasises its policy and value disputes with the liberal, democratic Euro-Atlantic community, and makes common cause with China, Iran and other states in what it calls the 'post-West' world as part of a wider global competition. Yet in more specific terms of Moscow's approach to strategy and war, this is one of the main reasons for the misdiagnosis of Russian war strategy through the last decade, with measures short of war being mistaken for measures of war.

Instead, it is more helpful to think of Russian strategy in war as being part of the *Western* family of traditions. Moscow may be a distant and wayward relation, but the family ties are there: in much of the late nineteenth and through the twentieth century, Russian culture and politics had deep European ties; military affairs were no exception. Certainly, an important distinctiveness in Russian war history exists – different wars were fought, and even wars 'in common', such as the two world wars, were very differently experienced. But there is also much that is universal and shared, and thus recognisable.

Clausewitz and Jomini, two thinkers at the heart of Western military strategy and philosophy, served as Russian officers, and have long exerted influence on Tsarist, Soviet and then post-Soviet Russian thinking about war. If we cannot really understand contemporary Western military strategy without reference to Clausewitz and the debates he stimulated, he is similarly influential and debated in Russia. Likewise, other Western thinkers and officers, including Hans Delbrück, Helmut von Moltke, Alfred Thayer Mahan and Basil Liddell Hart, have all exerted influence on Moscow's thinking about strategy and war.

In short, Russian thinking about and strategy for war are steeped in direct interaction with – and explicit reference to – European traditions. Consequently, Russian debates about the changing character of war and war strategy often directly echo those in the West. With these similarities in mind, we can recognise familiar themes and questions and analyse strengths and weaknesses the more easily to parse Russian strategy. And on the basis of such similarities, we can filter out the exoticism in our analysis, identifying important differences and what is distinctive about the Russian way in war. Simply, there is no need for mystification about Russian concepts such as the 'art of war' or '(strategic) *maskirovka*'.

With this in mind, this book focuses on analysing Moscow's strategy in war in the context of a longer-term trajectory to trace the tension between continuity and change. Rather than attempting to interpret these questions in terms of fluctuations in the reforms of the 2010s, or even the post-Cold War era, we must look to a 'long century', one that links the German wars of unification (1864–70) through to the 2030s. This allows us to track real continuity and change. Does a change in the state's leadership lead to a change in war strategy? Does victory or defeat in battle or war cause change? How long does change take?

In this way, we can see the echoes of persistent debates about strategy and war, and the ebb and flow of fashion and taboo. We see how analysis in the 1920s drew not just on World War I and the Russian civil war, but on the 'lessons' of the wars of 1864–70, and how those debates of the 1920s and 1930s were repeatedly revisited in the 1940s, 1960s, 1970s and 1980s, even as technology and society evolved. And we see how the reform and modernisation of the post-Soviet Russian military in the 1990s and 2010s continued to draw on these threads. It is this long trajectory that has informed Gerasimov's horizons since he was appointed Chief of the General Staff in 2012, and that is shaping planning for the future.

This longer trajectory allows us to examine the peaks and nadirs that the leadership and armed forces have faced, and what wars and technological development mean in theory and practice. Such a longer-term trajectory is indispensable: if we hope accurately to parse Russian debates, doctrines and strategy, we must be familiar with how the Russian military perceives and describes evolving threats and problems, and how strategists interpret the lessons of history, the dilemmas of geography and the challenges of bureaucracy.

With this trajectory in mind, we can turn to the evolution of Russian thinking, doctrine and strategy in war. During this long century, the central feature of Russian war thought is the tension between two forms of strategy in war that can be framed as a 'strategy of destruction' and a 'strategy of attrition'. This tension has shaped Russia's way in war in theory and in practice, as officials and experts have debated the implications and advantages offered by preparing for and waging short or long wars. It is within this context that we can begin to analyse and interpret questions of war preparation and mobilisation, the advantages offered by offensive or defensive strategies, the importance of creativity and initiative in Russian theory, and the persistent problems, doubts and difficulties the leadership and military face.

'Strategic culture' and a Russian 'way in war'

These themes fit into a wider, long-running set of debates about strategic culture and whether there are distinct national approaches to strategy making and war. Indeed, the war in Ukraine has stimulated discussion about 'strategic culture' in a new era in both the Euro-Atlantic community and Russia.[13] The idea of 'strategic culture' emerged during the Cold War as observers tried to illuminate how policy makers in Moscow would not necessarily come to the same decisions as Western policy makers, especially regarding the use of nuclear weapons. Today, this approach is largely associated with Jack Snyder's assessment of Soviet nuclear decision making (though Snyder himself later moved away from strategic culture as an analytical tool). Policy makers in particular states, so Snyder argued, were socialised into a distinctive and semi-permanent way of approaching strategic decisions.[14] In this way, strategic culture seeks to depict the (predictable) persistence of a state's strategic approach and interests that endure across time, shaped, even constrained by, traditions, values, habits and customs. Geography and history are considered to be essential ingredients that shape strategic culture.

Snyder was contributing to what was already a very rich literature that attempted to interpret the culture of Moscow's actions. George Kennan's 1947 article 'The Sources of Soviet Conduct' is today often referred to, but others, including Frank Roberts, the chargé d'affaires in the British Embassy in Moscow at the same time as Kennan, also made significant contributions. These thinkers examined Moscow's doctrine and policy, including approaches to war, to explore whether Moscow's conduct was 'reasonable' and 'calculable' and whether it was possible for the West to communicate effectively with Moscow.[15] And alongside Snyder, others made very useful contributions to the analysis of how cultural factors shaped Moscow's strategic thought and activity.[16] Studies of the Soviet way in war pointed to the preference for the offensive, for speed and surprise – and the 'lure of the single big, brief, and early strike'.[17] Still others offered stimulating assessments of cultural, intellectual and bureaucratic life, providing rich source material for interpreting Moscow's activity, from a tendency for major strategic undertakings to systemic challenges such as *bardak* (roughly, if not very satisfactorily, translatable as 'uncontrolled events').

Indeed, equally important in considering strategic culture – and whether Russia's is distinctive – is the human element, with a range of proclivities such as *bezalabernost* (sloppiness or an inability to work things through), *bezotvetstvennost* (irresponsibility), *nereshitelnost* (indecision), *neispolnitelnost* (non-implementation), *bezrazlichie* (indifference), *khalatnost* (negligence), *kolebanie* (vacillation) and forms of dishonesty in the chain of command (such as, but not limited to, *ochkovtiratelstvo*). At the same time as Snyder was writing on Soviet nuclear decision-making culture, the prominent British observer Ronald Hingley was exploring these other aspects. He noted that, 'as spectacular as Russian prestige undertakings can be, and formidable as the concentrated energy is which they can focus, no one familiar with the country could miss the antithetical and no less characteristic qualities of vagueness, laziness, casualness, unpunctuality and the like'.[18]

One can add further variations drawing on Russian culture; indeed, knowledge of Russian literature, film and music is especially useful in assessing Russian strategic culture and war strategy. One notion is *Oblomovshchina*. Drawing on Ivan Goncharov's fictional character Oblomov, this is characterised by a 'talismanic belief that putting things down on paper is the same as doing them', combined with an indifference to keeping to agreed schedules and actions and a fear of taking responsibility for decisions because of potential repercussions.[19] A second is *Shvondershchina*, drawing on the character Shvonder in Mikhail Bulgakov's novella *Sobache serdtse* (*Heart of a Dog*). Shvonder represents the personification of the Bolshevik government, but also a mediocre, obedient and ideological functionary, all too happy to resort to the powers of the police and security services.[20]

In the post-Cold War era, 'strategic culture' was challenged. Critics questioned what 'culture' means, how it takes shape, and the extent to which it can (coherently) be passed down through generations. Indeed, are there not multiple cultures within each state? Moreover, some observed that the lens of strategic culture, particularly as applied in political science studies, causes analytical rigidity: rather than exploring change, it seeks predictability through supposedly immutable cultural continuity.[21]

Nevertheless, despite this critique, since the 2010s the literature specifically on Russian strategic culture has grown, including in Russia.[22] For some, thinking in terms of strategic culture helps mitigate mirror imaging by framing a range of questions about how decision makers see the world. It is the context in which strategy is formulated and implemented, providing essential reference points. It can thus help to illuminate how different intellectual climates and thought patterns might manifest themselves across different cultures and distinctive approaches to conceptualising the past and future.[23]

Too often, however, this is little more than a cursory nod to snapshots of Russian history and assorted analogies. It has become separated from both Russian history and traditions and from contemporary context, and produces hypothesised, capability-based scenario assessments that entirely overlook cultural dimensions that shape and limit strategy.[24] Indeed, it often contains neither 'strategy' as complex process, nor 'culture' as an evolving sociopolitical and intellectual context with reference to the human element. The extant strategic culture literature posits an abstracted version of Russia and Moscow's strategy, with little to say beyond one-dimensional depictions of authoritarianism and corruption. Consequently, too often a sense of continuity becomes over-emphasised into a dismissive 'everything remains more or less the same', but without substance. This in large part explains Western surprise when Moscow renewed its assault on Ukraine in 2022, both at the extent of the use of force, and at the problems the Russian effort encountered.

Used with caution, strategic culture can help to interpret Moscow's way in war. This should include not only geography and history, but the messy complications that constitute strategy making, from indecision (*nereshitelnost*) to squander (*razbazarivanie*), and from mobilisation (*mobilizatsiya*) to seeking surprise and 'suddenness' (*vnezapnost*). In many ways, strategy, as we will see, is often an active process of 'measures to (re)take control of events' (*protivo-bardachnie meri* or *prekratit bardak*).

Historians have contributed to this strategic culture discussion, examining the idea of distinctive national 'ways of war'. Such approaches – also much debated – have worked, however, as explanations of the past with specific historical end dates, rather than attempts to forecast the future.[25] Nevertheless, one approach offers a productive method for interpreting contemporary Russian strategy in war. This draws on Basil Liddell Hart's work on the British 'way in war', delivered first as a lecture in 1931.[26] The individuality of Liddell Hart's approach, illustrated by the title 'way in war' (rather than way 'of' war), provides a useful example for our purposes because he focused on strategy making and the relationship between national policy and war. Strategy, he argued, began with state policy – how the British sought to harmonise state power to defend a global empire at a time of international change. For Liddell Hart, the 'British way in war' worked at two levels: strategically, with national policy linking economic and military interests and capabilities, and then operationally, though a limited or indirect approach on the least expected lines, using speed, surprise and mobility. This was a direct response to – and an attempt to find a way to avoid – the attritional fighting of World War I.[27]

Liddell Hart sought to establish strategic principles for specific contexts, and to create a more systematic explanation of the way Great Britain had waged war to protect and advance its interests. To do so, he linked the past to the present and the future, applying the context of the past for didactic purposes to understand the present and to inform an awareness of the future. Thus, 'strategy' and 'history' worked in a dialectical relationship, with digested historical experience shaping strategic theory and practice to meet contemporary needs and inform thinking about the future.

Liddell Hart's 'British way in war' has been subjected to extensive debate. The very first question posed by the audience following his 1931 lecture challenged his thesis, and the critique has continued ever since. Observers point out that Liddell Hart 'pondered' and 'plundered' the work of many others, including Winston Churchill and the British naval historian Julian Corbett.[28] Some criticised his approach to history. The late Sir Michael Howard, the doyen of war studies, argued that British strategy, especially in the twentieth century, had been the very *opposite* of what Liddell Hart asserted.[29] But Liddell Hart was not writing a history of British strategy. Instead, echoing Corbett, he was attempting to produce ideas to inform that strategy at a time of deepening crisis and changing international geography. In this way, we can see his 'way in war' as a means of engaging in a series of debates about the dilemmas London faced, in arguments that are reformulated across generations.

Importantly, Liddell Hart's approach is very illustrative of *Russian* strategy and war making, and illuminates how we can interpret it. His work is often cited by Russians themselves;[30] the Russian state, and particularly the military leadership, engages in a similar process of using history to shape strategic principles to address the dilemmas and challenges of a changing world. And Russian thinking about war has long embraced the idea of 'national' ways in war – while the 'science' of war is 'general', war doctrines must be specific to states.[31]

This has particular value, since national ways of war – whether depicted as 'blitzkrieg' or as US and British 'maritime' ways – have been repeated points of reference and criticism through the last one hundred years in Russian professional debate and official doctrine alike. Like Liddell Hart and Corbett, Russian officials and observers, including Putin, Gerasimov and many others, link the past to the present and future, didactically applying the experience of the past to interpret the present to inform an awareness of the future and thus shape strategic principles.

Applying history to strategy

History is an essential ingredient in interpreting Russian strategy and thinking about war. That said, this is not straightforward, so it is worth clarifying just what we mean by 'history' and how it plays a role. For many in the Euro-Atlantic community, the resumption of war in Ukraine in 2022 has reinvigorated a discussion about Russia's history. On the one hand, this has resulted in the drawing of analogies to argue that Moscow faces potential, if not impending, defeat.[32] On the other, the focus is on how the Russian leadership distorts history for political purposes. Western officials and observers have written about the 'amateur' and 'pernicious' ways that Putin 'cherry picks' the good parts of history, omitting the bad, to offer a particular narrative of Russian history. The broad consensus is that Putin not only distorts the historical record, but is often factually incorrect.[33]

Surely few can be surprised that a politician would use (and abuse) history to suit their own political ends – and it is clear that Putin and other senior figures do this. In official (Russian) history, there is a strong emphasis on what British historian John Plumb would have called 'the Past' – a 'living past', one used to sanctify the government, provide moral example and invest a sense of destiny and purpose. We should not confuse such myths with historically validated fact, neither should we be surprised that political leaders seek to use them.[34] Such an approach is the antithesis of much (academic) historical study in the Euro-Atlantic community today, where history is considered to be an intellectual process to discover what happened on its own terms. This even seeks to be destructive of 'the Past'. At one level, then, Moscow's 'use' of history is one of the reasons that the Euro-Atlantic community and Russia so often appear to live in different worlds, and we should be explicit about the different approaches to 'the Past' and 'history'.

There is also much to be said about (military) history more specifically, how it has evolved in the Euro-Atlantic community from a 'drums and guns' battlefield narrative approach towards a wider 'war and society' one,[35] and whether it is possible to draw 'lessons' from history. For some, history does not teach lessons. For others, there is a long tradition of looking to the past for philosophical counsel and exemplars.[36]

There are different communities of those writing about history in the Russian language. For all that there is an officially sanctioned version of history, reflected in the works of – for instance – Vladimir Medinsky, presidential aide and chairman of the Russian War Historical Society, there are others, writing in Russia and abroad.[37] And for its part, the Russian military explicitly draws on history for practical lessons. The tasks of the history of war include the education of the military and public and the struggle against falsifications of history. History is also explicitly used to generate creativity and initiative in officers by

imbuing a deeper grasp of the art of war.[38] Actually, it is rare
to find an issue of a Russian professional military journal that
does not include an article, case study or discussion about an
aspect of history, a war or a campaign, reflecting on traditions,
experiences and problems encountered and resolved, and rendering conclusions and lessons to advance contemporary war science.
Gerasimov's speeches and articles are full of historical references
and 'lessons', underscoring the (Russian) maxim that every war
has its own logic, and thereby that the logics of the wars of the
past can be examined and interpreted.[39]

Russian thinkers and officials underline the 'special role' of
history in shaping strategy and reform in force development and
organisational theory and practice. It is not the only ingredient:
others include data science and forecasting. But it is an *essential*
ingredient: Russian military leaders have long asserted that the
'lessons of history' have 'long-term practical value', and that a
knowledge of history is an 'essential stage in mastering strategy
and professional activity'. According to the late editor of the
publication *Voenno-istoricheskii zhurnal* (*ViZh*), 'no substantive question in any sphere can be resolved' without the study of history.[40]

The main object of Russian history of war is the study of
the theory and practice of the conduct of wars and of concrete
combat experience which allows the understanding of the
evolution of war strategy and its future development. As we
shall see, senior strategists persistently assert that history for the
sake of history loses purpose; instead it should provide evidence
for the development of laws of war, generalisations from war
experience which have theoretical and practical meaning for
the defence of the state and the development of the contemporary
art of war. For the Russian armed forces, the history of war has
long had a practical meaning, therefore: experience of the past

is used to orient the present and reflect on the future development of the art of war. Interpreting this approach offers a window into the view of the Russian leadership on the changing character of war: Moscow's strategic inheritance, the main reference points and analogies which serve as intellectual anvils. It provides the longer-term trajectory to contextualise, for instance, Moscow's interpretation of how and why wars start, the evolving content of the initial period of war and how technology influences war.

This is not one-dimensional – the discipline of history has suffered significant challenges, and there are extended and heated (and politically charged) internal debates between different communities over method and content. During the Soviet era, criticisms focused on 'cults of personality', 'subjectivism' and nihilism and 'negative approaches to the military past, including leaders and diminishing the activities of the command', and 'ignoring the experience of the Great Fatherland War'.[41] In the less ideological environment of post-Soviet Russia, historians have criticised 'cleansed and polished' and 'essentially superficial memoirs and historical literature' – the uniformity of politicised Soviet 'legends'.[42]

What we are looking for here, therefore, is a *historiography* of Russian strategy and war, the intellectual and cultural threads that shape its way in war. We are looking for the roots of debates and how ideas are revived, recycled and laundered – what is written in and what is written out: essentially, how the Russian leadership invokes, critiques and emulates their predecessors while looking to the future. This means recognising different communities within the Russian historiographical debate, and that Russian historical methodology differs from Western uses. The phrase 'history teaches us' has more practical relevance in Russia than in the Euro-Atlantic community. Without a knowledge of Soviet and Russian (war) history, it is not possible to parse debates or statements by senior officials today, who often refer implicitly and explicitly to history, using it as an anvil to hammer out contemporary reforms.[43]

This historiography helps us track continuity and change and recognise echoes through the decades. The echoes of the learning experience and debates of the 1920s and 1930s are audible in today's discussion, as are those of the debates of the 1940s, 1960s and 1980s. Explicitly and implicitly, the ghosts of Alexander Svechin, Mikhail Tukhachevsky, Sergei Gorshkov and Nikolai Ogarkov, among others, all haunt today's debate in Russia about the changing character of war as the current generation grapples with the dilemmas posed by shifting international geography and deepening crisis.[44] When Gerasimov noted in the 2010s, for instance, that wars are no longer declared but are prepared in secret in advance, and that the wars of today are not the same as those of previous eras, he echoed these predecessors, rather than propounding new major changes in definitions of war. And just as Soviet historians remarked in 1974 that the history of the Great Fatherland War was closely connected with that of their own era, so Gerasimov persistently referred to its lessons in the 2010s. This is essential for interpreting preparatory mobilisation measures, the choice of strategy in war, and operational measures such as surprise and deception.

Structure of this book

This book explores patterns in Moscow's strategic thinking about and experience of war to see what we might learn about Russian intent and practice, the better to address challenges today and tomorrow. It is intended, therefore, to offer an examination of how the Russian leadership has rationalised experiences of warfare during this 'long century' to shape a philosophy and war strategy to address what Moscow sees as its strategic dilemmas.

As such, though it focuses on Russian strategy, it also contributes to ongoing wider debates about the changing character of war and the re-emergence over time of persistent questions. These include thinking about the adversary, the lessons of history, and conceptual innovation and the role of technology. At the heart of the book, therefore, are a series of unresolved tensions, in the sense of the Euro-Atlantic community's relationship with Russia, between theory and practice, and between plans and implementation. To this list, we can add the unresolved tensions in the continental and maritime dilemma, and 'direct' and 'indirect' strategies. Rather than offering a resolution to these tensions, the book traces how they wax and wane.

The chapters are structured along chronological lines to reflect on the evolving development of Russian theory and strategy, and to match this to practical experience in the wars that Moscow has fought. Woven through this chronological discussion will be examinations of central themes in Russian war strategy, such as initiative and creativity, surprise and deception (including *maskirovka*), and the evolving roles of different services.

Likewise, I have woven some illustrative reflection on wider international conditions and domestic contexts into the chapters. If history is an essential ingredient in Moscow's way in war, then it is worth reflecting on how that discipline has evolved in Russia. And if technological innovation is an important aspect of the evolution of war strategy, we must reflect on the evolving condition of the scientific disciplines in Russia. So, while strictly speaking this is neither a general 'history' nor a 'technology' book, the health and vigour (or lack thereof) of these disciplines at different times are valuable considerations for understanding the evolution of Russian strategy in war.

This book uses a multidisciplinary approach deliberately to open up a vast potential canvas. In so doing, we will encounter a number of contested questions. Russia's uniqueness, for instance, is an article of faith for many inside Russia and beyond, and there is much to say about the political, cultural and philosophical aspects of this question. But too often this only serves to exoticise Russian war science and strategy, as reflected in much misunderstood concepts such as *maskirovka*, and the poet Tyutchev-style assertions that Russia cannot be understood with the mind.

Similarly, this book opens up the richness of Soviet and Russian history of war and strategic thought. In so doing, by examining historiography, it tests some long-held tenets about Russian military thought and practice. But there is much more to be said about the theories of specific commanders, and the wars and campaigns they waged: many interesting highways and byways can only be pointed to here.

So, some caveats are worth noting at the outset about what this book seeks to do and what goes beyond its remit. Given the contest between the Euro-Atlantic community and Moscow, the book attempts empathy to parse Moscow's thinking and actions. Empathy is not synonymous with sympathy: attempting to interpret how and why Moscow goes to war and uses its military as a tool does not denote sympathy with either its means or its goals. It means examining why others act in the way they do, and how a state does and does not work, neither rendering it as an abstract, nor essentialising or exoticising its actions. It is an antidote to mirror imaging and capability-based analysis, and an essential underpinning to any effective deterrence and defence policy.

Introduction

This is the purpose of using the 'way in war' approach. The study of strategy requires finding the best lens through which to examine political affairs from the perspective of those involved in making the decisions, shaping the plans and implementing them.[45] To be sure, the basis of good strategy is good anthropology and sociology,[46] but to this should be added geography, history, language and culture. This is important because the study of Moscow's strategy means delving into Russian interpretations of events. This has two consequences. First, this book is not intended as a 'military history' in the strict sense. It does not record and examine Moscow's strategic and war history in terms of the accuracy of details and an objective understanding of the reasons for why and how campaigns were waged.[47] Instead, it explores how and why Moscow's strategists framed the dilemmas and challenges they faced, how they interpreted war and the strategy required to win it. In other words, it sets out how Russian strategists perceive their world rather than an objective truth, and, to do so, it draws on both history and strategic theory as these strategists did to illustrate the evolution of Russia's way in war.

To do this, I focus primarily on the state and the key leaders, the views of the statesmen and soldier-thinkers who designed war doctrine and strategy and implemented it. These sources are treated with appropriate caution. For all the limitations of the memoirs and histories – their distortions, grievances and mistakes – they illustrate prevailing attitudes and narratives, fashions and taboos. Much like strategists elsewhere, Russian strategists can misdiagnose the conditions they face, and suffer from groupthink, dogma, confirmation bias and mirror imaging.

To reinforce this analysis, I draw on a wide range of official strategic documents, plans and speeches, professional books and journal and media articles, memoirs, social media, television series, films and music. Even so, we might observe that in tracing the historiography of Russia's way in war, there is an evolution in the available source material. The narrative of the Soviet era is better known, albeit with some important limits on the available factual evidence. This is in contrast to the post-Soviet era, in which there is more evidence available, albeit with less narrative clarity or consensus.[48]

The second consequence is that we must underline just how far apart the Euro-Atlantic community and Russia have grown since the mid-2000s. The relationship is now tantamount to one of strategic contest, one that both parties see potentially lasting throughout the 2020s.[49] The book starts from the position of there being obvious, long-running and fundamental policy and values disagreements, such that senior officials on both sides think that relations reflect a clash of polar opposite views. This is significant given that 'war' is understood by both the Euro-Atlantic community and Moscow to be the resort to armed force to resolve policy clashes. The lengthy list of disagreements, from NATO enlargement (indeed, the alliance's *existence*), to the annexation of Crimea, to mutual accusations of interference in domestic politics, and almost everything in between, is extensively covered elsewhere and needs no further rehearsal here.

This leads to the final caveat: this book focuses on continuity and change in Russia's 'way in *war*'. The focus of the analysis is at the strategic level, at the nexus of national politics, economy, society and the military. It explores Moscow's state strategy for war, so it does not look at Russian views of arms control or deterrence, nor diplomacy and measures of competition short of war, important though they are.

In the same vein, it explores doctrine and strategy and the quest for victory in major war, rather than what might be called a 'way in *battle*'. The book does not detail all the uses of the armed forces, from 'internal' deployments during the collectivisation process, to the suppression of protests and riots in the Soviet Union in the 1950s and 1960s, to 'contributions' to wars and conflicts abroad. Though it occasionally touches on evolving operational approaches and tactics, and some of the changing variety of actors involved, such as partisans and private military companies, it does not examine them in depth.

1

What is 'war' to the Russians, anyway?

If we are to examine the Russian way in war, we must begin by asking what 'war' is to the Russians. Or, more specifically, given the great variety of societal and personal experiences,[1] what war is to the Russian political and military *leadership*, and thus what this means in terms of national policy and war strategy. This illuminates why Moscow goes to war, how it seeks to win, and what escalation and defeat or victory mean. Finally, it helps to interpret whether (and how) Moscow's interpretation of war has changed, and the extent to which a Russian 'way in war' is familiar to Western observers, or is distinctively Russian.

The significance of the question is obvious: is Russia today, as some suggest, 'at war'? To differentiate between the annexation of Crimea in 2014 and the events of 2022, many Western observers describe Moscow's assault on Ukraine in 2022 as a 'full-scale' invasion or war.[2] But what, then, is the difference between 'war' and 'SVO' to Russia, and why does Putin insist on calling the assault on Ukraine the latter, while simultaneously asserting that there is a 'real war' being waged against Russia?[3] Does this difference matter? If a war is already underway between Ukraine and Russia, and NATO is in a 'pre-war' situation, and readying for a 'full-scale war' with Russia, what does this mean in practice?

At first glance, the answer appears straightforward. Moscow is waging an unprovoked and illegal war against Ukraine to subjugate that country, using extensive and often indiscriminate firepower to achieve its aims. Today's war against Ukraine – often framed as 'Putin's war' – is seen as one in a long line waged by a dictator in the footsteps of Hitler and Stalin; Putin is seeking to use a 'short, victorious war' to distract the population and boost popularity without having to implement necessary domestic reforms.[4] In this telling, the differences from Western approaches are highlighted – most obviously in command style and the widespread brutality and lack of concern even for the lives of Russian soldiers.

But given what is at stake, Clausewitz's encomium to judge correctly the kind of war on which we are embarking, not mistaking it for nor trying to turn it into something alien to its nature,[5] obliges us to dig a little deeper. We have seen how views of the war in Ukraine differ. Putin has referred to Russia's renewed assault on Ukraine in February 2022 as a 'pre-emptive rebuff to aggression' (*uprezhdayushchi otpor agressii*),[6] a view rejected by senior Western officials as 'absurd' and 'ridiculous'.[7] Differences were clear prior to Moscow's renewed assault. When German Chancellor Olaf Scholz observed that 'war in Europe has become unimaginable for my generation and we must make sure it remains so', for instance, Putin replied that 'we all witnessed a war in Europe that was unleashed by the NATO bloc against Yugoslavia'.[8]

At the military level, the question 'what is the nature and changing character of modern war' is perpetually debated by the Russian armed forces. Here, we find some apparent similarities, given the influence of Clausewitz (the 'great philosopher of war' or the 'Mahdi of Mass' and massacre), Liddell Hartian-style 'indirect' approaches to war, or regarding evolving 'generations' of war. Again, though, there are differences. The Russian military uses a specific vocabulary in which many terms do not have exact English translations. Moreover, the Russian debate about war is conceptualised in terms that do not resonate in the Euro-Atlantic community's discussion: 'wars of controlled chaos', US 'Trojan Horse' strategies and 'twenty-first-century blitzkrieg'. To this, we must now add 'special war operation'.

Defining 'war' and *voina*

Defining 'war' is important because it helps to clarify distinctions between Moscow and the Euro-Atlantic community, and also to determine what this means in practical terms for shaping Euro-Atlantic deterrence and defence. If the Kremlin insists that what is taking place in Ukraine is an 'SVO', what – if anything – does this mean for how it interprets its own actions in terms of state effort? What does it tell us about the connection between political decisions, military theory and war strategy? What does calling the campaign an SVO enable or prevent the Russian leadership from doing?

As we shall see throughout this book, Moscow has often made a distinction between '(strategic) operations', conducted without a mobilisation, and 'war', usually against a major state or coalition adversary that required extensive state-level effort. This distinction also emphasised the gap between political intent and military capability. The Russian leadership has sought on a number of occasions to use the military in an 'operation' to resolve a political problem; for their part, the armed forces recognise how an 'operation' can escalate quickly into a larger war. The Russian debate is therefore about whether 'lightning operations' work: there is often a political belief in their potential, but this belief sits uneasily alongside an intellectual recognition that they rarely deliver decisive results and that attritional campaigning often ensues.

The English-language discussion about 'war' is complex and multifaceted. It is untidy in the way we discuss the 'Hundred Years' War' or 'Thirty Years' War', and in the varied ways the word 'war' filters into the sociopolitical lexicon. The Vietnam war is not technically considered to be a war, since Congress did not issue a formal declaration of war; wars in Iraq and Afghanistan are often called, respectively, Operation Desert Storm and Operation Enduring Freedom. Western demobilisation and then demilitarisation after the Cold War – the 'peace dividend' – has reshaped society's approach to thinking about war; the language of war has spread far and wide ('culture wars'), but war as armed combat is generally seen as futile, even illegal.

The more formal discussion is similarly diverse, with extended debate about neologisms, 'new wars', and wars against drugs and international terrorism. Michael Howard argued that the declaration by senior officials that the US was 'at war' with terrorism was a natural but 'irrevocable error'. To misuse the term 'war' was not simply a legality or semantics: to declare that one is at war is to create a war psychosis expectant of decisive results, with the use of force being seen as the first rather than the last resort.[9]

The impact of what became an open-ended war against terror and the conflicts in Iraq and Afghanistan had such a deep impact on Western understandings of 'war' that by the early 2010s it was no longer easy to distinguish between war and peace.[10] Whereas previously 'war' was exceptional to 'normal' life, and shaped human experience into eras with a 'before' and an 'after', the war against terror was framed in a boundless way. Moreover, the war against terror blurred strategic thinking, elevating counter-insurgency operations to strategy, and framing wars as being 'of necessity' or 'of choice'. The lengthy war against terror was enabled by disconnecting the US public from the fighting: it became a government policy rather than a state of national existence, and 'war' drifted to the margins of political life as no deep sacrifice was called for and daily life continued largely undisturbed for the great majority.[11]

Indeed, Western thinking about war has undergone a major evolution since the end of the Cold War. Beginning with the Gulf War, the Euro-Atlantic community has deployed armed force on a number of occasions, achieving a number of quick, decisive victories. But the experience of the protracted deployments to Afghanistan and Iraq has served both to temper the resort to armed force, and the expectations of achieving political results from it. This experience has shifted the emphasis in the purpose of defence away from combat and towards security and deterrence. Experiences in Iraq and Afghanistan fostered a 'political and societal disengagement from the idea of victory'.[12]

Even as these wars were being waged, criticisms emerged about the underestimation of the potential challenge – senior officials suggested that the intervention in Afghanistan would accomplish its mission without a shot being fired – as well as poor intelligence, little knowledge of the enemy, groupthink in decision making, problems in command and control, and insufficient equipment and logistical support. Official inquiries followed.[13]

'War', then, is defined as 'premeditated, organised violence practised by one group against another', especially with political, ideological or economic drivers; it is the resort to armed force to resolve a clash of wills. It is characterised by

1. the use of force: 'Fighting is what defines war';
2. contention: if one party attacks another, the other must respond: 'This reaction means that possibly the most important feature of war is reciprocity', with the enemy having a vote and possibly adopting asymmetric or unpredictable responses;
3. a degree of intensity and duration to the fighting: 'scale matters';
4. those waging war not fighting in a personal capacity;
5. its being fought for some aim beyond fighting itself.[14]

We can take this further to explore 'ways', 'types' and 'categories' of war. First, the encounter of two armies on the battlefield in a cataclysmic clash has shaped a 'classical' Western cultural idea(l) of war. This reflects the centrality of the meeting of two opposing forces in a great battle – an honest, frontal and *decisive* clash – that lies at the heart of this 'Western way of war'. As we saw in the introduction, this is a contested idea, but is usually framed in manoeuvrist warfare terms, the effort to use technological superiority and tempo to defeat the adversary.

Second, although war is infinitely variable, including raids, sieges, battles and massacres, Western attempts to describe it have broadly resulted in two categories: 'small' wars and 'major' or 'total' wars. If the former encompasses a range of sub-categories which may be framed as 'irregular' warfare, the latter relates to those such as the two world wars. Such major wars are sometimes referred to as 'total' wars because the struggle goes beyond the battlefield to include political, social, economic and cultural fields. Such total wars involve the mobilisation of all the state's economic and societal resources to wage war against the entire enemy nation, demanding unconditional surrender. This has evolved such that wars without the resort to nuclear weapons are described as 'conventional' or 'limited' – though the limited nature of a war is not only a matter of degree, but of national perspective.[15]

Third, continuity and change are reflected in the attempt to define war by means of 'generations' that reflect technological and societal developments. Some Western observers chart four generations:

1. From the classical era to the nineteenth century, in which battles were fought between massed formations of manpower;
2. Evolution in the nineteenth century with the development of firepower with longer range and rapid-fire weapons;
3. Taking shape in the twentieth century, facilitated by technological advances that permitted mechanisation and enhanced communications, facilitating greater speed and manoeuvre and striking the enemy in depth; and
4. A decentralised form of warfare that blurred the lines between war and politics, combatants and civilians, and included non-state actors.[16]

These 'generations' are much debated, and they provide a platform for further debates over the impact of technology on the dominance of the offensive or the defensive, the usefulness of platforms such as tanks, aircraft and large naval vessels, and the value of surprise, concentration and dispersal of forces.

As in English, the Russian-language discussion about 'war' – *voina* – is both untidy and the subject of much debate. The Russian language also refers, for instance, to the Hundred Years'

What is 'war' to the Russians, anyway?

War (*stoletnaya voina*) and the war against drugs. Linguistically, the word 'war' filters widely into the media and the sociopolitical lexicon, often absorbing English-language influences, such as 'hybrid warfare' (transliterated as *gibridnaya voina*), information war, Cold War and so on; as elsewhere, the term 'war' is used (or avoided) politically, to galvanise support and to justify policies.

Likewise, the essence of war and the great range of its characteristic features, trends and developments in contemporary and especially future conflicts are the theme of constant debate among Russian defence and security circles. The changing character of war and the varieties of war, even the definition of war itself, are all themes open to deliberation in Russian war science.[17] A good illustration of this is how these themes have percolated throughout Gerasimov's speeches and articles throughout the 2010s, including in his now (in)famous 2013 article, in which he explicitly posed the question 'what is modern war?'[18]

As we shall see, though, Moscow's official views of war have long remained largely consistent. *Voina* is a sociopolitical phenomenon. It is a confrontation between states, an organised, armed struggle in the name of advancing political goals. This struggle takes various forms, including economic and diplomatic measures, but the main, decisive means are the armed forces. This emphasises that war is a state-level activity, determined at the national level, in which the leadership uses the full resources of the state. It is worth underlining, therefore, that in war the military is just one tool – albeit the most important.

The Russian MoD defines war (*voina*) as the

extreme form of resolving disagreements, characterised by the sharp change in relations between states, nations or other political actors, and the transition to the use of means of armed and other types of violence for the achieving of sociopolitical,

economic, ideological, territorial, national, ethnic, religious and
other aims. The content of war is *armed conflict*.[19]

A distinction is already clear, therefore: Russian war science
should be understood at two levels, debate and doctrine. Accepting
that there is constant, often dialectical debate about the changing
character of war and how it is waged, Moscow's official view
of war echoes Clausewitz, and can be distilled to mean the
transition to the use of armed violence to resolve a policy clash.

This has implications for our thinking about Russian strategy
and the use of armed power. It suggests that war (and warfare)
should be interpreted beyond the military/armed forces. In other
words, it is more helpful to think in terms of war as a holistic
phenomenon of which military power is just one, albeit the
most important, feature. Thus, where we find the term *voina*,
or its derivatives, we should think 'war', rather than 'military'.
This retains the emphasis on state-level strategic activity, and
creates a distinction between a state-level 'war' and a '(war)
operation'.

We can take this further: Moscow identifies different 'levels'
of war. Rather than reflecting the intensity of the combat, these
identify the extent of state effort – and thus offer guidelines to
interpreting mobilisation and escalation. They are

1. Armed conflict: an armed clash between states (international
   armed conflict) or between opposing sides in the territory of
   one state (internal armed conflict).
2. Local war: a war pursuing limited military-political objectives
   when military actions take place within the borders of the
   warring states and affect mainly the interests (territorial,
   economic, political, and so on) of those states.

3. Regional war: a war involving several states in the same region waged by national or coalition armed forces in the course of which the sides are pursuing important military-political objectives.

4. Large-scale war: a war between coalitions of states or major states or the world community in which the sides are pursuing radical military-political objectives. A large-scale war may result from an escalation of an armed conflict or a local or regional war and involve a significant number of states from different regions of the world. It would require the mobilisation of all the physical resources available and the spiritual strength of the participating states.[20]

Interpreting *voina* in this way offers valuable insight into distinguishing between types of war. For much of the modern era, *voina* has been synonymous with Great Power war. To all intents and purposes, this has meant that when Moscow's strategists considered war, what they had in mind was a decisive clash with the West, one that would involve mobilising the material and spiritual resources of the whole state and have global consequences.

Moscow has certainly used its armed forces to achieve policy goals in ways other than direct, decisive clashes with the West without formally calling them wars, though the definitional lines have sometimes blurred. Moscow did not consider its use of armed force to crush the Hungarian and Czechoslovak uprisings in 1956 and 1968 (the latter known as Operation Danube) to be wars, but instead as 'counter-revolutionary operations'. These were, in some senses, therefore, 'security operations' or versions of 'special operations'. Equally, in 1979, Moscow launched what it called a 'limited intervention to assist a fraternal nation' in Afghanistan.

While the initial operation delivered some success, Soviet forces became enmeshed in a decade-long counter-insurgency struggle. As the author Svetlana Alexievich put it, 'war is a world, not an event', and by 1981, with operations in Afghanistan underway already for two years, in 'ordinary life' they do 'not know or talk about it much': it was a 'war and not a war'.[21]

In the post-Cold War era, Moscow has launched operations that are referred to in general terms as wars but not officially designated as such. The Chechen war that lasted from 1994 to 2009 was a brutal and expensive struggle. As discussed in Chapter 5, Moscow launched it intending it to be a quick, decisive operation to 'restore constitutional order'. And, as discussed in Chapter 6, senior Russian officials assert that the confrontation between Russia and Georgia in 2008 might have been given the soubriquet the 'five-day war', but it was not really a war since the campaign was complete in three days and characterised by only limited combat. Officially, it was designated as a *prinuzhdeniye k miru*, a 'coercion to peace'.

Three points emerge from this. First, these examples may have been or become wars in practice, but are not officially designated as wars because of the limited level of overall state effort. Moscow did not initiate a mobilisation, and in some cases did not even allocate more funding to the armed forces. Likewise, as we shall see in Chapter 6, the interventions in Crimea and eastern Ukraine in 2014 and the Syrian civil war in 2015 are usually referred to as '(special) operations'.

Second, they reinforce the point that officially, in Moscow's view, war is not synonymous with military operations. War may be defined by the use of armed force, but it is more than armed combat: it is a sociopolitical phenomenon that involves state-level effort, including mobilisation. Equally, Moscow can use specific terminology for political reasons to deploy armed force and not consider itself to be at war, whatever the human implications or even the intensity of the fighting. The political context for the operation, therefore, is essential.

During the modern era, Moscow has achieved only mixed success in both wars and operations. Russia lost the Crimean war and the Russo-Japanese wars in the late nineteenth and early twentieth centuries, though on neither occasion did the state fall, and on both occasions statecraft quickly reversed the military results. If Moscow lost the Cold War contest, World War I remains its only strategic defeat *in war* in recent times, with defeat on the battlefield, revolution at home and the collapse of the state.

But the Russian leadership has found the military instrument to be unreliable and expensive. While the armed forces delivered rapid, decisive success in Operation Danube, they were unable to do so on other occasions, such as in Chechnya. This is for a number of reasons, as we shall see, including the state placing the armed forces in an unenviable position at the start of an operation or war. The record is mixed: attempted lightning blows have worked for Moscow, delivering quick political success; more often, though, they have led to an expensive, protracted struggle.

This leads to the third point: the Russian military discussion about war strategy evinces concern about the escalatory nature of conflict. Armed conflict or 'local war' can escalate quickly into a regional or large-scale war. This has coloured the debate about strategies of lightning wars, which are 'strategic operations' rather than wars, and which define the initial intent of Operation Danube, Afghanistan, Chechnya and Georgia, but which are complex and difficult to wield. Their difficulty heightens the risk of both escalation and becoming entangled in a long war.

By Western strategic definitions, as well as on a human level, Moscow's renewed assault on Ukraine is very obviously a war. There is some useful distinction to be made, however, between Moscow's use of the terms 'SVO' and 'war' that can shed light on what potential escalation looks like.

How to win a war, part I: the Russian art of war

What, then, is success in war, and how to achieve it? The MoD defines 'victory in war' (*pobeda v voine*) as

> bringing defeat to the enemy and the achievement by one of the warring sides of political and military strategic aims of the war. The direct result of victory is the cessation of military activity on the conditions of the victor, formalised by an international legal document – an act of surrender, agreement or truce, or peace treaty. The main characteristics of victory in war are success in conducting military battle, the destruction of the armed forces of the enemy and occupation of the most important parts or all of its territory … signs of victory are the collapse of economic potential, disorganisation of structures and functioning of organs of political power, the collapse of opposing political conditions and the loss by the population and armed forces of the moral ability to continue to resist. The source of victory in war is the concentrated combination of all material and spiritual capabilities of the state and effectiveness of their use as expressed in military power.[22]

Equally, 'defeat' (*porazhenie*) is defined as the 'impact of various forces and means of military conflict on the enemy with the result that the enemy either completely or partially (temporarily) loses the ability to fight'. In the 'military sphere, it is the destruction of the enemy armed forces in war, battle, an operation or engagement'.

Moreover, *porazhenie* is additionally defined as 'destruction', the result of action on the target of different types of weapons to 'decrease [the enemy's] ability to function down to the level where it loses the ability to work as designed, whereby it loses its combat capability'. Thus, *porazhenie* is relevant at the strategic and at the operational levels, featuring in phrases such as *ognevoe porazhenie protivnika* (the fire destruction of the enemy), which characterise the Russian military's debate about war fighting.[23]

If the debate is wide-ranging, therefore, war is, in official doctrinal terms, the result of a policy clash that defines the context and the initiation of armed hostilities, and success and failure in war can be reflected on a spectrum tracing the highest stages of success (political victory, which permanently resolves the policy clash and rules out any war of revenge), through military victory, and then into the negative with military defeat and finally complete destruction.[24] This indicates that purely *military* victory or defeat is insufficient, and is subordinate to the bigger *policy goals*. If the policy clash is not resolved, then war is likely to erupt again at a future date. Conversely, even though the military might be defeated, statecraft might mitigate or even subvert that military defeat.

The question then becomes 'how to win a war?', which leads us to the Russian art of war (*voennoe iskusstvo*): a 'theoretical and practical activity that involves the ability to create knowledge … preparing for and conducting military operations … where developed creative thinking and high organisational and strong character qualities are necessary for the commander'. It is about interpreting the changing character of war, and the evolution of forms and methods of warfare, providing a scientific basis on which military education and war doctrine and strategy are built.[25]

To interpret Russian thinking about war accurately, then, it is helpful to frame three categories in the Russian art of war: war science (*voennaya nauka*), war doctrine (*voennaya doktrina*) and war strategy (*voennaya strategiya*). These are interlinked and reciprocally interactive, which may be clumsily depicted as war doctrine setting tasks for war science, which in turn informs doctrine, which in turn informs war strategy, the experience of which in turn feeds back into war science.

War science is the system of knowledge concerning the nature, essence and content of armed conflicts and the facilities and methods for conducting combat operations with armed forces and their comprehensive support. It derives its findings from the study of geography and historical experience in war, training exercises, the physical sciences, technology and industry, data science and military forecasting. The findings of war science provide the foundation for war doctrine.[26]

If the idea of war science can be readily understood by Western observers, the term 'doctrine' is potentially a false friend. In NATO terminology, 'military doctrine' is developed to win specific wars. In Russia, however, it is framed at a higher, more philosophical level, and defined as 'establishing the essence, aims and character of possible wars', and as encompassing 'economic, technical, legal and other essential aspects of military politics relevant to the state for the preparation of war'. It is the state's officially accepted system of scientifically founded views on the nature of modern wars and the use of the armed forces in them. It has two interactive aspects, sociopolitical, elaborated by the political leadership, and military-technical, elaborated by the General Staff. It is as much an official philosophy as a doctrine, and subject to change. This change is caused less by new equipment or new methods; rather it depends on changed *conditions*.

Given changes in conditions, the state may decide to update existing doctrine, or, if necessary, replace it.

While war science is considered universal and relevant to all states, war doctrine is specifically designed for the distinctive realities of a particular state. Indeed, war doctrine is considered to be unique for each state, because the political, social, economic, cultural and geographical realities of states are never precisely the same.[27]

If war science is the foundation for war doctrine, then war doctrine guides war strategy in the fulfilment of practical tasks, and war strategy is the framework for the development of operational art and tactics. Russian use of the terms 'strategy' and 'war strategy' are also potential false friends for Western observers. From the late eighteenth century, French, German and then British interpretations of strategy focused on military command and the use of military engagements to achieve political goals; strategy was understood to be closer to the art of command. By the twentieth century, however, for those such as Basil Liddell Hart, strategy was the link between policy and military execution, the art of distributing and applying military means to fulfil the ends of policy and attain a better peace. As war and society became ever more complex, strategy became akin to statecraft and evolved towards terms such as 'grand strategy', which include political, diplomatic, economic, psychological, cultural, moral and technical factors. Two points of consensus in an otherwise contentious debate are that strategy must link theory and practice – it is the art of creating power, an executive process of implementing plans – and that it is difficult.[28]

This offers intriguing prospects for examining Russian definitions of strategy and comparing them to Western approaches. On the one hand, for instance, the Russian military generally interprets strategy more closely in principle to early British and French interpretations of strategy as the art of command.[29] On the other, although Moscow explicitly asserts its attempts to generate long-term strategy, 'grand strategy' is usually viewed as a Western concept.

At the state level, though, the definition of mobilisation (*mobilizatsiya*) is relevant in this respect. It defines a 'complex of state measures for activating the resources, strength and capabilities of the state for the achievement of military-political aims' (a definition nearly synonymous with Western definitions of grand strategy). Mobilisation emphasises the practical measures for the transition to a war footing of the country's military, economic and state institutions at all levels (general mobilisation) or some part thereof (partial mobilisation).

Mobilisation has two pillars, military and economic. The latter has been a vital pillar of Moscow's thinking about war – and what distinguishes 'war' from 'operations' through the last century. It involves the reorganisation and conversion of the industrial and natural resource sectors of the economy as well as transport and communications ministries to the service of the armed forces and the state for the conduct of war. Mobilisation – ordered by the president – can be carried out openly or secretly, and has two stages, preparation (*podgotovka*) during which the economy is prepared for war, and readiness (*gotovnost*), when war is imminent and the leadership brings the armed forces to full strength and deploys them.[30]

At the military level, the Russian armed forces have long thought and acted in broader state terms, to include political, economic, psychological, moral and technical factors as part of strategy: war strategy serves state policy.[31] As we shall see, Gerasimov and other senior officers continue to point to the geostrategic and geo-economic context in which they are seeking to shape strategy.

The Russian MoD defines war strategy as a 'component of the art of war, its highest sphere, which includes the theory and practice of the war activity of the state'. The contents of war strategy are

> based on the results of the evaluation of the state and of directions of development of war-political conditions, and on scientifically based goals, principles, directions and tasks, and the objective needs and real capabilities of the functioning and development of the war organisation of the state. War strategy is closely connected with the politics of the state and is directly dependent on it. Politics defines the tasks for war strategy and strategy provides their fulfilment. In war strategy, the main principles of the war doctrine of the state are given concrete shape where applicable to the military sphere.[32]

Thus, the central theoretical and practical questions address a range of matters including the leadership of the armed forces in peace and wartime, preparation of the aims and tasks of the armed forces in war, and military activities at the strategic level. It includes the content and methods for preparing and conducting the war as a whole, and the different forms of strategic activity. War strategy seeks to position the armed forces, therefore, and prepare them for the transition to war, including extensive consideration of how the armed forces relate to the socio-economic condition of the state and the state's mobilisation capabilities.

War strategy includes foresight: attempting to estimate the likely character and duration of future war, and consequently the preparation of moral-psychological, technical and rear-echelon activities of the armed forces and the preparation of the economy, population and territory of the state for war. The official definition continues with the point that it should include an assessment of the strategic views of leading states and coalitions, and their capabilities for preparing, unleashing and conducting wars and activities on a strategic scale.[33]

Three points emerge from this. First, the definition is explicit – state strategy and war strategy may be interactive, but war strategy is subordinate. Politics should guide the use of war strategy: because war and military operations are only a component of a political conflict, war strategy is a tool of state policy. This does not necessarily mean that there is complete harmony between state leaders and the professional military, as we will see throughout this book.

Second, Russian war strategy tracks the changing character of war, sketching a trajectory from the wars of the past through the present into the future. In this sense, Russian thought is Clausewitzian: the underlying nature of war is considered to remain largely consistent, while its character evolves due to shifts in technology, science, economics and society. This introduces a tension between continuity and change, since no two wars can be exactly alike. Following in a long line of Russian soldier-thinkers from imperial times through the Soviet era to today, Gerasimov is explicit about this.[34] This means that we must be careful when reading that Russian definitions of war have changed substantially in the post-Cold War era, or even the last decade. Sometimes, Western observers of Russian theoretical and definitional debates have become lost in debated semantics about 'war', beginning to dance on the head of a pin while overlooking both the official doctrinal definitions and practical realities.

The Russian professional debate about war has long framed strategy's development in stages from classical antiquity to today.

In so doing, it recognises periods of development and of torpor. According to one prominent Russian observer, the development of Moscow's war strategy has 'not been straightforward, with periods of stagnation, departure from traditional ways, breaks and stumbles: often on the eve of and during major wars, there were large-scale strategic miscalculations'.[35] In this way, Russian war strategy often has a contrapuntal feel, echoing Western military strategy while being framed against it. Alongside Tsarist-era strategists such as Genrikh Leer and Nikolai Mikhnevich, those such as Henry Lloyd, Clausewitz, von Moltke and Liddell Hart are among persistent reference points in framing the evolution of strategy, even as Moscow's political and military leadership prepared for potential war with the West.[36] Gerasimov has emphasised that Russia 'must be ahead of the enemy in the development of war strategy' to retain the initiative – Russian war strategy is interactive, and often incorporates lessons from the strategies of other leading states.[37]

And while Western thinking points to four 'generations' of war, Russian military theorists outline six subtly different generations. These can be characterised as follows:

1. massed formations and edged weapons;
2. gunpowder weapons;
3. rifled, breech-loading weapons;
4. automatic weapons;
5. nuclear weapons;
6. information-facilitated precision strike weapons.[38]

There are nuances to this, as we shall see. But this is the essential foundation if we are to reflect meaningfully on Russia's way in war and how it has evolved, what remains broadly consistent and what changes, as well as for any discussion about a 'new generation' in war, and how Moscow plots its way beyond the current fighting in Ukraine and reforms its armed forces.

The third point to emerge is that Russian war strategy serves as a bridge between theory and practice. As such, it has to encompass two directions: the development of a system of knowledge about war (especially in terms of foresight and forecasting), and the completion of practical activities for the prevention, preparation and conduct of war.[39] As a practical art, it is a very important component of military leadership – the leader's ability to apply the art of war. The Russian state and military leadership recognise the great difficulties inherent in strategy, and that theory often outpaces reality in terms of technological development and the challenges posed by organising state capacity and human proclivities.

If Russian strategic culture includes both innovation and indolence, speed as well as laziness and unpunctuality, resource as well as waste and squander, as widely reflected in military histories and cultural works alike, then *effective* strategy is leadership achieving the state's set tasks regardless. In other words, 'strategy' is well described as creative and energetic leadership to 'implement measures to take control of deteriorating events' (*protivo-bardachnie meri*) to overcome these conditions and achieve the goal.

How to win a war, part II: victory-delivering, lightning war?

In these terms, Russian state and war strategy has a deep European heritage. It is heavily influenced by the intellectual legacy of Hans Delbrück and the tension he described between one-blow or lightning war 'strategies of destruction' (also sometimes translated as 'annihilation' or 'throwing down') and 'strategies of exhaustion' (or 'attrition') in a longer war. In this context, debates about strategy have focused on how wars break out and how to achieve and sustain the initiative. At the heart of this is a concern about the 'mobilisation gap' between Moscow and its adversaries: for much of the last two centuries, the Russian political and military leadership has acknowledged that its adversaries could concentrate, deploy and commit their resources to war more quickly than Russia, thus seizing the initiative.

In turn, this has generated debate that often focuses on the periodisation of war – the 'threatening', 'initial', 'continuing' and 'final' periods – and what activities characterise each period. Changes in thinking about war and war strategy often relate to which measures apply to which period and the moving of some measures from one period to another. A significant shift is seen to have occurred when mobilisation measures were advanced from the 'initial' (*nachalniy*) to the 'threatening' (*ugrozhaemiy*) period (also known as the 'period of direct threat' [*period neposredsvenniy ugrozy*]). This is one of the most intensively debated strategic questions in Russian thinking about war, especially since the Great Fatherland War: questions of war preparation and conduct, the feasibility of achieving a knockout blow, mobilisation and the mobilisation gap (the potential advantage of other states in organising and deploying their capabilities faster than Russia), and therefore the potential decisiveness of the threatening and initial periods in seizing the initiative in war define strategic debate, doctrine and strategy.

With this in mind, in common with other European nations, Moscow has sought to understand and harness surprise and its exploitation to achieve decisive political results. This has evolved into an extended debate about seeking the knockout blow, often framed as lightning war or 'blitzkrieg', to avoid costly attritional war. Although the term became commonplace due to the successes of the Wehrmacht in the early stages of World War II, more recently blitzkrieg has become a controversial term. Historians observe that there was no official German 'Blitzkrieg' doctrine and that the Wehrmacht did not use the term: it is a vaguely defined, poorly used buzzword, myth or legend.[40]

Nevertheless, the balance between strategies of 'exhaustion' and 'destruction', the latter reflected in a search for the knockout blow, remains useful for our purposes in exploring the Russian way in war. Indeed, the Euro-Atlantic revisionist turn on blitzkrieg has not arrived in Russia. Struck by the horrors of Operation Barbarossa in 1941, blitzkrieg remains seared into the Russian (military) psyche, and has permeated Soviet and Russian thinking about the changing character of war ever since.

The idea of blitzkrieg features across the post-Soviet Russian professional military debate, with senior figures in the Russian defence establishment now asserting that Russia faces a new, 'twenty-first-century blitzkrieg'. Actually, blitzkrieg merits official definition where hybrid warfare does not. This definition is revealing, and worth citing in full:

A way of waging an aggressive war, founded on the suddenness and swiftness of actions that ensure the enemy's defeat in the shortest possible time, before he is able to mobilise and deploy his armed forces. The holistic theory 'Lightning War' was developed by German militarists in the early twentieth century and laid the foundation for the German war strategy in the first and second world wars. The theory substantiated the possibility of avoiding a protracted war, eliminating the struggle on two fronts, through defeating enemies one by one and achieving victory despite having fewer economic resources and smaller military potential through the sudden and massive use of the latest weapons and military equipment in delivering the first powerful blow.[41]

In this way (lower case 'b') blitzkrieg – lightning war – exists as a feature of general war science, and is applied to different wars and operations. It is a feature of Moscow's own search for decisive victory, rendered in Russian as *pobedonosnaya, molnienosnaya voina* (victory-delivering, lightning war). As noted above, therefore, the question is not about whether blitzkrieg – or rather *molnienosnaya voina – exists*. It is whether it *works*.

Indeed, there is a strong tradition in Russian war science that argues that such a strategy is fraught with risk, and that, instead, a strategy of exhaustion (*strategiya izmora*) and mobilisation is more auspicious. As with the lightning war strategy, this view had its roots in the nineteenth century, and was advocated by some in the interwar years, but gained strength after the Great Fatherland War. Alongside *molnienosnaya voina*, *strategiya izmora* remains a central point of reference in both professional debate and official definitions of strategy.[42]

We will trace the evolution of the lightning war strategy as a concept that comes into fashion or falls into taboo, and the way the Russian military debates its evolution as a concept, their doubts about it and its acknowledged difficulties. Indeed, examination of the tension between *pobedonosnaya, molnienosnaya voina* and its counterpoint, *strategiya izmora*, opens up the central themes of Moscow's way in war, and is the focal point of the most significant questions underpinning Russian war strategy: the 'mobilisation gap' and the importance of surprise, initiative, and time and space management, and the balance between combat-ready forces and mass mobilisation and the offensive and defensive. The renewed Russian assault on Ukraine in 2022 again brings the question of blitzkrieg to the fore.

2

Winning revolutionary war

World War I is the prime example of Russian 'strategic defeat' (*polnyi razgrom*) in the modern era. A series of defeats on the battlefield from February through December 1917 coincided with the accelerating collapse of Tsarist authority, leading to the Emperor's abdication in March, followed by the shift of power first to the Provisional Government and then to the Soviets. With revolution spreading and mutiny in parts of the armed forces, the loss of Riga in September showed that Russia was no longer capable of substantial defence. In October the Bolsheviks, led by Vladimir Lenin, seized power in the second revolution of the year; the Russian army began to disintegrate and could offer only token resistance to Germany and Austro-Hungary in February 1918.

The Soviet Republic was forced to sue for peace, but the ensuing Treaty of Brest Litovsk in March 1918 was punitive. Soviet Russia defaulted on all its commitments to its allies and ceded authority over great swathes of territory, including conceding the independence of Ukraine and the Baltic states, and the gains that Russia had made in the Caucasus. The extent of these concessions, combined with the collapse of the government and the eruption of civil war, differentiate Russia's defeat in World War I from other wars of the modern era.

Noteworthy, too, is how this defeat is portrayed today by Russia's leadership. Putin has stated that 'victory was stolen from our country … by those who called for the defeat of their homeland and army, who sowed division inside Russia and sought only power for themselves, betraying the national interests'. This theme of Russia losing from within is one to which he has returned, stating that the result of the war was not due to battlefield defeat, but because Russia was 'torn apart from within' – 'Russia declared itself a loser. To whom did it lose? To the nation that ultimately lost the war.'[1] So this catastrophic defeat continues to feature in state thinking.

Even so, the Brest Litovsk treaty was annulled in November 1918 when the Allies defeated Germany and the Austro-Hungarian Empire. Indeed, the treaty had served Russia's new Bolshevik leadership by providing some temporary relief while they waged the civil war against the remnants of imperial power. This quick leap is depicted by some prominent Russian state-affiliated observers today by the juxtaposition of two chapters – one on the Brest treaty titled 'woe to the defeated', but the very next as 'from defeat to victory – in just one step', since it laid the foundations for the 'victorious return of the western regions'.[2]

The respite brought by the treaty was somewhat ambiguous, since war continued to rage from central and eastern Europe to the Pacific. But it did allow the Bolsheviks to refocus their power in what became a particularly brutal contest for power. In summer 1918 the Bolsheviks imposed so-called 'war communism' to weaken the remains of imperial power and to introduce communist authority. This entailed the nationalisation and central management of all industry, state control of trade, the requisition of agricultural supplies and the rationing of food and martial control of the transport infrastructure.[3]

By then the Bolsheviks had established two other arms of power. First, in December 1917, the Bolsheviks established the All-Russian Extraordinary Committee (ChK, known as the Cheka) – the secret police – and waged a relentless campaign of suppression against internal opposition, including arrests and executions under Lenin's 'Socialist Fatherland in Danger' proclamation of February 1918. Over the next two years, the ChK became a substantial armed force in its own right, numbering some 200,000 by 1921, with arbitrary powers of arrest and execution, and it reflected what can be seen as a lasting division of 'war cultures' in Russian strategic culture between the armed forces and the internal security services.

The assassination of Moisei Uritsky and the attempted assassination of Lenin in August 1918 accelerated this campaign to what became known as the 'Red Terror', a 'wholescale and indiscriminate' subjugation of opponents of the revolution, real and perceived. The Bolsheviks were an isolated and minority-based regime, surrounded by enemies: the scale of the 'unbridled and disproportionate' brutality meted out by the ChK was because of the violent class nature of the war, and also a 'desperate reaction' against a ring of enemies, domestic and international.[4]

The Bolsheviks also formed the Workers' and Peasants' Red Army (Red Army) in January 1918 to wage the civil war, a complex and multifaceted series of campaigns against 'White' imperial armies, who were supported by interventions by the British, French, US, Japanese and Czechoslovaks, and then against national movements. By early 1920 the Red Army, led by Lev Trotsky, had largely defeated the Whites and their allies, and by 1921 the Red Army had defeated independence movements in the Caucasus and Ukraine. While some sporadic resistance continued into the late 1920s, the civil war ended in 1922.[5]

But the Red Army was not uniformly victorious. The Royal Navy's activity in the Baltic Sea had demonstrated Leningrad's exposure to external pressure. And in 1919 Polish and Soviet forces had skirmished over borderlands in Ukraine and Belarussia and Lithuania. In April 1920 Poland invaded Ukraine and captured Kiev. The Soviets, who saw Poland as a bridge to Germany to instigate revolution in Europe, launched a two-pronged counter-attack, the 'western' front through Belorussia and the 'south-western' front through Ukraine. Both offensives were initially successful, quickly retaking Kiev, before Polish forces counter-attacked in August in the battle of Warsaw, achieving the 'Miracle of the Vistula', splitting the Soviet fronts and driving the Red Army back into Belorussia.

Moscow sued for peace, and a ceasefire was agreed in October. The Peace of Riga followed in March 1921, dividing the disputed territories between Poland and Soviet Russia, though neither side paid war compensation, and Soviet diplomacy kept Ukrainian representatives out of the negotiations. The result, therefore, was more ambiguous than the battlefield results implied. Although the Red Army had been forced to retreat and Moscow had ceded some 200 kilometres of territory and failed to export revolution to Europe, Warsaw had also failed in its main war aims of seizing territory in Ukraine.

Eight years of war, revolution and war communism had left Soviet Moscow internationally isolated and the Bolsheviks in charge of a ravaged and exhausted country. Some 16 million people had died, and millions more had emigrated. Socio-economic conditions were close to collapse. Inflation was increasing, imports had ceased. Industrial production, debilitated by the breakdown of the transport system and a lack of supplies, was 20 per cent of 1913 levels; grain yields were half of pre-World War I levels. In 1921 severe drought exacerbated the situation, and widespread famine and disease ensued through into 1922.

Despite their victory in the civil war and the Red Terror, the power of the Bolsheviks remained limited. They anticipated international hostility, but popular indifference and opposition to their rule was widespread. Rebellions in the Tambov region and in part of the Red Navy at Kronstadt in 1921 – both forcefully crushed, the latter at considerable cost – instilled a lasting insecurity and opened the way to the use of force against fellow revolutionaries. Even as Lenin demobilised the Red Army and eased war communism, introducing the New Economic Policy in its stead, the leadership deemed that further war was inevitable. A war mentality shaped thinking regarding all socio-economic questions; as the Bolsheviks worked towards a dictatorship of the proletariat, militarised rhetoric characterised policy campaigns.

This revolutionary period offers considerable insight into the foundations of Moscow's war strategy. It reflects the blend of deeper, long-running continuity through persistent reform and change. It also reflects the consistent interaction with Euro-Atlantic strategic traditions. And finally, this revolutionary period was a fertile one for Moscow's thinking about war: a rich debate evolved over core strategic questions of doctrine and relations between politics, the state and the armed forces, and the roles and benefits of the offensive and defensive and, more broadly, strategies of destruction and exhaustion that provided reference points for the next one hundred years. They are still being cited today.

Soviet Moscow's view of war as armed struggle

The Bolsheviks deemed war to be an inevitable consequence of their seizure of power, one for which they had therefore to prepare. Although they intended that the revolution should initiate a wholly new state and a new era, there was a strong sense of continuity in thinking about strategy and war. This reflected a recognition that it was impossible summarily to revise all questions of war science from a void, in isolation from historical conditions. The Bolsheviks did not seek immediately to 'overthrow' all the old principles and create 'special proletarian strategy and tactics'.[6]

This was, in a sense, practical. While some commanders such as Mikhail Frunze and Mikhail Tukhachevsky had emerged during the revolution and civil war, a large percentage of the Red Army's senior officers were graduates of the Imperial Staff Academy, and had served as regular officers before joining, or being mobilised by, the Red Army. These imperial officers – known as war specialists (*voenspetsy*) – made a decisive contribution both to the Red Army's success in the civil war and to re-establishing military education (the Academy of the General Staff was created in December 1918). Together, these officers, including those such as Alexander Svechin, shaped the theoretical debates about future war that characterised the 1920s and 1930s, drawing on the Tsarist and European war theory inheritance and experience to shape a strategic philosophy. Indeed, not only did imperial Field Regulations remain in force until 1929, but even the first Soviet Field Regulations of 1929 were largely drafted by imperial officers. In 1929 the Soviet political administration investigated the extent of Tsarist influence in the military in terms of numbers of prominent officers: 198 of the 243 who were writing about military affairs were former imperial officers; of those writing about strategy and tactics, only 32 per cent were Communist Party members.[7]

Born in conditions of war, war communism and revolution, and on the basis of Marxist ideology, the Soviet leadership defined war as a social phenomenon in pursuit of political aims. War was the 'more or less lengthy condition of sharp conflict' between two or more societies or large parts of those societies, a conflict that was decided through the help of 'organised enforcement, usually the use of weapons'. The state should be organised for 'lengthy and planned' enforcement of its intent.[8] Two points emerge from this. The first was the strong and explicit reference to Clausewitz: war was the continuation of politics by other means, a tool of policy. This was shaped by Marxism, to be sure, which meant that war was conditioned by the class struggle: the historical and historico-economic conditions that gave rise to it, and which classes staged and directed it. War would be uncompromising and decisive until socialism was victorious worldwide.[9]

Initially, the Bolshevik intention to achieve a socialist system of society by eliminating the division of humankind into classes meant the export of socialism through revolutionary wars, waged by revolutionary classes. After the setback against Poland in 1920, this evolved, however, into an abiding concern with an imperialist attack, with some, such as Lev Trotsky, advocating the defence rather than the further exportation of socialism.[10] Nonetheless, other senior figures continued to assert that in certain conditions, Moscow could go on the 'offensive beyond the borders of our land'.[11] This represented a balance in Moscow's thinking between two likely types of war – an imperialist attack, and a successful socialist revolution in a major European nation that summoned the USSR's assistance. Through the 1920s and into the mid-1930s, the balance between these two types leaned heavily towards the former; only in the latter half of the 1930s would the USSR provide assistance abroad to the Spanish republicans, and by then the general emphasis was on war with Germany or Japan.

The second point is that through the 1920s, there was a broad consensus in Moscow that a war would require a prolonged and substantial commitment. In this, the Soviet emphasis on war not only as armed struggle, but as the concern of the whole state, was clear. As Tukhachevsky wrote, war in the current era ceased being the concern of one soldier-strategist, and was now in the hands of the government. War plans required the preparation of the armed forces and the strengthening of economic and political facets of the state, and depended ever more on heavy industry and technological development.[12]

This provided the basis for the definition of the art of war and war doctrine. The art of war was the art of organising the armed forces, the preparation for and then the conduct of war activities. Whereas Tukhachevsky emphasised state power in industry and technology, Svechin, who provided the official definition of the art of war, framed it in historical terms, highlighting the study of the evolution of wars to trace the dynamics of the shift from one form of armed force and method of waging war to another. This emphasised a sense of continuity – even in the late 1920s, the sources of thinking about the art of war, war science and doctrine were European and imperial strategists, such as Clausewitz and Tsarist generals Genrikh Leer and Andrei Zaionchkovsky. Indeed, in defining the art of war, Svechin paid particular attention to Napoleon, von Moltke the elder and Hans Delbrück.[13]

The official definition of war doctrine drew on Frunze's thinking, as the 'army's acceptance' of a given state's interpretation of the character of the construction of the armed forces, methods of combat preparation of troops, and their guidance on the basis of the state's view of the character of the combat tasks which lay before it and the means for their resolution. This was shaped by the 'concrete conditions' each state faced, which meant that war doctrine was specific to states, framed by the level of development of productive strength of that state.[14]

A 'unified war doctrine' or the 'integral commander'?

As the official definition acknowledged, in the USSR war doctrine was the subject of 'heated debate' in the early 1920s, with 'many mistakes', even 'doctrinaire nuances'.[15] The primary focus of this heated debate was over the need for a 'unified war doctrine' (*edinaya voennaya doktrina*). The question of the desirability of a unified war doctrine was in fact long-running: Tsarist officers had debated this prior to World War I. Frunze revived and advocated it in the early 1920s. A professional revolutionary, Frunze had been arrested and exiled by the Tsarist authorities before World War I, before rising to prominence in the revolutionary movement in 1917 and joining the Red Army in 1918. A successful commander in the civil war, he defeated White armies led by Admiral Kolchak and General Wrangel, and in 1920 became the authorised representative of the Revolutionary Military Council of the Republic of Ukraine and commander of the troops of the Ukrainian military district.

From 1922 Frunze rose to some of the most senior positions of political and military authority in the USSR, dominating the discussion alongside Kliment Voroshilov, one of the most prominent Bolsheviks and a close ally of Stalin. By 1925 Frunze was chairman of the USSR's Revolutionary War Council, People's Commissar for War and Naval Affairs, head of the Red Army's War Academy and a member of the Council of Labour and Defence. His role was to oversee the planning and practical organisation of the Red Army; in 1924 Tukhachevsky had been appointed his deputy, overseeing the theoretical development of strategy. In these roles, Frunze played a definitive role in shaping Moscow's thinking about war and implementing reform of the armed forces. Although he died from complications during what should have been routine surgery in 1925, he is still credited with creating the basis for a new Soviet approach to war, and the development of Soviet doctrine. His works were regularly republished throughout the Soviet era; indeed, alongside Lenin, his work was perhaps the most often and widely cited as an authority on war until the 1980s.[16]

Frunze argued that a unified war doctrine was necessary because modern wars were different to those of the past. Whereas in the past, wars had touched only a small part of a nation's society and involved detachments of regular forces, they now involved the whole nation: millions fought, and war affected all aspects of society. In such circumstances, he argued, the most important requirement was for the integrity and strict coordination of the state's preparation and conduct of war. The complexity of managing such a system went beyond the capacity of individual military leaders, and must represent the state as a whole.

The state should define the nature of the overall situation and war policy, designating its intent and developing a plan of action for the state as a whole. In so doing, the state decides the nature of prospective wars, and the overall approach to them, whether passive defence or active missions. This defines the organisational development of the armed forces, force structure and training. Such a unified war doctrine would be based on two pillars – the political and the military-technical. Within this, the military must assume an organisational form responding most fully to those tasks set by the state.[17]

Dissent came from many quarters. Military specialists disagreed, considering this to represent a tactical outlook on war. Others argued that there could be no such single doctrine, either in the USSR or elsewhere; the search for such a unified war doctrine was akin to searching for the Golden Fleece, a 'dream about celestial matters', rather than paying attention to 'fundamental principles'. While some agreed on the need for unity, that unity should be in formal, material preparation and organisation.[18]

The most substantial and sustained critique, however, came from Trotsky, then People's Commissar for Military and Naval Affairs. Trotsky deemed such a unified war doctrine – which he referred to as the 'Ukrainian theses' – to be 'theoretically incorrect and practically unfruitful'. Furthermore, such a doctrine was unnecessary, since the Party had already established a Marxist world view, and there was no need for another one from the military. Indeed, the abstractions of such a doctrine would only undermine Marxist propaganda by confusing soldiers about the possible kinds of wars to be fought, and was of secondary importance behind the need to address the practicalities of service. All told, Trotsky argued, the idea of a unified war doctrine was 'ridiculous' and smacked of dogmatism.[19] It would not be until after Frunze took over as People's Commissar for Military and Naval Affairs in 1925 that his view of the need for such a unified doctrine began to prevail, and, as we have seen above, by 1928 it was enshrined in official definitions as 'war doctrine'.

Emerging from this debate, however, was a broader acknowledgement of the need for the unity of state effort in war: since war tests all the economic and societal organisational forces of a state, the state must be able to act as a coherent whole in both preparing and conducting war. Tukhachevsky, among others, had initially rejected a political role in war strategy as an 'intrusion' on the commander-in-chief's complete authority when campaigning. But he accepted the need for harmony between state policy and war strategy – which was best achieved when exercised by one actor, which in the USSR's case should be the Council of Defence.[20] Tukhachevsky repeatedly returned to this theme, (slightly) shifting his initial explicit opposition to political interference. In the late 1920s he observed that 'politics directs war'. By 'creating the necessary economic, political and social resources ... politics resolves in the last resort the questions of organising the armed forces', and 'the conduct of the operation is entrusted to strategy, to the command of the armed forces'. He asserted that while war was a continuation of 'politics, at the same time ... the results achieved during the course of military operations can greatly influence the scale and forms of war'.[21] He subsequently offered the idea of a 'polemical strategy'. This would lay the foundation for a new doctrine and serve to integrate state policy and war strategy: rather than conduct war with only military force, his doctrine would offer a 'comprehensive and superior strategy'. This failed to convince supporters; critics observed that it was less an attempt to subordinate strategy to state policy than to adjust policy to strategy.[22]

Another version was offered by Svechin. One of the most prominent military specialists, Svechin had fought (and commanded) in the Russo-Japanese war and World War I, before joining the Red Army in the spring of 1918. One of the most significant figures of early Soviet thinking about strategy and war, he wrote the book *Strategiya* which shaped thinking at the time, and continues to influence Russian thinking today – indeed, the most recently published editions are entitled *Strategiya – the main work of Russia's Clausewitz* and are described as 'war wisdom' (*voennaya mudrost*).[23]

In *Strategiya*, Svechin framed the overall architecture of state activity in preparing for and waging war, setting out the hierarchy of state policy and state conditions in which military affairs take place. He placed primary emphasis on state policy in shaping the socio-economic conditions, emphasising that 'war is waged by the supreme authorities of the state, because the decisions which must be made by the leaders of a war are too important and critical to be entrusted to any one agent of executive authority'. The (military) commander-in-chief is not supreme, Svechin continued, because he does not 'direct foreign and domestic policy or the entire rear of the active armies, because he does not have all power over the entire state'. A strategist is only 'part of the leadership of a war, and sometimes decisions are made without his knowledge and sometimes against his will'. Real command meant the integrated leadership of the political, economic and military fronts, embodied by the highest political competence in state affairs, the holder of supreme power. This 'integral commander' (*integralnyi polkovodets*) is not an individual, but a collective.[24]

This said, Svechin acknowledged that experience indicated that there is no 'ideal' form of organisation of political leadership of a war, and that it is difficult to establish a politically and militarily satisfactory command organisation – bearable conditions for cooperation should suffice. Furthermore, he acknowledged the interactive relationship between state policy and strategy: responsible politicians, he argued, must be familiar with war strategy, and their decisions consonant with it. Strategists might criticise mistaken policies – 'mistaken policies bear the same pitiful fruit in war as in any other field' – but they could not escape the point that strategy itself is a projection of policy. War is a component of political conflict, so strategy, he continued, 'cannot exist in a vacuum without politics and is condemned to pay for all the sins of politics'.[25]

There is much more to be said about these substantive debates about doctrine and versions of the 'integral commander'. Other senior figures, such as Boris Shaposhnikov, who went on to become Chief of the General Staff, made noteworthy contributions to thinking about the relationship between policy and strategy.[26] But Moscow's view of war was strategic, a whole-of-state activity: unity and coordination between state policy and war strategy, and between the body politic, economic capacity and the armed forces, were considered essential.

Visions of future war

As the political and military leadership hammered out doctrine and the relationship between state policy and war strategy, they also debated visions of future war. As noted above, Moscow saw war as inevitable, and that it would be a decisive clash between imperialist and socialist systems. The military leadership spent considerable effort throughout the 1920s and 1930s reflecting on the likely shape of such a war as international conditions evolved. Two points of broad consensus emerged during the 1920s. The first was that any war would be protracted. The second was that it would likely be against a coalition of (Western) capitalist powers.[27] These scenarios took substantive shape in the second half of the 1920s, and especially from 1929 with the Great Depression across the capitalist states. It took more explicit form in the early 1930s, when Japan seized Manchuria and then when Adolf Hitler took power in Germany in 1933.

From the extensive discussion of a future war throughout the 1920s and into the 1930s, three versions stand out. First, Tukhachevsky oversaw a study that coincided with the 1927 war scare. This emerged in 1926 with the fall of the Polish government and rumours of British support for the return to power of Josef Pilsudski, especially after the May coup. This would shift the balance of power in Europe towards Great Britain, and represent a potential challenge to Soviet borders. By mid-1927 senior Soviet officials were asserting that Polish fascism, backed by imperialist powers, was challenging Moscow's authority in Ukraine. In May and June 1927 the British government had broken off diplomatic relations with Moscow, and the Soviet ambassador to Warsaw had been assassinated; in July Stalin accused the British government of preparing to wage war against the USSR.[28] This posed a potentially multifaceted challenge to Moscow: London could finance Warsaw, posing a continental threat, or it could use its naval power to launch a sea-based attack on Russian interests, blockading the economy or even conducting amphibious landings as it had during the civil war.

The 'reality' of the war scare has since generated much debate. Some argue that it was merely a figment of Moscow's imagination, others that it reflected an echo of the psychological trauma of 1919–20 with the Allied intervention in the civil war and war against Poland, and others still that while the record shows no intent on the part of the Western powers to attack Russia at the time, Soviet leaders were genuinely concerned about the potential for an attack. Moreover, as we shall see, it served to shift internal policy.[29]

Tukhachevsky wrote extensively on various themes of modern war and strategy, how the character of war changed according to socio-economic development and how strategy should accordingly evolve.[30] But his *Budushchaya voina* (Future War) study was perhaps his most substantive collection, and incorporated the work of other senior officers. It took nearly two years to complete, and was produced in over 700 pages in limited distribution, most copies of which were subsequently destroyed. Tukhachevsky underlined the significance of political and economic factors in planning for future war, and assessed the combat and economic potential of Western states, and possible scenarios. In so doing, he set out a concrete vision of future war on which to modernise the Red Army.

The study framed the great size of armed forces and the material demands that would be made by war, and shaped two main scenarios. The first was an attack on the USSR's western borders by neighbouring states, with Great Britain and France providing technological and financial support; the other was an attack by neighbouring states, likewise supported, on the USSR's western, southern and eastern borders. To wage such wars against coalitions, he argued, the USSR must fight with all the strategic, organisational and mobilisational consequences, since the struggle would be long, large in scale and one of exhaustion.[31]

A second study came shortly after. Written by Svechin, it offers considerable insight into Moscow's thinking about future war, and is also valuable in considering current circumstances. Svechin's assessment was the result of a deep analysis of past experience, economics and geography. Like others, Svechin considered that future war would likely be protracted and painfully attritional: it would test the socio-economic fabric of the nation. In 1930 he drafted a note to Voroshilov outlining his views of what such a war would look like. Like Tukhachevsky, Svechin deemed a future war against a coalition to be most likely: the coalition would seek the destruction of the Soviet state, creating in its stead an agglomeration of states that would represent a disguised colony. For Svechin, this coalition would be led by Great Britain and France, while the US, refraining from direct participation, would provide financial and material support and Germany would offer direct logistical assistance. The coalition would mobilise its financial resources and seek to assert the freedom of sea communications and deliver the attack to the south, especially the Donetsk basin, North Caucasus, using the national questions in Ukraine and Transcaucasus to strike at Soviet unity.

For Svechin, this posed a serious challenge, because the USSR would not within the following fifteen years be able to match the coalition's qualitative or quantitative superiority: the Red Army must accept that the coalition would enjoy technological superiority. Moreover, he used the scenario to argue that the Red Army paid too little attention to strategic defence, and to the dialectical relationship between the offensive and the defensive.[32]

A third reflection on future war – again offered by Tukhachevsky – came in 1935, as Soviet concerns about German power under Hitler grew. Rather than a scenario, perhaps, it was a clear identification of a looming challenge. He highlighted Hitler's pronounced anti-Soviet attitude, as well as his demands that the USSR weaken its western borders and that Paris refuse to cooperate with Moscow. Tukhachevsky reflected at length on German mobilisation capacity, the growth of military aviation and German views on modern warfare, underlining that the goal of Berlin's strategy would be to 'achieve a solution with mobile, high-quality forces capable of conducting operations before the mass was in motion'. Tukhachevsky quoted senior German figures to emphasise that 'rapid mobilisation, as well as the rapid advance of troops, will play an exceptional role', with the intent to use fast-moving troops and aircraft to 'disrupt the enemy's mobilisation'. Tukhachevsky was explicit: this pointed to the need, when preparing for war, to be 'guided by other scales in time and space than those that military history has taught us'.[33]

This version of future war was depicted in the propagandistic 1938 docu-film *Esli zavta voina* (If Tomorrow There is War). The film showed assorted (German-speaking, European) fascist forces launching a sustained, surprise attack on the USSR. Having weathered the initial assaults, the Soviet authorities – government, Party and Stalin – declare war, and launch a massive counter-offensive using large quantities of modern, specialised equipment. Long-range aviation strikes enemy airfields and transport infrastructure, and, after sustained artillery barrage and deception measures, tanks launch long-distance attacks, seeking decisive engagements, with airborne assault forces being used to prevent the enemy from using reserves. In its finale, the film shows the proletariat in enemy towns and industrial centres rising up to overthrow the fascist authorities.[34]

Strategies for waging future war: destruction or exhaustion?

This debate about future war was rooted in interaction with Euro-Atlantic thinking about strategy and war, characterised by critical reflection on the lessons of World War I and the emergent role of technology and its influence on warfare. While the Soviets drew on Marx, Engels and Lenin, Clausewitz remained at the heart of the debate.[35] Many of the debates directly echoed European questions, whether about the role of cavalry, motorisation or mechanisation, or about the feasibility of achieving success with a 'lightning blow', designed as a war of short duration to defeat an enemy in one massive attack.[36] Nor was this purely a theoretical debate: there was direct military-to-military cooperation with the Reichswehr,[37] and Moscow bought Western tank designs.

This interaction had a number of threads. In part, the debate sought to consider war at the strategic and operational levels: what the war had shown about the capacities of an industrialised nation at war, and how to avoid attrition and restore movement and decision on the battlefield. But in equal measure, it was about interpreting the strategies of likely enemies in that war – Great Britain in the late 1920s, Germany from the mid-1930s onwards – and also a means of achieving leverage in internal politics, as adversaries were smeared with advocating foreign or counter-revolutionary traditions. This all reflected a blend of admiration for, but disagreement with, Western thinkers. The works of J. F. C. Fuller, Liddell Hart, Gifford Martel, Charles de Gaulle, Giulio Douhet and von Moltke the elder were published in Russian and much discussed. Recognising the value of the mechanisation aspects of these works, Soviet officers were also critical. Vladimir Triandafillov, for instance, critiqued foreign (and Soviet) military writers who advocated small, professional, motorised armies. 'It is barely possible to take seriously ... naïve' assertions that such forces could conquer modern states: such an army, having invaded deep into an enemy country, would risk isolation if it were not immediately supported by a stronger army.[38]

Tukhachevsky acknowledged that Fuller (and Liddell Hart) had attempted to weave together the experience of the past with an understanding of the development of technology to offer 'progressive thoughts' on future war, and that in his work there are 'many interesting thoughts on the actions of tanks'. Nevertheless, he stated that Fuller's reasoning was 'endlessly confused', and that he hated and feared the USSR, before criticising his views on small but mobile armies in big wars – such an army would be 'simply crushed', Tukhachevsky stated.[39]

Others sought to build on the legacy of Clausewitz, von Moltke and Hans Delbrück. Svechin, for instance, elaborated on his discussion of the connection between state policy and war strategy in terms of the balance between a strategy of destruction and a strategy of exhaustion. In so doing, he asserted that these two approaches flowed directly from the dynamics of state politics and conflict – again emphasising that state policy and strategy must be 'strictly coordinated'. In this way, he argued that it was the task of state policy to define a future war as not only a 'strategy' of destruction or exhaustion, but a 'war' of destruction or exhaustion. Only on this basis could the state then elaborate the appropriate strategy to achieve the required goal; this choice of strategy was of great importance for guiding the activity of the armed forces, but even more so for guiding political conduct and economic preparation. A war of destruction, he argued, could be conducted primarily by means of supplies stockpiled in peacetime. Equally, a large state could base a war of exhaustion exclusively on the work of its industry during wartime.

Furthermore, he suggested that the political, economic and geographical context for the war was essential in determining the choice of approach. The dissimilarity of two opponents – which he illustrated with reference to Great Britain and Russia as maritime and continental powers respectively – meant waging a war of exhaustion. Equally, if great distance was involved, or the two parties were equally balanced in military capability, a war of destruction would not be possible: a war of destruction required clear superiority in weapons and personnel, something that the USSR's then socio-economic situation did not permit.[40]

This led to a prolonged and heated debate, during which Tukhachevsky was particularly critical of Svechin's approach not only for 'inconsistency', 'passivism' and 'simplification', but for preaching 'strategic decadence' and 'reducing the role of revolutionary wars to strategic thrusts'.[41] For his part, Tukhachevsky thought that industrialisation and innovative force concepts could remedy the USSR's then quantitative and qualitative shortfall, and argued for the more offensive approach of a war of destruction. Victory, he argued, could be achieved through a surprise offensive to destroy the first echelon of enemy forces, disrupt mobilisation and destroy vital power centres through an initial blow. Mechanisation and technological development, he argued, would provide the means for such an attack.

Tukhachevsky's attack on Svechin would have consequences not only for Svechin personally, but for the wider debate among the armed forces, as discussed below. In terms of policy, however, Tukhachevsky won the debate, and Soviet forces began to move away from an attritional approach towards one prepared for destruction through the early 1930s. But this debate set the stage for extended reflection on two important issues. The first related to the transition to war and a war's first or initial period. This encompassed the sequence of events regarding the declaration of war, mobilisation, deployment of forces and major military operations. In the mid-1920s Svechin wrote of the 'pre-mobilisation period', which took place prior to the war; and of mobilisation as a prolonged, continuous process rather than a single event. Even the mobilisation of the Red Army at the beginning of the war could only be considered the first echelon of a mobilisation, he argued. 'In future', he continued, 'we should anticipate an even greater level of activity in the pre-mobilisation period', including 'extensive economic measures'.[42] Again, this reflection on pre-mobilisation and the transition to war would continue throughout the 1930s, most notably in Georgi Isserson's 1940 book *Novye formy borby* (New Forms of Struggle).[43]

The second issue was the development of a series of sophisticated theories that sought to blend Marxist ideology with technological development and industrialisation. The theory of 'deep battle' (*glubokiy boi*) – using motorised and mechanised forces to penetrate the enemy's tactical defences – emerged in the late 1920s, and was followed in the early 1930s by 'deep operations' (*glubokie operatsii*). This latter envisaged high-speed offensives by massed tanks with air, air assault and artillery support to penetrate the enemy's tactical defences. The first blow would neutralise defences to the maximum depth possible, to facilitate a rapid expansion into the enemy's operational depth, disrupting mobilisation and preventing the enemy from reorganising their defences. Surprise, speed, firepower and constant pressure through the use of reserves to achieve decisive superiority at the critical time and place meant that the Red Army would be able to retain the strategic initiative, encircling enemy forces and destroying them.

The development of deep battle and deep operations should be seen in the light of Euro-Atlantic debates about strategy and war – Fuller and Liddell Hart, among others, were often referenced – and in the context of a possible looming war with the West. This represented the eventual success of Tukhachevsky and those who advocated offensive operations to seek decisive victory, and was reflected in the Field Regulations of 1936. Describing those Field Regulations, Tukhachevsky repeatedly used the term 'lightning' to describe the preparation and conduct of an offensive blow that would shock weakened capitalist states, a decisive blow that would deliver total victory.[44]

But if those such as Voroshilov believed that mechanisation and technology meant that war could be won with little bloodshed, Tukhachevsky was explicit about the likely costs and potential dangers. He stated in early 1937 that operations would be 'inestimably more intensive and severe than in the First World War', and that offensive operations in the 'initial period of war can last for weeks'. Moreover,

> as for the blitzkrieg that is so propagandised by the Germans, this is directed towards an enemy who doesn't want to and won't fight it out. If the Germans meet an opponent who stands up and fights and takes the offensive himself … the struggle would be bitter and protracted; by its very nature it would induce great fluctuations in the front on this or that side and in great depth. In the final resort, all would depend on who had the greater moral fibre and who at the close of the operations disposed of operational reserves in depth.[45]

State mobilisation and the 'new' Red Army

The leap from the Field Regulations of 1929, which recognised technological inferiority, slow mobilisation and the large scale of operations – and thus a need for attrition – to the Field Regulations of 1936 was not just the result of theoretical development. It happened because of a substantial shift in the wider state context, one which did much to accelerate the capacity for war, but also set in motion processes that would disaggregate Moscow's strategy.

We saw above how the war scare of 1927 drove thinking about what future war would look like. In practical terms, though, it served to underpin a complete transformation in Soviet life which would provide the foundations for the emergence of a new Red Army by the mid-1930s. This began with the first Five-Year Plan and collectivisation in 1928, which simultaneously reflected concern about enemies abroad and at home, and constituted an attempt to launch a decisive effort to build communism.

The first Five-Year Plan sought economic independence and to improve society's technological base. In that sense, it was not synonymous with defence or rearmament, but given that its goals included industrial self-sufficiency and a heavy industrial base, it provided the conditions for the Red Army to begin to modernise alongside other sectors. And by the early 1930s the drive to rearm had become explicit. The implementation of the Five-Year Plan therefore characterised Moscow's thinking about strategy and war and its 'strategic culture'. It reflected the increasing militarisation of the USSR, with the economy being guided towards serving the build-up of the security services and armed forces. Indeed, in the 1930s, in terms of economic mobilisation planning, the USSR embarked upon the most ambitious and comprehensive prior preparation of its economy for war ever conducted: an economy of 'total preparation for war'. According to one Russian specialist, Stalin created 'a unique system for the preparation of the economy to mobilise for war'. This system proved so powerful that its influence was felt even in post-Soviet Russia, seventy years later.[46] Indeed, it reflected the militarisation not just of the economy, but of politics and society also, effectively shaping a Soviet mobilisation capacity. This had ramifications across society. On the one hand, there was an active increase in the role of paramilitary and civil volunteer organisations to assist in the process of collectivisation and industrialisation. Military imagery and the rhetoric of 'fronts' accompanied this drive to impel socio-economic change. On the other, 1928 was the year in which Soviet tolerance for non-Marxists and old bourgeois specialists expired. From 1928, and especially from 1931, the Communist Party exerted full control over intellectual life: *partiinost*, the Party line, or the truth as established by the Party, demanded the militarisation of all disciplines. It reflected, effectively, a permanent mobilisation mode.

In this context, the 'historical front' became subordinated to party politics, and non-Marxist historians were subjected to a sustained repressive campaign of harassment and arrests, one that accelerated from 1931; even the Marxist historian Mikhail Pokrovsky fell from grace, his students repressed. Echoing other intellectual and cultural fields such as literature, Soviet history in many ways suffered an (involuntary?) 'inability to create' and fell into 'silence'.[47] Stalin's 1938 book the *History of the Communist Party of the Soviet Union (Bolsheviks): Short Course* became the only official guide to history.

Science and industry followed a similar path. Throughout the 1920s physics and engineering flourished, in part through drawing on Western ideas: 'Fordizm' and 'Taylorizm' became standard terms in Soviet industrial circles as they sought improved labour productivity. In 1928, however, the campaign to replace bourgeois specialists with Marxist proletarians began, combined with a growing role for the state in the conduct of science. This meant that although the state provided extensive material support for research and development, there was also a strong ideological influence. In 1928 the Shakhty case was the first show trial since 1922, with 53 engineers arrested and charged with economic sabotage. Forty-five were found guilty and either imprisoned or executed. This was followed by the Industrial Party trial, in which scientists and economists were accused of attempting to wreck Soviet industry.[48] Research was stifled, pseudoscience flourished; as with historians and novelists, the lives of whole communities of scientists and engineers were ruined by repression.

This intellectual context is significant because it formed essential conditions for the armed forces. The armed forces suffered in much the same way as historians and scientists: the move from bourgeois specialist to Red specialist was felt there as well. Even in the mid-1920s, Svechin lamented the state of Soviet history of war: its current state, he argued, 'does not satisfy the most modest desires of strategy' and was 'scientifically prostrate'.[49] Given the ideological framework of *partiinost*, this did not – *could* not – subsequently improve. Although the 1920s were a time in which Soviet thinking about strategy and war flourished, it too began to chill in the late 1920s: Tukhachevsky's political smearing of Svechin was a good example. Many thinkers in the armed forces, too, were affected by *partiinost*; some three thousand commanders, mainly former Tsarist officers, were arrested in the late 1920s and early 1930s.

The combination of sociopolitical mobilisation and a huge, crash industrialisation effort provided the Red Army with the numbers and materials it needed. The Red Army doubled in size from 1929 to 1937, and established first mechanised brigades and then mechanised corps through the early 1930s. This sense of an industrialised, mobilised Soviet Union capable of the mass production of specialised modern weaponry was depicted in *Esli zavtra voina*. But the ideological framework and punitive cultural-intellectual environment would have a lasting effect on both history, that essential ingredient in shaping strategic philosophy, and also on scientific development, which, over time, would impinge on Soviet technological development.

Waging lightning war

The 'old' Red Army had waged a short, successful campaign against China in 1929. Using a blend of diplomacy, propaganda and a substantial force of some ten divisions led by Vasily Blyukher, Moscow launched a major offensive that overwhelmed a much inferior Chinese force in two stages between August and November. The Red Army was able to carry out a successful encirclement operation with broadly successful use of aircraft and tanks.[50] But it was not until the second half of the 1930s that the newly modernised, re-equipped Red Army was deployed in a series of campaigns that would put the new theory, reflected in the Field Regulations of 1936, to the test.

The first of these deployments was to assist Republican forces in the Spanish civil war in 1936. Although the USSR did not directly participate in the war, it sent substantial material and personnel support, including tanks and aircraft, and senior officers as advisors, including Nikolai Kuznetsov and General Dmitry Pavlov, with the latter in command of a Soviet tank brigade. While it was participation in a war rather than a war waged directly by Moscow, the Spanish civil war would have immediate and lasting effects on the Red Army. Following his combat experience, Pavlov returned to the USSR unenthusiastic about the viability of the Red Army's new mechanised and tank formations, deeming them to be too vulnerable and unlikely to be able to defeat entrenched defences. Appointed commander of the Red Army's armour, and then to the main military council, he advocated and oversaw the reorganisation of tanks into an infantry support role.[51] Thus began the unwinding of the theoretical developments achieved by 1936.

Subsequently, Voroshilov would oversee the waging of four campaigns at great geographical distance from each other within eighteen months. The first was in summer 1938, when Moscow deployed the Red Army against a Japanese border incursion. This represented the first major combat in what had been a sustained series of escalating border skirmishes between the USSR and Japan since the early 1930s. Stalin and Voroshilov ordered the Red Army's Far Eastern Front to combat readiness and, in August 1938, Blyukher again organised and led a substantial force, launching repeated assaults on Japanese forces in the battle at Lake Khasan. Eventually the Japanese sought an armistice, but limited logistical supply, poor training, preparation and reconnaissance and poor coordination in battle meant that the Red Army had suffered heavy casualties and was unable completely to dislodge the Japanese from their defences. The Far Eastern Front was dissolved and reorganised into the Red Banner Army; Grigori Shtern, a veteran of the Spanish civil war, replaced Blyukher, who was arrested by the NKVD in October, tortured and executed in the Great Terror with some of his subordinates.[52]

The contest with Japan continued, however, and fighting resumed in spring 1939, culminating in the battles at Khalkhin Gol. In June 1939 Voroshilov appointed Georgi Zhukov to inflict a decisive defeat on the Japanese. Zhukov oversaw a major logistical effort to build up armour, artillery and aircraft. Having achieved overwhelming material superiority, Zhukov then launched a surprise offensive deep into the Japanese rear, achieving first the encirclement and then the destruction of Japanese forces in a twelve-day campaign.[53]

In many ways, this represented the first real use of the thinking that underpinned deep battle and deep operations. The decisive victory was the 'birth' of Zhukov's subsequent stellar career as a commander:[54] decorated with the first of his four Hero of the Soviet Union medals for the campaign, within eighteen months he would be promoted to Chief of General Staff. Success was achieved despite a number of problems, from the complex logistical and supply environment to ineffective reconnaissance and flawed command and control; it was an example, indeed, of strategy as *protivo-bardachnie meri*. It came at such a high cost in equipment and casualties – perhaps some 25,000 of a force of 57,000[55] – that internal Soviet analysis concluded that the concept of deep battle was flawed, and advocated instead methodical advance by massed infantry with close artillery, aircraft and tank support.

As Zhukov was launching his offensive at Khalkhin Gol, Moscow was elsewhere in the throes of signing the Molotov–Ribbentrop pact with Germany, a non-aggression treaty with secret protocols agreeing to divide Poland and the Baltic states between them. The day after peace with Japan was concluded, Moscow launched the Red Army into another campaign in Poland.[56] Moscow mobilised some half a million troops and four thousand tanks to be organised into three army groups. Voroshilov directed the forces to launch decisive lightning strikes, and, given the Red Army's overwhelming material superiority and Polish forces fighting a two-front war, the campaign was completed within a month.

Even so, the Red Army's success was tempered both by having seen the Wehrmacht's campaign, and by its own inefficient performance. The campaign was characterised by familiar problems. Mobilisation was hasty but incomplete at the time of the offensive, partly because some equipment had to be transferred from the Far East and arrived late, partly because many of those mobilised were not ready for combat by the time they were deployed. The campaign itself was marked by poor preparation and reconnaissance, poor command and control and coordination between different services, logistical trouble, and comparatively high casualties.

Once again, very shortly after the completion of the 'lightning' Polish campaign, Moscow deployed the Red Army against Finland in what became known as the 'Winter War'.[57] Relations between Moscow and Helsinki had become tense in early 1938 when Moscow began to demand that Finland cede control initially over islands in the Gulf of Finland and then, in autumn 1939, over other, larger tracts of territory in the name of enhancing Leningrad's defences against a possible German attack. Helsinki refused Moscow's demands, and in November Moscow denounced the non-aggression pact between the USSR and Finland and launched an invasion, with Stalin ordering that the attack be conducted and concluded as quickly as possible, expecting victory within five to six weeks.

Although the Red Army achieved strategic and operational surprise, the initial assaults foundered on the Mannerheim Line to such an extent that the high command was obliged to halt attacks for six weeks to reorganise. The Soviets renewed their offensive in early February 1940, and applied overwhelming force to capture the Mannerheim Line. In mid-March Helsinki acceded to Moscow's demands, agreeing to a peace settlement that ceded extensive territory, including land still occupied by the Finnish military and of considerable economic value, and compensation costs.

If the campaign had yielded more territory than Moscow had demanded in November 1939, it also revealed what by now was a very familiar set of problems in the way Moscow deployed its armed forces. The first was the gap between the state and the armed forces: the General Staff had anticipated Finnish resistance and prepared a comprehensive operations plan, but Stalin initially ignored this, instructing the commander of the Leningrad military district, Kirill Meretskov, to conduct a short campaign with little preparation. In terms of the campaign, poor planning and reconnaissance meant that there was little detailed information about Finnish defences. Logistical support was constrained not only by very limited infrastructure, but by Moscow's decision not to declare war, which caused confusion between civilian and military authorities over the mobilisation of transport facilities. Poor command and control and tactics meant that the initial assaults were badly coordinated frontal assaults. The consequences were appalling losses – some 390,000 dead, missing or wounded. As one observer put it, the single cause of Soviet victory was attrition.[58]

Two further points are worth making about the Winter War. First, it is often cited by Western commentators as an analogy for today's struggle between Russia and Ukraine, whether in terms of Finland holding off Moscow at great cost, or ceding territory.[59] The war is also cited by Russian officials and observers. Putin has stated that the Soviet leadership went to war to 'correct the historical mistakes they had made in 1917': the border was too close to Leningrad, which posed a potential threat. He added that the first months of the campaign were 'very peculiar, bloody and ineffective on our part. Then everything fell into place … we reorganised, began to act differently, concentrated significant forces and resources … and the other side felt the full power of the Russian state.'[60]

Second, Helsinki resumed hostilities in the Continuation War (known in Russian as the Finnish front of the Great Fatherland War). The Finnish attack coincided with Operation Barbarossa in June 1941 and initially made significant advances, reclaiming territory lost in 1940 and moving into Soviet territory. The Soviets launched a major counter-offensive in summer 1944 which drove the Finns from these positions, leading first to the Moscow Armistice and then the Paris Peace Treaties of 1947, in which Helsinki ceded all territory in accordance with the 1940 agreement, further territory on the Barents Sea and Gulf of Finland, and paid $300 million in war reparations to the Soviets.

Finally, while Moscow was deploying force in these campaigns, the Red Army was facing another, yet more serious test. While not exactly a war, this test would wreak more losses on the Red Army than its campaigns in the Far East and Poland combined. It would also serve to entrench the reversal of the theoretical development of the late 1920s and early 1930s, and, as discussed in the chapters below, would have long-term effects on Moscow's strategy and war-making capacity, becoming one of the principal reference points for explaining the disasters of 1941 and 1942.

As we have seen, even from its earliest days, the Soviet leadership could be ruthlessly repressive, including against the armed forces: following the crushing of the Kronstadt rebellion by Tukhachevsky, Lenin imposed much tighter discipline on the body politic, expelling or jailing the opposition, and the navy suffered a sustained punitive repression of those serving in its ranks. As with society more broadly, the armed forces continued to suffer as this strict atmosphere became more repressive towards the end of the 1920s under Stalin, the brutality of collectivisation and the growth of the prison camps. In 1931, for instance, the 'spring' case resulted in a large number of arrests, including of senior officers who had served in the Imperial Army, among them Svechin, Andrei Snesarev and Alexander Verkhovsky – all of whom were playing significant roles in shaping and developing Soviet war theory.

But even this repressive atmosphere paled in comparison with what would befall the Soviet body politic and armed forces from the mid-1930s. In 1934 Sergei Kirov, a member of the politburo, was murdered. Stalin used this as a pretext to eliminate all remaining opposition and further consolidate power. This reached a peak between 1936 and 1938, during which period the People's Commissariat of Internal Affairs (NKVD), first under Genrikh Yagoda (1934–36) and then under Nikolai Yezhov (1936–38), conducted a vast campaign of arrests, imprisonment, torture and executions against politicians, including the senior Old Bolsheviks who had been part of the Bolshevik movement before 1917 and the majority of Lenin's politburo, intelligentsia and ethnic minorities.

From late 1936, but particularly in mid-1937, this campaign hit the armed forces. Tukhachevsky was arrested in May 1937, charged with spying for Germany and establishing a Trotskyite military conspiracy. He faced secret military tribunal in June, alongside seven other senior officers, including Boris Feldman, Iona Yakir and Ieronim Uborevich, and was executed shortly thereafter. Presiding over the tribunal were Shaposhnikov, Budyonny, Blyukher and seven other senior officers; of these ten who sat in judgement, only Shaposhnikov, Budyonny and one other would survive the subsequent repressions.

This tribunal initiated a deep and sustained assault on the armed forces.[61] Three of the five marshals were executed, as were fourteen of the sixteen army commanders, and sixty of the sixty-seven corps commanders. Some 35,000 junior officers had been arrested by the time the Great Terror slowed down in 1938. Svechin, Snesarev and Verkhovsky, who had survived in 1931, were now among the dead, as were many other soldier-thinkers. (For their parts, both Yagoda and Yezhov were also arrested and executed.)

The leadership of the armed forces had suffered a devastating lightning assault from within at the hands of the NKVD. This reflected the power of the NKVD, which by 1936 was some 150,000 strong, and well equipped with armour and aircraft. If the two forces had previously viewed each other as competition for resources, the Great Terror served to engender a deep and lasting distrust between them. In some ways, this might be said to have fully established a duality of war cultures in Russia.

Within eighteen months, those who had drafted and shaped the Field Regulations of 1936, and therefore those who understood how they should work in practice, were either languishing in prison or dead, their work discredited by association. Those who were not imprisoned or executed were still affected by the repression. As one senior Russian observer has put it, with the Great Terror many military and political thinkers were excluded from intellectual life: Soviet thinking about strategy and war 'made no advances, and in many cases rolled back entire decades'. Consequently, a 'nuanced' understanding of the interplay between theory and practice was 'almost lost for good'.[62] Those who remained at the most senior levels – Voroshilov, Budyonny, Pavlov and the like – were those who had opposed the mechanisation of the armed forces or argued for a reorganisation to emphasise massed infantry with tanks and artillery in support roles. At lower levels, morale and initiative were undermined, with widespread alcoholism, indiscipline and suicides.

Sophisticated theory?

This, then, was the context in which Moscow and the Red Army was campaigning. The military leadership might have developed sophisticated theory, but that theory was just part of, indeed was dependent on, wider conditions. The campaigns reflected persistent problems, all of which were anticipated by some of these senior theoreticians: the political leadership placed the armed forces in a difficult position, and there were problems in command and control, interoperability and logistics. To this could be added the persistent underestimation of the enemy, poor planning and reconnaissance, and flawed tactics. In all these campaigns, Moscow's armed forces suffered comparatively heavy casualties.

Only some of the problems could be resolved by theory. Good theory was one thing, but much depended on the state as a whole, in terms of coordination across the state and how the state actually deployed force. Often, Moscow wielded its military tool in ways that prevented the effective implementation of the military's theory. Equally, within the armed forces, disciplinary problems – low morale, corruption and waste, alcoholism – all eroded the leadership's ability to effect reform and implement theory. Nevertheless, two important points emerge from this period regarding the development of Russian war theory.

First, although there were obviously some very fine, sophisticated theorists – Shaposhnikov, Svechin, Triandafillov, Tukhachevsky and Anton Kersnovski among others – this high level
was far from uniform. While some successful combat commanders
became prominent thinkers about war, notably Frunze and
Tukhachevsky, the relationship between theory and combat
command success was uneven. Some theorists, such as Georgi
Isserson, were unsuccessful as combat commanders. Furthermore,
apart from Shaposhnikov, these sophisticated theorists died before
their time or suffered at the hands of the state: Frunze died
during surgery in 1925, Triandafillov was killed in an air crash
in 1931, and Svechin and Tukhachevsky were among the many
who perished in the repression.

Alongside these soldier-thinkers were officers who were
successful combat commanders rather than theorists: Zhukov,
the Red Army's rising commander, who was learning how to
command modern forces in combat, for instance, and Semyon
Budyonniy. The latter had gained his reputation as a combat
commander during the civil war, but proved unable to adapt
to the changing character of mechanised warfare, opposing
Tukhachevsky's modernisation effort. His success as a combat
commander waned; other senior officers voiced more or less
oblique criticism of his intellectual and, over time, combat
prowess.[63]

Another was Voroshilov, one of Stalin's closest allies, who
had commanded an army during the civil war, and had, with
Stalin, defended Tsaritsyn (later called Stalingrad). While his
contemporaries acknowledged his personal bravery, in the late
1920s, amid the debate and political tussle for influence, opposition
to Voroshilov appears to have sought to discredit him in the
politburo for 'incompetence' and being 'unfit to direct the Soviet

war machine'.[64] Subsequently, senior Russian soldier-thinkers have offered scathing assessments of Voroshilov. Colonel General Dmitri Volkogonov, who became head of the Institute of War History in 1985 and was widely anticipated to become Russia's first Defence Minister in the early 1990s, considered him to be an 'utterly mindless executive with no opinion of his own', giving his full support to Stalin without a thought, and Tukhachevsky's distinct intellectual inferior, as demonstrated by his command performance in Finland. Volkogonov observed that Voroshilov's major book, *The Defence of the USSR* (1937), contained nothing on national defence, war strategy, operational skills or tactics; his works were 'superficial, agitational' and concerned only with propaganda in the 'traditional Communist vein'.[65]

Budyonniy and Voroshilov were both political appointees in the wake of the revolution and civil war. They were appointed marshals in 1935 – and were the only two of the five marshals to survive the Great Repression; indeed, both played major roles in that repression against the theorists. It is hard to find better examples of *Shwondershchina*. Following the Winter War, Voroshilov's command career stalled and he was replaced as Defence Commissar by Semyon Timoshenko, though he remained a prominent political figure. Budyonniy was removed from combat command in 1941 following the disastrous failed defence of Kiev, and although he retained senior posts, he was moved further and further away from real command.

Second, while sophisticated thinkers wrote theory, it remained for that theory to be widely accepted. As we have seen, Svechin lost the argument with Tukhachevsky by the early-to-mid 1930s; but after the Great Repression began, association with the ideas of Tukhachevsky and his team after 1937 was perilous. Even those theorists who survived the repression found that their work fell on deaf ears: as a prominent officer later observed, Isserson's *Novye formy borby* anticipated developments, but was at the time largely ignored, though in the early 2010s Gerasimov would explicitly refer to the themes of this work.[66]

Furthermore, sophisticated theoretical works might have been written, but educating the wider officer corps and armed forces as a whole to implement them proved difficult. On the one hand, this was because of the broader lack of higher education across the new officer corps, both during the early 1930s as the Red Army expanded quickly and especially after the Great Repression. Just 7 per cent of those officers who remained had a higher military education.[67] Some of this was reflected in the 1934 film *Chapayev*, with the commander, a civil war hero, having to correct and educate his officers and brigade commanders regarding how to organise battles and where the commander should position himself.[68]

On the other hand, problems of implementation were due to the methods of military education and training. Russian historians have pointed to a 'theoretical bias' in teaching, for instance, which the Red Army inherited from the Tsarist era. This meant that classes in applied tactics did not immerse officers in a simulated real combat situation but limited them to assessing examples from military history and classroom tactical problems: officers were trained to memorise a number of templates for situations, rather than independently assessing situations. According to one Russian observer, teaching 'forgot that the purpose of studying tactics was not to prepare a military scientist, but a commander, not an expert analyst for the quiet of the office, but an organiser and leader of battle'. Officers graduated, therefore, with insufficient mastery of the technique of organising a battle.[69]

Furthermore, teaching styles tended to focus on detailed particulars, rather than looking at the whole. Military education focused on providing a 'careful, jewellery finish of some minor detail to a crudely crafted whole'. Teaching suffered from 'forgetting' that the army and navy are 'systems' (*bessistemnost*), and from a lack of discipline in thinking and a negligent or not fully seen through (*nedodelannost*) attitude to combat training.[70] As we shall see below, these are recurrent concerns.

The disaggregation of Moscow's strategy

The late 1930s, therefore, were a time of considerable change for Moscow's armed forces. The 1936 Field Regulations reflected theoretically innovative and sophisticated ideas about how to wage war – often developed in interactive debate with wider Euro-Atlantic thinking – and these were substantively resourced by the state. The British Field Marshal Archibald Wavell observed the Red Army's exercises in 1936: 'the army has made great strides in equipment and in education, and its spirit and bearing are impressively good', he noted, and 'relations between officers and men appear excellent'. 'A very great deal of money is spent on the army, and the officers are, as a class ... one of the most privileged in Soviet Russia.' Even so, he thought that 'in tactics it seems doubtful if similar progress has been made, from what we saw they seem somewhat clumsy and old-fashioned'. He concluded that 'the Soviet army would be formidable inside its own frontiers but much less formidable outside'.[71]

Doctrine and strategy were not yet fully aligned: the effects of theoretical and technological modernisation were not felt across the whole Red Army, creating an archipelago effect of strength and modernity in some areas amid conditions of continuing obsolescence. Nevertheless, Tukhachevsky had overseen the modernisation of Moscow's armed forces, the establishment of a 'new' Red Army, based on mechanisation, firepower and mass, and a broader sense that a major war loomed.[72] But the people who oversaw the armed forces by end of the 1930s were Voroshilov and Budenny: it was they who featured prominently in *Esli zavtra voina*, with the decisive strikes being delivered on horseback. And, as we have seen, by that time countervailing processes in the state and within the military were already undermining modernisation. The state's reassertion of control led to a deliberate effort to reshape the body politic as a whole, imposing wider intellectual *partiinost* at exorbitant human cost. This produced a prolonged repression that peaked in the Great Terror, a substantial part of which included the destruction of the command structure of the armed forces and the discrediting of the designers of war theory. Simultaneously, the state leadership had committed the armed forces to a series of campaigns without appropriate preparation, resulting in poor performance, again at appalling human cost.

Consequently, by late 1940 and early 1941, the Red Army was traumatised and in disarray. Indeed, the repressions continued: by this time, a total of 40,000–45,000 officers had been arrested, of whom some 15,000 were executed, the remainder imprisoned. Morale was low: failures of discipline, suicides and accidents were prevalent; drunkenness was so pervasive that a special order against it was decreed in December 1938.[73]

Equally, in the wake of its experiences in Spain, the Far East, Poland and Finland, the command instigated another series of structural reforms. In November 1939 the main military council ordered the disbanding of the mechanised formations, establishing motorised divisions in their stead. And the nature of campaigning in Finland served to divert thinking about operations from deep battle to how to break down deeply entrenched fortifications. This led both to intellectual debate about overcoming permanent fortifications and a training regime that emphasised accumulation of forces, engineering and gradually breaking down defences. For some Russian observers today, the defeat of the Mannerheim Line represented a 'unique feat (of arms) in world practice'.[74]

But the Wehrmacht's success in Poland and then Western Europe in 1939 and 1940 provoked another rethink among the Red Army's command and, in July 1940, another reorganisation of the armed forces to re-establish mechanised corps and tank divisions and retrain commanders. In December 1940 the military leadership held a major conference to debate doctrine and strategy. During this conference, the main theme was the need for readiness for an intense and protracted war. Zhukov and Timoshenko attributed German success to surprise, the shock of powerful blows against weak and irresolute opponents: such a collapse would not happen to the USSR, echoing Tukhachevsky's early 1937 view. Thus began a shift towards the strategic defensive and another process of attempting to build to scale, with the defence industry producing large quantities of equipment combined with a substantial increase in the active duty strength. The problem, they suggested, was not a new style of warfare, but rather how the USSR could bring sufficient material and manpower to bear in what would be a prolonged, attritional war.

3

Operation Barbarossa and the Great Victory

The power of the lightning blow in war was demonstrated by Operation Barbarossa, the offensive launched by Germany against the Soviet Union on 22 June 1941. The defining example of 'Blitzkrieg', certainly as far as Moscow is concerned, this offensive and the subsequent war scarred the USSR and has influenced Russian state and war strategy ever since. Even today, it colours war science, doctrine and strategy.

The four years of war that followed Operation Barbarossa were waged from the Arctic to the Black Sea, from the Volga to Berlin, and set the stage for the Soviet war against Japan in Manchuria in 1945. The Great Fatherland War was fought on a vast scale and with unprecedented intensity as the Soviet Union mobilised millions of people both to fight and to sustain the economy. The costs of such an effort to achieve victory were likewise unprecedented in destruction, socio-economic dislocation and loss of life and limb.

Consequently, the war was transformative. On the one hand, waging it transformed the Red Army into a modernised, well-equipped and battle-hardened force, capable of sophisticated, simultaneous large-scale offensives. And, on the other, the results of the war created new global strategic conditions as the USSR sought to establish buffer and client states to preserve the fruits of victory, and subsequently perceived and faced rather different sets of challenges and threats. Indeed, in the wake of the war, Moscow's horizons shifted from the regional to the global.

Nevertheless, if the war was in so many ways transformative, important threads of continuity remained visible. Continuity was reflected, for instance, in the Soviet leadership. Stalin, of course, remained paramount, and much of the senior leadership team remained in position throughout the war and into the post-war era. Continuity was also visible in terms of how the war was waged: the Red Army built on, adapted and implemented pre-war doctrine reflected in the 1936 Field Regulations, and continued to endure many of the same practical problems that it had faced in the 1930s. Above all, Operation Barbarossa served to amplify the long-running debate between the search for the knockout blow and the need to wage a strategy of exhaustion. This debate remained connected to – though usually in political tension with – debates also underway in Western militaries.

The Great Fatherland War: the transformation of the Red Army

The Soviet experience of the Great Fatherland War is often framed in three periods.[1] During the first, lasting from 22 June 1941 to 18 November 1942, Germany held the strategic initiative. During this catastrophic period for the Soviet Union, German forces advanced first, within six months, to Moscow, Leningrad and Rostov and, then, in 1942, to Stalingrad on the Volga and the Caucasus. The Soviet pre-war army was virtually destroyed, losing some 75,000 tanks, 123,000 guns and mortars and suffering some 6.4 million 'permanent' casualties – those killed or missing in action, those who died of wounds or were taken prisoner. During this period, the Soviet Union began to reorganise its war-fighting capability. The fighting was extremely intense, and while the period was one largely of overall Soviet retreat, the Red Army did mount a number of counter-offensives and inflicted significant damage on invading forces.

The second period, during which the strategic initiative shifted to the Soviet Union, lasted from 19 November 1942 through autumn 1943. It began when the Soviets launched their winter campaigning with Operation Uranus, to encircle and destroy German forces at Stalingrad, and Operation Mars, to encircle and destroy the German 9th Army near Moscow, through the battle of Kursk in July–August 1943. This period of Soviet revival and consolidating success saw growing production of equipment and the restructuring and modernisation of the armed forces.

During the third period, from after the battle of Kursk in autumn 1943 through to the end of the war in 1945, the Soviet Union held the strategic initiative. This began with a series of strategic offensives initially referred to as 'Stalin's 10 blows' which lasted through 1944. These defeated Germany's allies, drove German forces back and positioned Soviet forces for the final offensives in 1945, first from the river Vistula to the river Oder, and then the assaults led by Marshals Zhukov and Ivan Konev into Germany to capture Berlin.

The Red Army's renaissance through the war reflected a blend of familiar and persistent problems as well as developing strengths. One of the strengths was the ability of the state to balance mobilisation on the two pillars of socio-economic and military power. The Great Fatherland War reflected the sense of 'war' as a multi-dimensional state-led activity, with the economy playing a vital role in sustaining and then increasing arms production.[2]

At the outset, military preparations were limited by the strategic situation in which the Red Army found itself. The armed forces were still amid a major re-equipment and reorganisation process following the experiences of the Great Terror and the Winter War, and the doctrinal reassessment that began after Germany's successful invasion of Poland. While Stalin had permitted some redeployment of forces in summer 1941, in June he did not permit the armed forces to take up combat positions as Operation Barbarossa loomed. Rejecting intelligence reports, Stalin continued to seek to deter Hitler and to avoid moves that could be interpreted as a provocation. Consequently, although Zhukov and Timoshenko sought to persuade Stalin to order forces in the west to high alert, this came too late and Soviet forces were taken by surprise; most of the intended recipients in front line positions did not receive the directive to move to combat positions before they came under fire.[3]

During the war itself, there were familiar problems regarding strategic command and control. At the outset, the strategic leadership took time to cohere; an absence of overall military command led to mistakes in troop control.[4] The strategic leadership of the Stavka, with Stalin at its helm, persistently misunderstood the relative capabilities of the opposing forces, overestimating Soviet strength and underestimating that of the Germans. Accordingly, the Stavka ordered the Red Army to mount overly ambitious offensives which it could not carry out. Nikita Khrushchev later recalled that Stalin was 'very far from an understanding of the real situation which was developing at the front'. In a mood of 'nervousness and hysteria', Stalin would not listen to his senior military officers, interfered with actual military operations 'causing our army serious damage', and issued orders which 'could not help but result in huge personnel losses'.[5] If in 1941 front line commanders implemented standing orders that resulted in counter-attacks at corps level that were vigorous but often suicidal, in 1942 and 1943 the Stavka ordered offensives that culminated too soon, leaving the Red Army open to German counter-attacks.

Such offensives during the first two periods were often poorly prepared. Support and logistics, especially beyond railheads, were inadequate and unable to meet the requirements of warfare at such a scale. This resulted in problems coordinating mobilisa-tion and the organisation of rear services, as well as the tardy delivery of ammunition, food and other supplies.[6] This combina-tion led to ill health, crime, poor discipline, pillaging and theft.[7] Logistical challenges remained throughout the war, up to and including the assault on Berlin.[8]

There were also problems in the chain of command. Nikolai Vatutin, who commanded the Voronezh front during the battle of Kursk and then the offensives into Ukraine in 1943, stated that it was 'easier to beat the adversary at Kursk than to overcome the indolence, laziness, lack of understanding and at times even resistance of my own commanders at every level'.[9] Sergei Shtemenko described command mistakes and friction during the planning of Operation Bagration in 1944, with commanders 'haranguing' subordinates, with the failure to give clear instruc-tions leading to confusion and 'muddled answers' in reply to the senior command's demands.[10] Others described the prevalence of violence in the chain of command, with Soviet generals and officers 'cursing' and 'beating their subordinates all the time'. According to Khrushchev, Stalin condoned – even demanded – that his commanders strike his generals. 'For the majority of marshals' in the Great Fatherland War, it was 'simpler to shoot even a lieutenant or captain than to thrash him', but 'only Budyonniy ... allowed himself to beat up rank and file soldiers'.[11]

Recognition of many of these problems only emerged subsequently, and often implicitly, in Soviet strategic analysis. Later still, they emerged in the form of film and fiction. The author Vladimir Voinovich satirised – among other things – the chain of command, the lack of communications and coordination of troops and logistics, the incompetence of commanders, and especially the implementation of instructions. Voinovich caricatured, for instance, a general's promotion and the way that 'of all possible decisions he invariably makes the most stupid one'. And he had a colonel say that the 'main thing is to say "Yes, Sir!" when you're supposed to, then afterwards you can disregard the order'.[12] More abrasively, Viktor Astafev, himself a veteran of the war, later published the novel *The Cursed and the Killed*, in which he portrays the malnourishment, exhaustion and incompetence and violence in the chain of command, and the costly brutality of combat.[13]

Altogether, this meant that even as the Red Army began to achieve some spectacular victories, these continued to be accompanied by partial or complete failures. If Operation Kutuzov in summer 1943 reaped success with the capture of Orel, the Orsha offensives through that autumn and winter were an expensive failure, and the commander, Vasily Sokolovsky, was relieved. Similar examples occurred in the campaign on the Ukrainian front: the crossing of the Dnieper river in late 1943, while successful in overall terms, cost many lives.

Likewise, the successful final assaults in April and early May 1945 came at a very high price. Zhukov's opening frontal assaults on the Seelow Heights were so expensive that there was concern that his forces would be spent before the actual storming of Berlin was launched. Ramming his forces on to Berlin with inadequate reconnaissance and inefficient use of artillery and aircraft led to failures that 'drastically thinned' his forces. All told, in three weeks the battle for Berlin resulted in some 305,000 killed, wounded or missing, and the loss of over 2,000 tanks; the capture of Brno cost another 280,000 killed and wounded.[14]

Nevertheless, the Red Army's performance improved during the war, such that it was able to impose total defeat on Germany and its allies. Building on the doctrine and experience of the 1930s, and incorporating analysis of that experience, the Red Army shaped sound strategy and increasingly accepted the need for adequate preparation, including thorough reconnaissance, comprehensive deception measures and the pre-arranged cooperation and concentration of forces. Consequently, the Red Army was ever more able to implement coordinated and simultaneous offensives to build cumulative strategic offensives at scale, seeking to encircle and destroy strategically important formations.

Especially in the third period, the Red Army became adept at launching and sustaining first successive, and then simultaneous and incessant offensives along the whole front, reallocating resources from offensive to offensive to mask intent and then conduct cleaving blows to separate German army groups from each other and to destroy them in turn. These offensives used deception and surprise, and massed firepower combined with weight of numbers to achieve overwhelming operational and tactical superiority; the momentum that such offensives generated facilitated penetration into the enemy's strategic depth. The main aim was the destruction of the enemy's forces and ability to resist; in Zhukov's words, to 'smash' the enemy 'completely', 'to swamp the enemy in a sea of fire and metal', to secure the 'complete defeat' of Nazi Germany, and to 'force unconditional surrender – military, economic and political'.[15]

These operations restored confidence and provided the basis for the Soviet strategic offensive in Manchuria in August 1945. The assault on the Japanese Kwantung Army posed numerous challenges for the Red Army, from regrouping large forces across the USSR from Europe, to its conduct in complex territory, across vast distances, mountain ranges and deserts. Drawing on the doctrinal heritage of the 1930s and developed in the Great Fatherland War, the offensive was based on an innovative, carefully organised plan that demanded imagination and initiative at all levels. The Soviet leadership sought surprise and the deployment of an overwhelming preponderance of forces at critical points on multiple axes to achieve momentum into the enemy's strategic depth. The offensive, which was anticipated to last for two months or more, was to be sustained by the incremental commitment of additional forces in phased sequences.[16]

In the event, when the offensive was launched on 9 August 1945, the Red Army quickly overcame the Japanese forces. Achieving strategic and operational surprise in the timing and direction of the offensives, Soviet forces were able to collapse the over-extended and unprepared Japanese defences. The Red Army advanced 900 kilometres in eleven days, pre-empting Japanese defensive moves and overwhelming resistance even ahead of schedule. In fact, as the Trans-Baikal Front's diary noted, there were no major battles, and the Soviet armies 'did not realise their fire and shock power'. Heavy rain and difficult terrain complicated logistics, but the Japanese forces 'proved significantly weaker' than Soviet intelligence anticipated, and, with outdated and insufficient equipment, they could not have hoped to win 'any kind of serious modern engagement'.[17] Having suffered from a strategy of destruction in 1941, Moscow delivered its own version four years later, a *pobedonosnaya, molnienosnaya voina*.

Facing a new historical era

Victory in Europe and in Manchuria resolved some strategic dilemmas, but it also created new ones. Internationally, Soviet power appeared greater than ever. The defeat of its main adversaries west and east, leading to the occupation of large parts of eastern and central Europe and an established presence in the Pacific, meant that Moscow had a much larger – even global – strategic horizon. This was offset by an immediate and sharp deterioration in relations with its wartime allies. Already in early 1946 this tension began to brew into what became known as the Cold War. In March 1946 Winston Churchill met President Truman in Missouri and gave his 'sinews of peace' speech, declaiming how the shadows of war and tyranny were falling over the world. Stalin replied that the speech was characteristic of Hitler, and that Churchill and 'his friends in the United States' were presenting the non-English-speaking world with an 'ultimatum': recognise British and US dominance or face war.[18] The tension between West and East intensified through a series of crises, the first major one being the Soviet blockade of Berlin in 1948–49, and, at the same time, the building and then the establishment of the North Atlantic Treaty Organisation (NATO) from 1948 through into the early 1950s, and then the Korean war.[19] For Stalin, confrontation and even war with the West seemed inevitable.

Soviet power now faced a very different kind of threat. On the one hand, although it retained substantial armed forces even after demobilisation, it faced a nuclear-armed opponent while not possessing such capabilities of its own. On the other, although the fruits of victory provided buffer zones and client states, the USSR's maritime flanks were once again very exposed to Western sea power. During the war, the United States and the British Empire had again demonstrated an awesome capability to carry the fight across thousands of miles to strike their enemies. These same powers had, of course, intervened in the Russian civil war, and they were already again demonstrating the potential of such power: the US Navy deployed, for instance, to the Black Sea in 1946.[20] As the US Secretary of Defense James Forrestal stated, the US could out-produce the world, control the seas and strike inland with the atomic bomb.[21]

Domestically, Moscow also faced dilemmas. Stalin's power appeared to be at a high point: he wielded vast and unchallengeable influence. Yet the Soviet Union was exhausted after the war. The scale of infrastructural destruction and loss of life was unprecedented, and the post-war reconstruction effort absorbed significant resources.

If the war had caused widespread shortages, the USSR was then struck first by drought and after that by famine from mid-1946 to 1948. The winter of 1946–47 was the worst in living memory across Europe. In these conditions, the Soviet leadership embarked on a complicated demobilisation process, one characterised by delays in the handing over of infrastructure from military to civilian control. Altogether, this created a complex and difficult socio-economic situation, with a combination of demobilised soldiers facing unemployment, a post-war spike in childbirth, widespread homelessness and hunger, and large numbers of maimed veterans and orphaned children.

Furthermore, Stalin's dominance was characterised by an attempt to consolidate power at home (and in Soviet-occupied Europe) through the assertion of intellectual and cultural conformism, an emphasis on the West as a threat, and continued repression with renewed waves of arrests. Indeed, the immediate post-war era was marked by episodes such as the 'Leningrad Case' (1949–50): six senior officials were arrested, investigated and shot, and hundreds of other party officials and public figures were fired, arrested, imprisoned or exiled. By the early 1950s, the prison camp population had grown to some 12 million; the consolidation of the camp system reflected the consolidation of the whole state and economic system.[22] This affected the military, as the repression struck both returning prisoners of war and senior officers alike. Certainly, those who had fought for the Germans faced severe punishment. General Andrei Vlasov, captured by the Germans in 1942, defected to them and raised the Russian Liberation Army. Recaptured by the Soviets in 1945, he was tried for high treason and executed in 1946, along with other senior officers who had served with him.

Equally, the author Varlam Shalamov described the plight of mid-ranking and junior officers and soldiers taken prisoner by the Germans in *Major Pugachov's Last Battle*: denounced during the war as traitors by the Soviet authorities, they faced military tribunals after it. Then 'ship after ship delivered ... former Soviet citizens who were "repatriated" directly to the far north east', the mines and the hunger. Indeed, Shalamov depicts how Major Pugachov had encountered Vlasov's men while a prisoner of war: with their 'manifesto' that the Soviet government saw them as traitors, 'it was no wonder' that so many men from the

German prisoner-of-war camps had joined the 'Russian Army of Liberation', he observed. Pugachov himself had not believed it until he had 'made his way back to the Red Army'; now, in eastern Siberia, he could see that 'everything the Vlasovites had said was true'. The *Pugachov* narrative context may differ from *Ivan Chonkin*, but the conclusion is remarkably similar: large numbers of Soviet troops are deployed to attack a small group of other Soviet soldiers in operations characterised by difficulties of transport, logistics and command, including confusion and punitive scapegoating. As Major General Artemyev says as he prepares to launch the final attack, 'I tell you I'm not joking when I say I'm waiting for my orders. I'll be lucky if I just lose my job.'[23]

Even those senior Soviet officers who had delivered victory lived in an atmosphere of fear and repression from early 1946 through to the mid-1950s. This was not only a matter of the Party's criticism of Zhukov and his demotion in 1946. The 'Aviation Case' resulted in the dismissal, arrest and imprisonment in 1946 of both Minister of Aviation Aleksey Shakhurin and Chief Marshal of Aviation Alexander Novikov. Air Marshal Sergei Khudaykov, deputy commander of the Red Air Force, was arrested in 1946 on charges of espionage, imprisoned for four years and then shot.[24]

Nor did the navy escape. In 1947 Nikolai Kuznetsov and other senior naval officers were arrested and investigated; Kuznetsov was demoted, the others imprisoned. And in 1953 the so-called 'Doctors' Plot' affected society at large and the military in particular, since senior officers were among those seen as potential victims. This was just one of several similar episodes at the time, including the 'Crimean Affair', the latter an alleged effort to make Crimea a Jewish autonomous republic and turn it into a springboard for Western imperialist adventures. Recalling the Leningrad and Doctors' affairs, Khrushchev later said that 'Stalin's version of vigilance turned our world into an insane asylum in which everyone was encouraged to search for non-existent facts about everyone else': the investigative methods were 'beat, beat and once again beat'.[25]

Nikita Khrushchev and the 20th Party Congress

To a degree, Stalin's death in 1953 ushered in a shift in Soviet politics. A power struggle led first to the arrest of Lavrenti Beria, first deputy chairman of the Council of Ministers and the head of the NKVD. Found guilty on a series of charges, he was shot before the year was out; the Doctors' Plot evaporated, and some rehabilitations and reappointments began, including those of Novikov, Shakhurin, Kuznetsov and Zhukov. Over the next three years, Khrushchev emerged as leader and then began a process of 'de-Stalinisation' at the 20th Party Congress. Indeed, this Congress – the first since Stalin's death – was a major event, revealing shifts in how Moscow saw the world, and shaping strategy and thinking about war.

If there were shifts in the landscape, however, the strategic dilemmas faced by the Soviet leadership became more pronounced. Internationally, while Moscow established the Warsaw Pact in 1955 to balance NATO, and expanded Soviet political and economic influence across the Middle East, Africa and Asia, the tensions of the Cold War and a series of crises highlighted the limits of Soviet capacity on the international stage. Moscow was able to do little beyond making threats, for instance, during the Suez (1956) and Lebanon (1958) crises.

Moreover, Soviet defence plans were challenged by Western technological developments, first through the threat posed by carrier strike forces, then through the developments of nuclear submarines (USS *Nautilus* was launched in 1955), and then, from 1956, by the US's development of the Jupiter and Polaris ballistic missile programmes. This latter development meant that Soviet forces would face a major challenge in the initial period of any war with the US. To cope, the USSR would need to adapt its forces to be able to control those seas that US nuclear submarines would use, to defend forward positions and destroy US strike fleets.[26]

Within Moscow's sphere of influence and domestically, social instability and economic problems also imposed dilemmas on Moscow. Protests in East Germany in 1953 obliged Moscow, after some deliberation and hesitation, both to reverse policies and to send in Soviet forces to crush the riots. In 1956 the de-Stalinisation process – especially the political atmosphere engendered by the 20th Party Congress that year – contributed to a wave of protests, first in Poland and then, in October, in Hungary. Once again, Moscow vacillated before sending in troops to destroy the movement.

Domestically, the Soviet leadership continued to face socio-economic challenges, especially the need to continue reconstruction; there were still severe shortages of consumer goods, even of housing and food. Under Khrushchev, this entailed a shift of resources to civilian sectors and something of a release of intellectual life. Under Khrushchev, the Soviet leadership put their faith in modernisation through the large-scale application of technology. The 20th Party Congress reflected this: Khrushchev promoted nuclear power, and Igor Kurchatov spoke, reflecting the influential role of nuclear scientists, physicists and engineers.

Science still faced the wider context of Soviet (political) life: an ideological and centralised bureaucracy that subdued innovation and dissent, and that combined repressive measures with demands for technical progress and productivity. The *sharashka* scientific and technical prisons of the 1930s had resulted in valuable technical advances, including military aircraft, and continued to play a role in the military's development after the war.[27] Nevertheless, Soviet post-war science benefited from a large number of trained graduates emerging into industry, supplied with substantial resources officially guided towards attempting to overcome comparative technological inferiority to the West. Soviet science enjoyed a high degree of prestige, and by the mid-1950s this effort began to reap rewards, contributing to Soviet technological development and paying dividends for military modernisation.[28]

Stalin's support for nuclear science was a result of his view that the USSR must prepare for inevitable war, so he prioritised the development of the atomic bomb, dedicating considerable resources to it and silencing those who opposed 'new physics'. Soviet physicists became among the world's leaders in nuclear physics.[29] Moscow tested its first atomic device in 1949, which led to a sustained period of development and the testing of hydrogen bombs in 1953 and 1955. From the mid-1950s, these tests were carried out using modernised delivery systems, including the R-5 medium range ballistic missile (1954–56). In August 1957 the Soviets launched the R-7, the first intercontinental ballistic missile. Reflecting the dual purpose of such technological development, the R-7 had both military and civilian purposes. For the military, it carried a thermonuclear warhead; in its civilian capacity, it served to launch Sputnik-1 in October 1957. This nuclear and missile development would have major implications for thinking about war and war strategy.

The sense of intellectual ferment characterised and emphasised by the 20th Party Congress also reached historians. As we saw in the previous chapter, history had existed as if frozen in a block of ice since the late 1920s/early 1930s. Stalin had imposed a path through his *Short Course* text, and the Party had exerted a deliberate and systematic effort to bring history under its control. Following Stalin's death, though, a community of historians began to emerge with implications for thinking about war and strategy. This revival – or, more accurately, slight thaw – in history as an intellectual discipline was reflected in the first large community discussions since 1928, and in articles in the journal *Voprosy istorii*, and was characterised by debates about the method and purpose of history. Khrushchev underlined this at the 20th Party Congress, calling for the correction of historical errors and the reconsideration of the events of the civil war and the Great Fatherland War.

The 'Burdzhalov affair' of 1956–57 reflected the ambiguities of post-Stalin political-intellectual life in the USSR. Eduard Burdzhalov, deputy editor of *Voprosy Istorii*, advanced serious criticisms of Stalin and historical science. He called for a closer look at the early years of the Great Fatherland War, now that more than a decade had passed since it had ended, and asserted that the task of history was to explain historical facts, not to hide them. Both he and Anna Pankratova, *Voprosy Istorii*'s editor, were subjected to an intense, hostile political campaign, and ousted from their positions. Nevertheless, a sense of revisionism continued and stimulated the discipline: from 1956 the Institute of History of the Soviet Academy of Sciences began to expand,

and from 1957 new historical journals were established. A sense of a new direction – albeit contested – was shaped by historians such as Arkady Sidorov, and this growth was sustained by veterans (*frontoviki*) who after the war had pursued a historical education. This revisionism was characterised by debates about historiography and the immediate relevance of the past to the present. The Burdzhalov affair set in motion a series of debates that beset Soviet history for the next fifteen years.[30]

This, then, was the context in which the historical study of war existed, and in which some of what we might call the 'infrastructure' for the use of history in shaping war strategy took shape. In 1949 the Office for the Study of Modern Warfare was established under General Shtemenko, apparently with connections to the Historical Administration of the General Staff. Likewise, the editorial board of the journal *Voennaya mysl* included several members of the Historical Administration of the General Staff. Major General Nikolai Talensky, chief editor of the journal, emphasised that the 'combat experience of the Red Army is and will be in future the fundamental and decisive factor which determines the development of peacetime military art for many decades'.[31]

Even so, the political-intellectual environment after the war meant that the study of the history of war was limited to propaganda, rather than contributing in a professional sense to the work of the Soviet armed forces. As it did for history and other intellectual fields, the Party set the guidelines for the historical study of war. The journal *Voenno-istorichesky zhurnal*, established in 1939, had been closed in 1941 with the outbreak of war and remained so. And the pervasive sense of repression meant that while Stalin was alive, it was courageous to examine the Soviet experience of the Great Fatherland War, particularly the first period: even a purely military analysis would have revealed Stalin's mistakes.[32]

Only after the 20th Party Congress did historians and military strategists began to dig into these questions:[33] some candour was permitted in memoirs, war histories and operational accounts. And in 1959 *Voenno-istorichesky zhurnal* was relaunched, and Pavel Zhilin appointed editor. This should not be taken too far: the Party retained control and insisted on *partiinost*. In 1957 the leadership even threatened to shoot writers at the first sign of Hungarian-type troubles. And in response to this revisionism, a counter-movement would gain strength in the early 1960s. But the foundations were laid for a Soviet version of what we might today call 'applied history': the application of experience and the past to contemporary problems. These shifts shaped the intellectual atmosphere in which war science and strategy formed.

The evolution of war strategy: from 'permanent operating factors' to the initial period of war

Although Moscow faced a new era and new challenges, there were no major revisions to war strategy in the late 1940s. War remained defined as a social phenomenon, organised armed struggle between classes or states in the name of economic or political goals: 'in its nature', war is the 'continuation of politics by means of violence', and the armed forces the main instrument for its conduct. The Marxist-Leninist and Stalinist underpinnings of war and strategy were emphasised: the class nature of war, the threat posed by imperialism and the view that only with the destruction of capitalism and the victory of socialism would the threat of war disappear. It was considered inevitable. War strategy was officially defined as the study of the leadership of all the armed forces of the state, and the preparation for and conduct of war as a whole by the highest echelons of command.[34]

The lack of revision of war strategy was due partly to technical limitations. The post-war demobilisation served to improve the Soviet armed forces – the chain of command retained the best officers, there was a shift towards mechanisation and armour in the balance of forces, and efforts were made to modernise logistics and communications, to rectify problems encountered in the war. For the first five years, Moscow focused on the move to full mechanisation and modernisation and absorbing and consolidating the lessons of the Great Fatherland War into doctrine. This meant sustaining massive conventional forces superiority over the adversary, and defeating them with fast, decisive ground actions. Equally, for some years the Red Army, renamed the Soviet Army in early 1946, did not have atomic weapons. While they did test an atomic bomb in 1949, the Soviets still lacked the means to deploy it until the mid-to-late 1950s. It was not until the mid-1950s, therefore, that nuclear weapons supplanted tanks as the central strategic weapon; even then, they were absorbed into the existing structure of the strategic and operational thinking of World War II. Nuclear weapons would blast a gap in the adversary's defences which would be exploited by massive conventional forces advancing at speed into the enemy's depth.[35]

But this situation was also due to a high degree of intellectual conformity, not to say paralysis. After the war, Stalin dominated Moscow's strategic landscape, including military affairs. This is well reflected in the 1949 film *Padenie Berlina*, in which Stalin towers above the military, making the key decisions during the war. There is much to be said here about culture more generally, especially given the context of censorship and how the regime used film to consolidate official narratives and reassert Stalinist orthodoxy. Shot in 1946–47, the film featured a score by Dmitri Shostakovich, and it was rumoured that the script had been edited by Stalin. Yet it is noteworthy here because of Zhukov's relegation to a bit part player in the capture of Berlin, and the way that the war as a whole was portrayed. Anglo-American audiences might recognise the representation of German Nazism as a universal ideology seeking to take over the world and install its own order, and Berlin's desire for Soviet natural resources. Less familiar, though, would be depictions of the British Empire and the US actually *helping* the Germans, both by delaying the opening of a second front and especially by the representation of British business supporting German metal production.[36]

Conformism shaped the wider intellectual and cultural context, and the military continued to face significant repressive measures. Stalin left little room for the military to shape policy or establish its own 'doctrine'; questioning Stalin's views and Party orthodoxy, even being seen to pose a potential challenge to Stalin, would result, as we have seen, in repression. So, the command lived in a 'barren period', one in which Stalin's personal favour counted for more than ability, imagination or experience. Imaginative thinking about the implications of modern weaponry was stifled by orthodoxy.[37]

That orthodoxy framed preparations for long war and a strategy of exhaustion was reflected in basic Soviet sociopolitical and economic strengths. For all that the Red Army had regained its confidence in the offensive and delivered a strategic knockout blow against Japan, the strategy of destruction as reflected in blitzkrieg and the search for a surprise knockout blow was taboo. The USSR had suffered greatly from surprise. But the surprise achieved by German forces in 1941 had not determined the war's outcome, and after the war the Soviets criticised the Germans for their reliance on surprise – not only an underestimation of Soviet power, but tantamount to adventurism. Senior officers including Zhukov criticised German plans for their lack of attention to reserves, for subordinating everything to a strategy of the invading single echelon. Such a venture could not, in the view of these officers, have secured victory in a war between two major powers. If Soviet war science asserted that Western powers were still seeking a blitzkrieg-type destruction of the USSR, 'every tenet' of Soviet war doctrine opposed the conclusion that such a strategy could lead to a quick, decisive victory: major war would necessarily be a long struggle, decided by the material and morale potentials of the warring parties. Such a war would be characterised by massive, extended land campaigns, even after a nuclear exchange, and would be won by a series of successive campaigns of annihilation.[38]

This, indeed, was how the Manchurian war was seen. As one Soviet colonel pointed out, it exemplified a 'genuine lightning war, not at all like the myth of the lightning war which was created by the German General Staff ... victory was achieved by the decisive defeat of the enemy by means of successive blows of increasing strength'.[39] Here is the distinction in Soviet thinking between German 'blitzkrieg' and Moscow's *molnienosnaya voina*.

This view of a long war was based on the 'permanently operating factors' (*postoyanno deistvuyschie faktory*) that decided the outcome of wars. Stalin had set these out in February 1942, partly as an attempt to portray German successes as only temporary and to encourage the belief that the USSR could still win due to its ideological and material strengths.[40] In practice, though, these factors served as the manifestation and reference point of Soviet war doctrine until Stalin's death over a decade later, first to deny that Soviet strength could be overwhelmed by the Germans, and then later to deny that the Soviets could be defeated by US atomic weapons. The 'permanently operating factors' broadly reflected the importance of the stability of the rear, and encompassed the economic, political and morale potential of the state: this provided the war-making potential, giving the combat forces the wherewithal to fight. They included the morale of the army, the quality and quantity of divisions, the armaments of the army, and the organising potential of the command personnel. These were contrasted with 'transitory factors' which might be important at some stages of the war, but were not decisive in determining the outcome. These included a favourable strategic position, advance preparation and pre-mobilisation, combat experience and surprise.

This formulation of permanently operating factors was widely repeated in all serious Soviet discussion about war into the mid-to-late 1950s. In 1955 Talensky stated that Soviet war science did not deny the significance of temporary factors, but that it relied on the permanently operating factors to which the 'decisive role' belonged. The terminology began to shift, but the emphasis often remained on the economic, political and morale potentials of the warring parties. Industry and transport to ensure mass production and uninterrupted supply were the keys to ensuring victory in a long war: determined armed struggle still meant dealing the enemy blows of ever increasing strength, and, to that end, all the forces of the people and resources of the country must be organised continuously to step up the war effort.[41]

In this sense, for a decade after the Great Victory, Soviet views of future war were largely a projection of the Great Fatherland War on to the future. If the enemy might have some technological advantages, these could be overcome by the basis of Soviet sociopolitical and economic strength. This debate was in counterpoint to, and, in a sense, interactive with, technical and doctrinal developments in the West, not least as proposed by those such as Liddell Hart, who wrote of a revolution in warfare and about blitzkrieg.[42] In large part, this was because Moscow anticipated a Western attack on the USSR in the shape of another blitzkrieg-style assault. Indeed, after the Great Fatherland War, the US and the British Empire were often described as having similarities with German fascism in their quest for world domination by force; the US was seen to be echoing the German reliance on surprise through an atomic blitzkrieg against the Soviet Union.[43] Any attempt by the West would be met with a strategy of exhaustion and repeated hammer blows leading to Soviet victory and the final destruction of imperialism.[44]

Stalin's death did prompt a shift. For Khrushchev it was a 'major dividing line' and 'all sorts of concerns about the security of our country and the need to modernise our army crashed upon us'. He was scathing about Stalin's role as commander in the Great Fatherland War, in attempting to blockade Berlin and in his refusal to send decisive aid to North Korea. Consequently, Khrushchev believed that he had inherited a situation in which the Soviet Union had already suffered two big military setbacks since 1945.[45] And over time, a combination of an evolving domestic intellectual context, a changing international context and technological development led first to a series of modifications and reforms. Then, in the second half of the 1950s, it led to a growing reconsideration of future war, in which Khrushchev himself played a significant role, rejecting conservative military views, advocating technological solutions and seeking to restrain defence spending.

On the one hand, Khrushchev's leadership emphasised a move away from Stalin's view of the inevitability of war towards 'peaceful coexistence'. While the USSR would continue to seek to advance socialism in the Third World, war with the capitalist West was no longer inevitable since the Soviet Union was both strong enough to defend itself and its economic success would show the path to a socialist future. On the other, while local conflicts were acknowledged, large-scale war against the West remained the primary, almost exclusive focus for war science, and thinking about future war was characterised by a move back towards a renewed emphasis on the importance of the initial period of war and surprise.

Discussion appears to have begun almost immediately after Stalin's death, with a re-examination of all areas of war science in the light of technological development, leading to a series of reforms overseen by Zhukov. This was prompted by the realisation that the US and Great Britain had capabilities that meant that they could begin the war by striking deep into the Soviet rear. Rather than providing the strategic resilience for combating a land invasion, Stalin's permanently operating factors – the state's mobilisation resources – would now be the first target of the enemy's long-range strikes. By 1955 this discussion had begun to include a re-examination of the role and value of surprise in modern warfare by senior officers such as Pavel Rotmistrov, who had commanded at Kursk and then in Operation Bagration in 1944, and would go on to be Assistant Minister of Defence and then, in the early 1960s, Chief Marshal of the Armoured Forces. These officers continued to reject the idea of relying on surprise, as the Germans had in their blitzkrieg: any attempt to destroy a Great Power by a surprise lightning blow, even with powerful modern weapons, was still adventurism, and a long war would still be the outcome, won by the side with superior socio-economic potential.

Nevertheless, they did acknowledge that technological developments had greatly increased the importance of strategic surprise in war, such that unexpected blows could now be made against strategic targets. Not only should planning take this into account, therefore, but developing new approaches such as forestalling strikes was necessary. Rotmistrov even conceded that in certain cases surprise attack with masses of new weapons could provoke the quick collapse of a state with a low resistance capability because of basic failures of its socio-economic structure and an unfavourable geographical location.[46] In this sense, he echoed Tukhachevsky's observations of 1937: blitzkrieg might work against a small state, but not a large, resilient one.

This stimulated a debate throughout the rest of the decade. The basic definitions of strategy remained much the same: strategy in war 'directly depends on politics' which it implements: politics sketches out the general aims of armed struggle and defines tasks for the preparation of the state for war, including the necessary means for strengthening the armed forces. Strategy examines the changing conduct of war, including studying the likely adversary's economic, morale and military capacities, and, in war, emerges from political aims and concrete strategic conditions. Politically, war strategy may have been 'fully in line with the class and national interests of the people', but in concrete content, Soviet and bourgeois war strategies 'reveal common moments' in that they reflect common objective laws of war.[47]

At the same time, the realities of a revolution in military affairs – reflected in nuclear weapons and missile development, combined with communications, reconnaissance and over-the-horizon guidance systems programmes – were recognised to be causing radical changes in the character of war. For some, such technology could not change the fact that war depended on economic, political and morale factors. Technology might quicken moves within war, but it could not quickly destroy the massed armed forces of a whole state: the very scale of a people's war, conducted across tremendous territorial space, would ensure that all major wars would, in all likelihood, be drawn out.[48] For others, though, these new conditions meant that while the permanently operating factors remained an important basis – economic organisation being of decisive significance – war science should not restrict itself to 1942's factors: such factors were not set once and for all, and science and surprise should be added to the list of permanently operating factors.[49]

This debate about strategy was overseen and conducted by a group of senior officers that was only slowly evolving. Despite the repressions, there was a strong sense of continuity among the senior command, and the military's role in the state even grew as more senior officers joined the Central Committee in 1956. Those who had overseen the waging of the Great Fatherland War and Manchuria remained in command throughout this period, though the leadership evolved. Although not a military man, Khrushchev himself, of course, had considerable experience in the Great Fatherland War, and, having taken power, played an active guiding role in shaping military thought and strategy. Zhukov and Kuznetsov, demoted under Stalin, were returned to senior positions under Khrushchev, before again falling from grace and losing their positions in 1956–57. Others, such as Rokossovsky, Konev, Shtemenko and Sokolovsky, were also retired or demoted by 1960. Even so, Shtemenko would regain seniority during the 1960s, and, as we shall see in the next chapter, Sokolovsky would oversee a major work on war strategy in the early 1960s.

Those who replaced them also had lengthy experience, having likewise fought in the Russian civil war, the wars of the 1930s, the Great Fatherland War and Manchuria. These were part of a group who had served with Khrushchev, campaigning in winter 1942–43 and then on the Ukrainian front: Sergei Gorshkov replaced Kuznetsov, and Rodion Malinovsky replaced Zhukov in 1957. Others, such as Semyon Ivanov, who had served at Stalingrad and Kursk, and in Manchuria, also rose to prominent positions in 1959, and, like Gorshkov, would have long and influential careers through even into the 1980s. Recognising the growing importance of technical skills in a period of accelerated scientific development, Malinovsky also began to promote technical officers, advancing the careers of those who would later emerge to prominence, such as Nikolai Ogarkov, who in 1957 became Deputy Chief of Staff of the Far Eastern Military District prior to attending the General Staff Academy.[50]

Surprise: deception, cunning and 'suddenness'

The debate about surprise takes us into noteworthy aspects of Russian war science. It formed part of a renewed focus on the initial period of war as being potentially decisive, and reflected the longer-term recognition of the importance of seizing and holding the initiative in war. Victory was still to be achieved by the destruction of large groups of forces, which remained the paramount aim of strategic operations: smash through the defences and exploit the situation with an increasing torrent of forces to force the enemy into a hopeless position. Once forces were annihilated and resistance was broken, the capture of strategically significant objectives and territory would be a useful by-product. These, indeed, were the lessons of 1944 and 1945: the strategic offensives of the second, but especially the third period and Manchuria became the model for how to conduct deception and surprise with strategic regroupings of forces; Manchuria demonstrated what could be done with the initial period of war and how to win a quick victory with a theatre offensive.[51]

Achieving the initiative – and therefore creating the conditions for gaining momentum – was done through a combination of deception and leadership to impose 'suddenness', *vnezapnost*, at strategic, operational and tactical levels. 'Suddenness' is defined as

actions that the adversary does not expect, allowing him to be taken by surprise and contributing to the achievement of success in battle, operation, and sometimes, war as a whole. One of the principles of war art. Suddenness is achieved by the secret movement of troops, the leading of the adversary into false conclusions about intentions, the keeping secret of operational plans, the unexpected use of new weapons and equipment and methods of warfare unknown to the adversary; the choice of unexpected areas of concentration of main efforts and the pre-emption of the adversary in the delivery of strikes, speed of manoeuvre, decisiveness of actions. Suddenness can be complete or partial, and depending on the scale, strategic, operational or tactical. Suddenness can be used at the beginning of a war and during it.[52]

This would create the conditions for paralysing enemy decision making, collapsing the enemy's defences in stages and thus penetrating into strategic depth. This 'suddenness' – sometimes referred to as 'unexpectedness' (*neozhidennost*) – is an essential feature of Russian war strategy, and so requires some consideration.

Deception and surprise had long been an important ingredient in Russian military thought and strategy. But it was during the Great Fatherland War that deception had become a mandatory feature of every operation, its importance emphasised because of the dilemmas of concentration and dispersal imposed by the modern battlefield. To achieve breakthrough and exploitation required the concentration of sufficiently superior forces, yet the concentration of such large force groupings took time and rendered them vulnerable to detection by improved reconnaissance and destruction by firepower of increasing range and lethality.

The Red Army had gone to considerable lengths, therefore, to achieve deception during the second and third periods of the Great Fatherland War. Zhukov may have underlined its importance for the victory at Stalingrad,[53] but this was a complex learning process, one that included numerous problems, flaws, lapses and failures. Yet by the third period of the war, the Red Army was routinely confusing the Germans with decoys and causing them to miss regroupings and force concentrations, and thus the direction of the main blows and the timing of offensives. The enemy was kept guessing, and German defences were therefore thinned out just where the next offensive was to take place.[54] Consequently, the Germans missed each substantial strategic offensive. Instead of facing acceptable force ratios, therefore, they found themselves facing 5:1 Soviet superiority at operational level and 8:1 or 10:1 at the tactical level. Perhaps all the more important, deception caused the Germans to deploy their forces and reserves poorly at the strategic level, undermining overall resilience and flexibility, weakening the defence as a whole, and facilitating a cascading chain reaction of breaking down the defence.[55]

Deception – *obman* – paralyses the enemy's will to resist and ability to enact an organised defence, and therefore leads the enemy into making mistakes. *Obman* is generated by a combination of two elements: *maskirovka* and *voennaya khitrost*. *Maskirovka*, from the French term *masquer*, to mask or conceal, is defined in Russian war science as

> a complex of measures with the purpose of concealing troops (forces) and objects (facilities) from the enemy and leading him into mistaken knowledge about the existence, location, composition, condition, actions and intentions of those troops (forces) and also the plans of the command, a type of combat support. *Maskirovka* helps to achieve the suddenness of the action of the troops (forces), to maintain combat ability and to increase survivability.[56]

Maskirovka is, therefore, essentially organisational combat support. It involves a wide range of measures, including camouflage and concealment, disinformation, decoys, reconnaissance and operational security. Successful *maskirovka* depends on comprehensive detailed 'phoney' plans, each with a strict timetable and to be delivered simultaneously with the real plans. It is a highly complex process, one that requires considerable effort and resources: it requires substantial forces to deploy sufficiently credible 'decoy' offensives, including diverse and extensive equipment and troop numbers, and it must be coordinated across the armed forces, even the defence sector as a whole, while maintaining strict information security.

This very complexity renders it very difficult both conceptually and in practice. Successful *maskirovka* is resource-intensive and demands consistent innovation and sophisticated organisation by well-trained officers who have a subtle understanding of the enemy. While it might be an essential ingredient in Russian war science and strategy, therefore, the Russian military recognises the challenges that *maskirovka* poses. Routine or predictable efforts or poorly resourced measures render it vulnerable to counter-measures by the enemy. Imperfectly coordinated measures, including through overly tight information security, undermine the effectiveness of its delivery and thus of the offensive as a whole.[57]

The other element of deception, *voennaya khitrost* or 'war cunning', is officially defined as the

> art of leading the enemy into error about the true intentions and plans for the fulfilment of tasks. War cunning is used in the aim of achieving suddenness and the creation of favourable conditions for the destruction of the enemy. War cunning in battle and operations first and foremost presumes keeping secret the intentions of command, the dispositions of troops and offering the enemy a false understanding of intentions of command, the movement of troops, their location and condition. It is the use of unexpected methods and ways of acting.[58]

If *maskirovka* is deception as performed by organisations, *voennaya khitrost* is deception as carried out by the commander. It is reflected in the commander's ability to provoke the enemy into making mistakes and acting in a rash and unconsidered way. It requires the commander to be able to learn from personal combat experience and to take unusual decisions and see them through. It is synonymous, therefore, with the art of war, and the ability to achieve decisive results in the shortest time with the least losses.[59]

A nuclear revolution?

In many ways, 1945 represented the pinnacle of Moscow's war strategy – it was a practical business, learned the hard way. The campaigning in both wars was characterised by familiar challenges and strengths, from problems in logistics and the chain of command to the coordinated deployment of suddenness, force and firepower at scale. But the experiences of those years have been mined ever since for examples of how to achieve command and control and deception.[60]

War strategy evolved in difficult conditions. Material resources were limited as the state sought first to rebuild after the war, and then to prioritise civilian sectors. Furthermore, for most of the period, as we have seen, the intellectual atmosphere strongly discouraged the challenging of orthodoxy. This meant that the emphasis for much of the period was on Stalin's 'permanently operating factors'. Despite the successes of Manchuria in 1945, which the Soviet military considered to be a 'real lightning war', the balance in the debate between a strategy of the (surprise) lightning blow and a strategy of exhaustion lay with the latter. As far as the Soviet military was concerned, another Western blitzkrieg would be met – and defeated – by a strategy of exhaustion.

During the second half of the 1950s, however, this notion began to evolve as senior officers began to debate the value of surprise, and the question of the winnability of war in the initial period. As we shall see in the next chapter, this initial period would become a particular focus. By the end of the decade, this debate, strongly influenced by the recognition of a scientific technological revolution, had developed to such an extent that surprise and the initial period of war were recognised to be of growing importance. Together, these shifts represented a new stage in the Soviet outlook on war, a ripening of debates underway since Stalin's death, and a shift in the tension from a long war fought by massed armed forces towards the potential for a shorter war.

Indeed, in 1959 there was another reappraisal of doctrine and another round of structural reform with the establishment of the strategic rocket forces as a command. These shifts were set out in a series of speeches by Khrushchev through late 1959 into early 1960. In a memorandum on military reform in December 1959, he argued that the USSR had won good positions in the international arena, and should exploit the favourable situation by continuing to reduce its armaments and emphasise missile building. 'We must make this a rational army', he argued, one 'without superfluity' – and that meant a combat-capable army that met the requirements of guaranteeing security while lightening the load on the budget. Maintaining a large army while simultaneously possessing hydrogen bombs and missiles for both long- and short-range combat did 'not make sense', and simply meant 'lowering' Soviet economic potential. Malinovsky was thus tasked with shaping proposals for the reduction of the armed forces, and a conference of military commanders convened to discuss practical measures.[61]

During a speech on 14 January 1960, Khrushchev proffered a different view of future war as a result of a revolution in military affairs, in which new weapons should replace conventional ones.

Operation Barbarossa and the Great Victory

Nuclear weapons were now the main means of conducting warfare, and large standing armies were, he argued, both an extravagance and becoming obsolete. He again emphasised that economic considerations compelled a shift to missiles, and a substantial reduction both in ground forces and the role of the navy.[62] The following day, the Supreme Soviet adopted a law on a significant reduction in the armed forces of the Soviet Union.

4

Winning a war in the nuclear age

If Khrushchev's speech about a revolution in military affairs announced a major change and new stage in strategy, it was the consequence of discussions and shifts that had taken place over nearly seven years.[1] It reflected structural changes to the armed forces, including simultaneously the establishment of a new service, and a real and sustained effort to reduce the size of the Soviet conventional forces. Additionally, it underlined the re-emergence of an emphasis on firepower rather than numbers. For Khrushchev, who actively involved himself in the formulation of war strategy and exerted considerable influence on it, it was the size of the arsenal, not the size of the army that counted: large conventional forces were both a burden on the state budget and obsolete. He deemed an ocean-going navy to be an extravagance, large surface ships being good only for firing salutes.[2] Equally, the age of the tank was over: tanks would disappear from war forever, so they should no longer be built.[3]

The consensus that a war between major powers would be long was changing. As we saw in the last chapter, a shift was already underway, opening the door to renewed discussion about surprise and suddenness, and the suggestion that war *could*, in theory at least, be short: seizing the initiative during the initial period of war could be decisive, and, especially against a regional power, a state could quickly achieve its political goals. Equally, those such as Malinovsky were arguing that war between major powers would inevitably be a nuclear rocket war which would be destructive for all humankind – which meant that there could be no victor.[4]

Actually, a confluence of external and internal developments soon threw the new approach into doubt. On the international stage, Soviet confidence was undermined by the election of John F. Kennedy, and Washington's build-up of its forces: the development and deployment of Minutemen and Polaris missiles, combined with an expansion of the US Navy and special forces, contributed to the ability and willingness of the US to challenge Moscow. Moscow's own poor strategic coordination and technical deficiencies amplified this challenge. The Soviet navy in the late 1950s and early 1960s could not support Moscow's ambitions further afield because the state authorities rejected the military leadership's plans as being too provocative, and because technical problems in early nuclear submarines limited their ability to deploy force. As tension between the USSR and US grew, therefore, it became clear to Moscow that US superiority required careful reconsideration.[5]

Domestically, the way Khrushchev sought to drive war strategy and reshape the armed forces resulted in growing opposition. Partly, this meant the passive resistance of a bureaucratic system opposed to change. He himself acknowledged that his proposals were 'fed into the labyrinths' of the commissions, where there would be 'a lot of talk, speeches and verbiage', and initiatives would be 'dissipated'.[6] Equally, however, among the military opposition began to grow. In 1960 Sokolovsky resigned as Chief of the General Staff and Konev retired, both protesting troop reductions. The Cuban missile crisis led to further tension between Khrushchev and the high command: the General Staff's view was that the crisis had brought the world to the precipice of nuclear war.[7] Matvey Zakharov, who had replaced Sokolovsky as Chief of the General Staff, was reassigned to head the General Staff Academy; soon after, critical of Khrushchev's interference in military affairs, he went into early retirement.[8] By 1962 Malinovsky too was 'tiring' of yet more troop reductions and officer dismissals, and was critical of the way that Khrushchev had approached the Cuban missile crisis and then sought to deploy the military to crush the Novocherkassk protests in June 1962. 'One should not treat the army that way', he objected.[9]

This confluence of international and domestic developments, including a yet further effort to reduce defence spending, reached such a point that the Central Committee – with Malinovsky playing an active role – removed Khruschev from all posts and retired him in October 1964. Khrushchev's replacement, Leonid Brezhnev, dramatically changed the context for the military. Brezhnev himself was familiar with the defence sector, having served on the Central Committee first as deputy head of the political directorate of the army and navy, and then, since 1956, as the politburo member in charge of the defence industry and the space programme. And whereas Khrushchev had asserted that he did not trust the appraisals of generals in matters of strategic import, Brezhnev and Malinovsky were more in harmony. Brezhnev renounced Khrushchev's approach, halting the reductions, and instead devoted immense resources to strengthening the armed forces. Brezhnev also trusted Malinovsky's views on military matters: the latter was essentially given a free hand, and wielded considerable influence until his death from cancer in March 1967.[10]

Thus began a generation of dynamic development in which Moscow emerged as a real global actor. During this period, Moscow's thinking about strategy and war evolved as the political and military leadership wrestled with the challenges posed both by a changing international landscape and by the implications of scientific and technological advances. Focus fell on what victory in war would look like and how to achieve it in the nuclear era. This debate about modern war and the complex battlefield was pioneering, with much (ongoing) mutual emulation and interaction between East and West. Theory and practice in operations and wars fought by the Israelis, British and the US, as well as operations waged by Moscow, again highlighted the tension between the benefits of strategies for short, decisive war or those for waging a prolonged war of exhaustion. This resulted in another period of flowering in Moscow's thinking about strategy and war, reflected in seminal work, the influence of which can still be felt today.

War in the nuclear age

The change in approach initiated by Khrushchev in 1960 did not reflect a substantive alteration in Moscow's understanding of war. As before, war was understood to be a sociopolitical phenomenon, a tool of policy. War was still part of a whole, and that whole was politics, and 'quite obviously, armed struggle is what characterises war'. The definition of war as 'violence between states ... armed combat for definite political goals' remained valid.[11] Although there was some distinction between types of war, such as local wars and wars of national liberation, the main focus remained on war as being between the USSR and the West: a decisive clash between systems that would be global in horizon and require the mobilisation of the material and spiritual resources of the state.

Where it did imply change, however, was in terms of strategy, and especially war strategy. This provoked a sustained debate about the periodisation of war, escalation, and the roles of nuclear and conventional weapons. The central question over strategies of destruction or exhaustion, and whether a war could be short or would inevitably be long, permeated discussion.

Vasily Sokolovsky made a principal contribution to this effort to shape a modern strategy. Although he had retired in protest in 1960, Sokolovsky remained a prominent and influential figure in military affairs, considered one of the most knowledgeable senior officers.[12] He had joined the Red Army in 1918, and a long and distinguished career had followed, including at the battle of Kursk and with Zhukov at the battle of Berlin. After the war, he first became commander of the Soviet group of forces in Germany, then, in 1949, First Deputy Minister of the Armed Forces. In 1952 he was appointed Chief of General Staff. His edited volume *Voennaya strategiya*, published in 1962, was the first substantive Soviet attempt to reflect on strategy and war since Svechin's *Strategiya* in the 1920s, offering an officially sanctioned interpretation of the revolution in military affairs. Indeed, *Voennaya strategiya* offered a sustained examination of questions from the character of modern war to the hierarchy of the state and how military capabilities should connect with other aspects of state power. It reflected at length on the historical roots of war strategy, comparing and contrasting Soviet and Western war strategies. The volume also dwelt on the preparation of the country to repel aggression, the organisation and development and command of the armed forces, and the conduct of war.

In general terms, although Sokolovsky and his colleagues considered the laws of strategy to be objective and to apply to the same degree to all belligerents, there was no single strategy or war doctrine applicable to all states. A state's history, geography, national and political traditions influenced the character of its war strategy. Sokolovsky and his colleagues reviewed the work of foreign strategists such as Liddell Hart, and accorded specific strategies to different states: Great Britain's, for instance, was the 'concept of the strategy of indirect action'. During World War II, they asserted, the Anglo-American alliance waged a strategy of exhaustion against both Germany and the USSR.[13]

The strategic hierarchy that Sokolovsky and his colleagues elaborated was very clear: state policy was the pinnacle, from which all else flowed. State policy should set the guiding idea and coordinate all the tools of state to create favourable conditions for war strategy by mobilising the maximum resources and preparing diplomatic, economic and political morale measures. State policy set the most propitious moment to start the war: if the armed forces were the decisive tool, this also underlined the importance of diplomacy, economics and political morale. Diplomacy was essential for shaping wider international conditions. The economic conditions were essential for providing the material means that the state and armed forces had at their disposal and for replacing what were expected to be heavy losses in early combat. The political morale of the people was essential for domestic stability and ensuring resilience in the face of the initial blows.[14]

State policy therefore guided a complex and dynamic web of activities of which war strategy and armed struggle formed just one part of the whole, albeit the defining one. The priority of state policy was underlined – it played the leading and defining role: state policy and war strategy were neither equal nor synonymous. Nonetheless, Sokolovsky and his colleagues did emphasise the reciprocity both among the various tools of state policy, such as between the economic and military domains, and between the individual domains and overall policy. This unmistakably emphasised war as a whole-of-state activity in which the armed forces and armed combat played the decisive role; successful results were to be achieved by the defeat of the enemy's armed forces and the disruption of their economy.[15]

Sokolovsky defined war doctrine as 'the officially approved system of concepts and fundamental problems of war'. It reflected the system of views accepted by the state on the evolution of future war, the state's attitude to war, and the measures necessary to prepare the country economically and spiritually for war, and to address the problems involved in organising and preparing the armed forces and the methods for conducting war. In turn, war strategy encompassed the means and methods for preparing the armed forces for war and then waging it. It reflected a 'system of theoretical knowledge dealing with rules governing war as armed combat for definite class interests'. It is based on 'consideration of military and political conditions', the economic and morale potential of a state, the interpretation of the enemy, the impact of science and technology on the emergence of new weapons, and the use of past war experience as the state leadership sought to interpret the future of war.[16]

Two of these aspects deserve attention here. First, Sokolovsky and his colleagues focused on developing war strategy based on the experience gained from wars and military operations in the past. They reflected on Tsarist strategists Suvorov and Kutuzov, Mikhnevich and Leer, and gave sustained attention to Moscow's experiences of the civil war and the Great Fatherland War (some 50 pages were dedicated to the latter, including the defensive campaigns of 1941–43). Their assessment was often critical, as they noted errors, problems and shortfalls. During the civil war, for instance, command and control had proven problematic, with a lack of coordination between fronts. During the interwar years, insufficient attention was paid to the strategic defensive, especially the problem of withdrawing troops from enemy attack, and there was no correct assessment of the initial period of war. When Germany did strike in 1941, the higher leadership had prepared poorly, failing to organise sufficient strategic reserves and to deploy forces correctly, and giving only belated instructions. In short, problems of command in the initial period of war resulted in the costly loss of the initiative to the adversary.[17]

These lessons of recent experience were relevant to shaping strategy for the future because of the second aspect – the growing impact of scientific development and the creation of new weapons. According to Sokolovsky and his colleagues, the appearance of nuclear weapons and missiles had 'structurally changed' war strategy: war was now much more destructive and deadly, and was waged on a much greater, even 'unlimited' geographical scale.[18] Indeed, war strategy in this context had evolved into one of missile and nuclear strikes into the enemy's depth, along with the simultaneous use of all branches of the armed forces to achieve the complete defeat of the enemy and the destruction of their economic potential throughout their entire territory. The boundaries between the front line and the rear were now erased. Whereas previously war strategy and operations had sought to defeat or weaken enemy armed forces and therefore capture vitally important administrative and political centres, thus leading to victory, now massed missile bombardments would simultaneously strike both the armed forces and targets deep within the state in a single, continuous process. Whereas previously the main problem had been the breakthrough of deeply echeloned defences and strong fortifications, now missiles obviated this. For Sokolovsky and his colleagues, therefore, positional warfare was a thing of the past.[19]

This had many implications for strategy. Most important, though, was that with these modern weapons it was possible to achieve decisive results in a short period of time. Indeed, although Sokolovsky and his colleagues acknowledged that it was possible that war could be protracted,[20] they repeatedly underlined the possibilities for decisive action in a short period, especially in a war's initial period. The new weapons enabled the swift defeat and destruction of the enemy's armed forces and economic potential throughout their entire territory, and thus the elimination of one or multiple states from the war, *even if they had large territories and large populations.*[21]

Voennaya strategiya illustrated, therefore, that by the early 1960s the debate had leaned away from long war thinking and strategies of exhaustion towards thinking once again about seeking to land the lightning knockout blow. As one senior Soviet officer put it, these were years of 'nuclear euphoria'. In the view of the General Staff, a nuclear war could not only be survived, but it could be won, and won within ten days.[22]

New and updated editions of *Voennaya strategiya* were published in 1963 and 1968, and the volume received international attention. Many of the central theses of the volume – war as armed struggle, the dominance of state policy over war strategy, as well as the importance of the reciprocity between them and the significance of effective connections between the state and military leaderships, and the radical impact of new weapons on strategy – would continue to underpin Moscow's thinking long into the future.[23] Even so, the volume sparked sustained and critical debate at home, not least for its failure to give due attention to the 'continuity of the best traditions of the Russian national military school', for insufficient critique of the conditions of the late Stalin era, and for the unsatisfactory attention accorded to the role of the ground forces.[24]

Voennaya strategyia therefore served as a lightning rod for debate on three interrelated themes for the next twenty years: the balance between nuclear and conventional weapons, the role of the initial period of war and the role of sea power. This debate meant that already by the mid-1960s the discussion was again shifting, especially regarding questions about the character of a future war, and whether it would be short or long.

The return of conventional war in the nuclear age

In the first few years of the 1960s the consensus was that war would begin with a massive, surprise nuclear attack, but, as one Soviet officer put it, the problem of the duration of the war remained of great importance for understanding its character.[25] By the middle of the decade, though, the state and military leadership were considering other potential scenarios, including the need to prepare the state for protracted war. While the main concern remained the immediate use of nuclear weapons, thinking began to include the role of modern conventional weapons.[26]

This was partly because of shifts in strategic approach in the West and improvements in technology: in the mid-1960s, NATO debated and then adopted a more flexible approach to war, including with conventional weapons. And in 1967 the third Arab–Israeli war demonstrated the problems Soviet equipment faced against modern Western conventional weapons. Khrushchev later suggested that the Israeli victory in just six days meant that, 'in effect', Moscow had 'suffered a defeat'.[27]

Equally, this was because of the different tasks facing Moscow. Although tensions with the West eased with détente from the mid-to-late 1960s through much of the 1970s, Moscow faced problems in the socialist world. In August 1968, after political efforts to limit reform in Czechoslovakia, Moscow deployed overwhelming force to crush the Prague Spring. Moreover, Moscow's relationship with China had deteriorated to such an extent that in 1969 border skirmishes broke out between them. Indeed, such was the threat posed by China, as far as Moscow was concerned, that Brezhnev and Chief of General Staff Andrei Grechko oversaw a significant growth in the deployment of Soviet armed forces to the east.

This shift towards reintroducing thinking about and capacity for conventional war was gradual, but it continued and became well established by the mid-1970s as the military command began to see that the conventional period of a war might last not just for hours, but for days. The emphasis began to shift away from massive retaliation with nuclear weapons towards their more flexible use; by the end of that decade, the General Staff considered that an entire war might remain conventional.[28]

This had two consequences. First, in the mid-1970s, the leadership took the decision not to use nuclear weapons first.

Indeed, by 1977, although concern remained high among the political and military leadership about the serious potential threat of a surprise US attack, there was consensus that nuclear war would be simultaneously futile and catastrophic – and could not be won in the sense of war being the continuation of politics.[29]

The second consequence was the reaffirmation of Moscow's understanding of war as the continuation of politics by forceful means: the use of the armed forces to achieve political and economic aims. Although war was characterised by various forms of struggle, including economic, political and diplomatic, military action was the principal form.

The hierarchy was reiterated: state policy sets out the main tasks, and military affairs both result from and serve it. The 'leading role of politics with respect to war strategy lies in the fact that politics defines the objectives of war, determines the methods for conducting it, focuses war strategy on tasks and creates the conditions for accomplishing them, mobilising the necessary material and human resources'. Likewise, the economic and sociopolitical structure of the state have a 'determining influence' on the nature and substance of war strategy: the country's economy provided the material basis for a state's fighting ability. To be sure, there should be reciprocity between state policy and war strategy: state strategy must correspond to the military potential of a state: 'correct' strategy was a 'prerequisite' for victory; without it, the armed forces would suffer defeat. But war strategy was reaffirmed as the expression of state policy.[30]

Likewise, war doctrine still reflected the system of views of a state's military policy, addressing both the sociopolitical and military-technical aspects of this policy. While war science was guided by general laws common to all, senior officers reiterated that war doctrine and strategy were necessarily specific to nations, reflecting their unique sociopolitical, economic and geographical circumstances.[31]

Much of this was a restatement of long-established views. Yet there were important nuances. On the one hand, the explicit emphasis on war as a state-level activity, a sociopolitical phenomenon that required economic and political resilience as well as powerful armed forces, indicated a shift in emphasis towards war potentially being not just conventional but *protracted*. While it remained the case that a nuclear war would probably be comparatively brief, the military leadership observed that taking into account the enormous potential military and economic resources of belligerent coalitions, it could well be *protracted*. Economic and sociopolitical resilience was therefore the basis for sustaining a long war: if war broke out, it would be an uncompromising clash with decisive political and strategic goals. It would also be global in character, and, because of its destructiveness, would make maximal demands on the economic and spiritual resources of the belligerents. Military actions could continue for a long time, and the belligerents should be prepared to continue the struggle in the face of enormous losses; war would be a severe and prolonged crisis.[32]

On the other, it underlined the 'specifically' (*sugubo*) defensive nature of Moscow's war strategy. The emphasis had shifted from the offensive to 'repelling the aggressor' and 'defeating him utterly by means of decisive operations'. While the offensive remained the basic type of strategic operations, the importance of the defensive was acknowledged, and likewise that defence on any scale must be active to create the conditions for going on to the counter-offensive to achieve the complete destruction of the enemy.[33]

The initial period of war – strategies of lightning war and exhaustion

This discourse reflected the ongoing tension in Moscow's thinking about the advantages of offensive and defensive, and also the significance of the initial period of war. Debate focused on the dynamic interaction of three sets of questions: the characteristics of how different states waged war, the complex processes of entry into war, including mobilisation plans, and the changing character of war.

Throughout the 1960s, Sokolovsky and his colleagues had underlined the 'extraordinary' importance of the initial period of war. The combination of nuclear-armed missiles and both sides seeking maximum results in a decisive war meant that the initial period would be the 'main and decisive period', and would 'pre-determine the outcome of a war as a whole'. This emphasised the significance of even the first few moments of a war: a war could be won in that initial period. This had major consequences for Moscow's understanding of strategy and war. The ability of both the state and the military to prepare, organise, mobilise and deploy material resources and the armed forces in time was cast into doubt, since the threatening period of war – when preparations would be made before a war was initiated – was now obsolete: the mobilisation, concentration and deployment of forces was now done in advance of the war.

Actually, in this way, Sokolovsky's collective of authors sought to adapt the formula about the duration of a war. 'The most important factor determining the duration of the war', they argued, 'will not be the time during which it is conducted, but the effectiveness made at the very beginning.' The more effectively a state used the weapons and forces accumulated before the war, the greater the results it could achieve at the very beginning of the war and the more rapidly victory could be attained.[34]

One of the most prominent figures in this debate was army general and professor Semyon Ivanov, who, by the late 1960s, had become head of the General Staff's Voroshilov War Academy. Born in 1907, Ivanov had volunteered for the Red Army in 1926. Decorated in the Winter War against Finland, he served as Chief of Staff on different fronts in the Great Fatherland War, including at Kursk and the crossing of the Dniepr river in 1943. For his contribution to planning the Manchurian campaign in 1945, he was decorated Hero of the Soviet Union. After the war, Ivanov served as military district chief of staff before being promoted to Deputy Chief of the General Staff in 1959 and head of the Main Operations Directorate. In this role, he led Operation Anadyr to transfer weapons to Cuba.

Like most others, Ivanov's detailed analysis of the initial period of war drew on the diverse experiences of World War II and the different national styles of the belligerents. These experiences demonstrated that the role of the initial period had meaningfully evolved, and was now characterised by new content. The war had revealed a persistent trend to shift the preparation for conducting the deployment and first operations beyond the limits of the actual war itself to the pre-war period: what had previously taken place in the initial period – mobilisation, concentration and deployment of forces – now took place *before* the war, in the threatening period. This meant that some of the belligerents sought to achieve strategic goals even in the first attacks, using surprise and maximum force from the outset, and therefore that decisive encounters between the main forces now took place nearer to the start of the war. Success, he argued, depended on surprise and achieving air superiority on the main axes of attack, with rapid penetration into the enemy's rear to create favourable conditions for manoeuvre in operational depth. This led to the seizure of the initiative in war; once one side had seized it, it was extremely difficult for the other to recapture it.[35]

To shed further light on this essential question, Ivanov examined the participants' strategies. Using the lightning war approach, he argued, the Germans, Italians and Japanese had sought to achieve a crushing knockout victory before their adversaries could mobilise and use their economic potential. Great Britain, France and the United States had instead adopted strategies of exhaustion, only conducting static defence in the initial period of war, and waiting for the most favourable moment to apply decisive effort. This strategy relied on achieving the economic and moral exhaustion of the adversary; such a strategy sought to determine the war not in the initial period but in the final period: victory went to the side that could withstand the effort.[36]

Ivanov was critical of both strategies: the Germans overestimated the importance of the initial period, the British, French and Americans underestimated it, relying on an 'uncritical' and 'obsolete' dogma from their experience of World War I. Both were guilty of 'technicism', overestimating the capabilities of technology. And by placing their faith in small, well-equipped armies, both approaches were 'divorced' from the reality of the economic and financial strains of creating and maintaining forces for wars between major powers.[37] In wars between the capitalists, he observed, the aggressors may have been able to achieve their primary goals, and sometimes their ultimate goals in the first operations. But in the Great Fatherland War, German surprise did not have the paralysing effect it had realised elsewhere: the Red Army had not been destroyed in the initial operations, and German forces had not been able to penetrate into the most important political and economic centres.[38]

Blitzkrieg, Ivanov asserted, only could achieve victory over a militarily and economically weak enemy, and then only when that enemy had limited territory and low morale and political unity. Faced with large nations with considerable military and economic potential, a large landmass and high morale and political unity, blitzkrieg failed entirely, even when the aggressor achieved important results in the initial period. Nevertheless, for Ivanov, war *could* be won in the initial period: the strategic operation against Japan in Manchuria reflected a 'true' lightning campaign, a classic campaign combining suddenness, decisiveness and sweeping, deep operations to crush the enemy.[39]

The sea power of the state

The third theme that emerged from *Voennaya strategiya* was the changing role of maritime power in Moscow's strategic thinking. The emphasis that Sokolovsky and his colleagues placed on the fundamental changes occurring in maritime operations because of the possibilities offered by the development of an atomic, missile-carrying fleet was shared by senior naval officers.[40] But this was only one part of the story behind the significant technical development and numerical growth of the Soviet navy during the 1960s and 1970s.

Winning a war in the nuclear age

In fact, the role of maritime power and the navy in Moscow's thinking had considerably evolved since the end of the Great Fatherland War, and the development of the fleet reflected shifting strategic concerns. The most obvious of these was the changing nature of the threat. Before and during World War II, Moscow's main adversary had been Germany, a clearly continental challenge: the struggle at sea was not decisive, and the navy took a secondary role. After the war, however, the primary opponents were the USA, Great Britain and their allies in NATO: essentially strong maritime powers. These were opponents who had long-developed national strategies for war at sea. Western powers used an oceanic strategy as a basic concept of war doctrine, with the oceans providing launch pads for highly mobile, covertly acting carriers of long-range strategic missiles. Such forces were capable of inflicting in a short time tremendous damage on land installations far from the coast. The combination of a changing international situation and the influence of scientific development on military capabilities meant that conditions were thus very different. The importance of the sea, and of the struggle on the sea, would only grow.[41]

This required a completely different strategy, one that simultaneously highlighted the initial period of war and raised the importance of the Soviet navy. The path was certainly not smooth. Stalin had favoured developing the navy, but Khrushchev abandoned or reversed his plans to build a large surface fleet in favour of atomic submarines. Nevertheless, by the late 1960s the Soviet navy had reached a size and capability unprecedented in its history. This growth took it from being a force essentially dedicated to coastal defence to one with a global horizon, one that sought to challenge Western forces on the world's oceans. In 1970 the Soviet navy conducted the worldwide Okean exercise with 84 surface warships, some 80 submarines, 45 auxiliary and intelligence ships and a large contingent of naval aircraft; one senior officer stated that 'now we call our navy an ocean-going fleet, and this is correct'.[42]

Sergey Gorshkov was largely responsible for this emergence on to the world stage and the new and innovative naval approach. Born in 1910 to school teacher parents in the imperial civil service, Gorshkov joined the navy in 1927, attending the M.V. Frunze Naval Academy. Graduating in 1931 alongside others such as Vladimir Kasatonov, he went on to play an active role shaping and conducting Moscow's naval strategy until his death in 1988. He was appointed captain first rank after just ten years of service, and then, in October 1941, rear admiral, commanding the Sea of Azov flotilla. He had extensive wartime experience – commanding the largest Soviet amphibious landing of the war, the defence of Novorossiisk (1942), the reactivation of the Sea of Azov flotilla (1943), and supporting the westward advance of the ground forces (1944–45). This meant that he worked with some of those who after the war would become the most important political and military leaders, including Khrushchev, Malinovsky and Andrei Grechko, who succeeded Malinovsky as Minister of Defence in 1967.

Promoted to admiral in 1953, Gorshkov replaced Kuznetsov as commander of the Soviet navy in 1956 and was again promoted, this time to fleet admiral, in 1962. Under Khrushchev, he protected classes of surface ships as best as possible during the time of cuts, and then, under Brezhnev, oversaw a significant expansion of the fleet's capabilities and activity. As a commander, he believed in exacting discipline in the implementation of orders.[43] An intelligent, articulate officer, albeit brusque with fools, Gorshkov was 'distinguished by a strong sense of purpose and a gift for winning over both political and military officers'.[44]

Gorshkov set out his thinking in a series of articles examining the evolution of sea power published between 1972 and 1973 in the Soviet navy's journal, *Morskoi sbornik*, and then in his book *Sea Power of the State*, first published in 1976. Having built the navy and then shown in 1970 what it could do, Gorshkov sought to position the navy as both a strategic and a military asset: a means of advancing Moscow's power and in the context of the 'restatement' of military doctrine that took place under Grechko in the mid-1970s.

War, he emphasised, was the continuation of politics – military action could not be divorced from the goals of those politics which were being advanced through means of force. In that context, while all services contributed to victory in war, it was now the navy that was best capable of ensuring and promoting Moscow's interests in peace and war. Like no other service, he stated, it was the navy that could protect the state from beyond its borders and promote its economic and military power beyond its borders.

Moreover, if navies were at the forefront of diverse forms of armed combat, they now offered a means of changing the course and outcome of an armed struggle, even in continental theatres. Their freedom of movement and ability to concentrate powerful groupings meant that they could achieve surprise and deliver strikes from the sea. According to Gorshkov, therefore, the Soviet navy had evolved from being an operational-strategic level actor and defensive factor in war – a coastal action fleet – to a strategic asset, one that would seek to destroy the enemy navy in fleet-against-fleet action, and also strike the enemy's military-economic potential on land, in fleet-against-shore operations against vitally importance centres of economic, administrative and political power. Navies were therefore capable of decisively influencing the course of a world war.[45]

The military technical revolution

Gorshkov summed up this evolution of Soviet strategy and thinking about war by noting the inherent tension of continuity and change: Soviet strategy and military affairs continuously developed, but the essence of their fundamental direction remained unchanged. This tension was underlined in 1976 when Grechko died. His replacement, Dmitry Ustinov, was a civilian who had for a decade overseen the military industrial complex. In turn, Ustinov promoted Nikolai Ogarkov to Chief of the General Staff in January 1977. These appointments confirmed the shift away from using nuclear weapons as the first resort towards shaping a strategy for fighting conventional war, even in the nuclear era. This also reflected, as Ogarkov later acknowledged, the need for the armed forces to shift from quantity to quality, to reshape the large Soviet military into a smaller strike force based on advanced technology.[46] This was partly because, by the late 1970s, Moscow considered the huge armed forces and defence expenditure to be a burden and sought new ideas for defence: the military no longer enjoyed the same unquestioned economic priority it had enjoyed in the 1960s.

This situation was also a result of NATO's improving capabilities and the emergence of another level in military technological development, especially in automated command and control and powerful long-range precision weapons. This reflected evidence from the Yom Kippur War in 1973, which showed the growing lethality of anti-tank weapons as well as shifts in US thinking about war to the effect that a conventional war could be won in Europe by increasing the firepower of heavy divisions. By the mid-1970s prominent US thinkers were reconsidering their posture in Europe and the applicability of lessons from blitzkrieg-type warfare. Altogether, this situation obliged Moscow to rethink how it would seek to wage and win a conventional war.

Consequently, Ogarkov, aided by a team in the General Staff's department of development of war art led by Andrian Dani-levich,[47] shaped a vision of war that combined a dynamic, high-speed offensive into the enemy's strategic depths while simultaneously ensuring a strong defence and protection of the rear. Ogarkov's vision drew extensively on past experience and Moscow's strategic theoretical inheritance, and he sought to implement truly innovative reform by the early 1980s. As a result, Ogarkov became one of the most prominent Soviet war strategists. Often considered to be the father of the modern revolution in military affairs, and to have overseen the period of greatest post-war innovation, he was something of a rarity: the first military engineer to be appointed Chief of the General Staff. Born in 1917, he joined the Red Army in 1938, and graduated from the Military Engineering Academy in 1941. He served throughout the Great Fatherland War, before being appointed to divisional and military district commands. In 1968 he was promoted to First Deputy Chief of the General Staff, and in 1974 to Deputy Minister of Defence and chair of the state technical commission. His tenure as CGS was marked by his reformist vigour, but also by his disputes with the political leadership. He opposed the Soviet intervention in Afghanistan in 1979, for instance, and the imposition of martial law in Poland in 1981. Nevertheless, he also took responsibility for those decisions: in 1983, as the military's public face, he defended the shooting down of a Korean passenger aircraft by the Soviet air force.

For Ogarkov, future war consisted of a complex system of interdependent, large-scale simultaneous and successive strategic operations, including operations in continental theatres. Such a war – even if it remained conventional – would be a decisive, destructive clash, since modern conventional weapons could now inflict damage akin to that of weapons of mass destruction. And if such a war remained conventional, it would likely be protracted. It was simply impossible for an aggressor to achieve a knockout-blow first-strike victory.[48] This emphasised the significance of the political and social aspects of war doctrine: the political mission of war must fully correspond to the war potential of the state and methods of conducting military actions. Re-emphasising that war strategy is shaped by and serves politics, Ogarkov also underlined the dependence of the armed forces on the economy, since the economy conditioned the ability to fight a long war.[49]

Achieving victory in such a war meant the continued examination of past experience, different national strategies and Moscow's own theoretical inheritances. Ogarkov noted, for instance, the German theory of blitzkrieg and Liddell Hart's strategy of indirect approach. And although he criticised the Soviet leadership of the 1930s for not elaborating thinking about the strategic defensive and the initial period of war, Ogarkov argued that technological developments had created suitable conditions for adapting the theory of deep operations to modern conditions. The expanding range and destructive power of weapons both facilitated surprise and meant that effective strikes could be delivered across the whole depth of an enemy's state without having to increase significantly the quantity of forces for the assault. So, the attacker could now quickly shift the centre of gravity into the enemy's rear: for the first time in history, the entire state would be immediately involved in combat action.

This blurred the lines between the offensive and the defensive. To defeat strategic enemy groupings, the offensive – exploiting deception and suddenness – was to be characterised by powerful bombardment and air assault, combined with a high-speed assault by operational manoeuvre groups deep into enemy territory to neutralise NATO's nuclear weapons and disrupt command and control and logistics. The shock and speed of the assault would also mean an intermingling of forces, which would reduce the number of targets for any NATO nuclear strikes. If the offensive remained the core strategic operation, defence and retention of important territory was also important. Strategic defence was to be active, though, to create the conditions for going on to the counter-offensive to achieve the complete destruction of the enemy.

Ogarkov emphasised the introduction of precision-guided weapons, automated command and control, and the establishment of self-sufficient inter-service strategic groupings under unified command in each of four strategic directions. He sought to reorganise the armed forces into highly mobile, constant readiness groups and established training and large-scale command exercises such as Zapad 81 to test his concepts. In so doing, as one prominent Russian officer noted, Ogarkov turned the General Staff into the brains of the army. Equally, Ogarkov generated resistance within the system and garnered influential opponents. He developed 'deep disagreements' with Defence Minister Ustinov over the intervention in Afghanistan, and over procurement and the organisation of the armed forces. His vision also demanded a reorganisation and fine tuning of the armed forces that the military industrial complex and services alike sought to resist and sabotage. Parts of the ground forces resisted the attempt to move away from Great Fatherland War era approaches, and there were extended disputes about reforming and reorganising the air force and air defence forces based, according to Gareev, on 'narrow departmental interests'. Furthermore, Ogarkov was less inclined to support the major development of the navy than Grechko had been, leading to tension between him and Gorshkov.[50]

Conservatism, stagnation and the difficulties of implementing the vision

The complexities of strategy making limited, and, in the end, undermined Ogarkov's efforts. Some of these were longer-term, contextual problems. As we have seen, history was very much at the heart of thinking about war and strategy, whether in terms of the role of services such as the navy, or the periodisation of war and how to interpret the influence of technological development. This was reflected in the publication of Pyotr Pospelov's six-volume history of the Great Fatherland War, which emphasised the magnitude of the Soviet war effort and aimed to counter Western books that examined the war (including Liddell Hart's work). It was also reflected in the rehabilitation of those who had suffered in the repressions of the late 1930s, including biographies and the republication of their works.[51] More importantly, though, it was reflected in how history was now woven into MoD thinking. All the senior leaders – Sokolovsky, Bagramian, Gorshkov, Grechko, Ivanov, Ogarkov – used history as the intellectual foundation on which to build their arguments. The Institute of War History was established by the MoD in 1966, associated with the faculty of history of the USSR in the Academy of Sciences. Led by Pavel Zhilin, the institute actively contributed to the debate, publishing many books and articles.

Much of this was history as past experience, history put to practical use in the service of the development of doctrine and strategy. The military technical revolution required a view of the future, but for the senior military leadership this was only possible by interpreting the historical structure of the development of strategy and war. As Sokolovsky said, 'history for the sake of history loses its purpose'; history was to demonstrate propositions and confirm new laws.[52] The study of the history of war was intended to apply practical experience and evidence to theoretical development.

Equally, this took place in an evolving cultural and intellectual context. As we saw in the previous chapter, history had begun to re-emerge after Stalin's death, and this continued into the 1960s. Pokrovsky was rehabilitated in 1961, and historical revisionism took shape in the 'hour of methodology' as historians sought to modernise the discipline. This was reflected in the work of those such as Isaak Mints, who argued for the immediate relevance (*aktualnost*) of historical writing to contemporary affairs, and Alexander Nekrich, a *frontovik*, whose 1965 book *1941 22 Yunya* offered a critical reassessment of the Great Fatherland War and of Stalin, claiming that without Stalin's Great Terror of 1937, there would have been no tragedy of 1941.[53]

From the mid-1960s, however, the Soviet sociopolitical context became more conservative, a process underlined and accelerated by the Prague Spring. During this time, the writers Yuli Daniel and Andrei Sinyavsky were convicted of anti-Soviet agitation in 1966. For historians, the picture was little better. In 1965 the orthodox historian Sergei Trapeznikov was appointed to head the Central Committee's department of science and education institutes, and oversaw campaigns against revisionist historians, with many, including Nekrich, demoted, ostracised and silenced. This had a deep and prolonged effect on professional historians: even during the late 1980s and Gorbachev's reforms and burgeoning interest in history, professional historians remained largely out of the fray. The military was not exempt from this context: Sokolovsky's criticisms of Stalin and the interwar years made in the first editions had been excised by 1968. Some criticised Sokolovsky and his colleagues for insufficient attention to Tukhachevsky, Svechin and Shaposhnikov, even in the early 1960s. But despite the rehabilitations,[54] Lenin, Marx, Engels and Frunze remained the main points of political and military reference; it was only by the mid-to-late 1970s that senior officers such as Ogarkov were explicitly weaving Tukhachevsky's work into official strategic thought in a substantive way in his discussion of deep operations.[55]

History may have been central – essential, even – therefore, but it was put to service in a very particular intellectual environment. Official versions of the Great Fatherland War and World War II published under the names of Grechko and Danilevich throughout the 1970s were rejected by *frontovik* writers such as Astafyev for 'lacking all reality from the view of a soldier ... I was in a completely different war'; the history was 'falsified and cooked up'.[56]

If the sociopolitical context was characterised by conservatism, the economic context was sliding towards a stagnation
which impinged upon scientific and technological development.
Moscow certainly sought to drive science and innovation
through a significant increase in spending, investing heavily
to expand the Soviet system's capacity to create sophisticated
indigenous technology. But a range of problems stifled this
effort.

This was due to the state of the economy as a whole. Under
Brezhnev, living standards stagnated, and the economy was
characterised by slowing industrial growth, inflation, bottlenecks,
inefficiency and waste. The records of the meetings of the
Secretariat of the Central Committee reveal a wide range of
persistent socio-economic problems. Investigations revealed serious
disciplinary problems, from theft and squander (*razbazarivanie*)
to drunkenness at work and absenteeism. Dilapidated equipment and shortages of spare parts and materials across the
economy combined with a lack of training in personnel led to
many accidents, causing thousands of injuries and fatalities.
Enterprises not only failed to fulfil their output targets, but
manufactured poor-quality products, while simultaneously often
engaging in illegal manufacture – including in metallurgy and
arms manufacture. This may have caused the leadership 'very
serious concern', but regional trades union councils diluted
disciplinary measures.[57]

Furthermore, if the leadership complained of *vedomstvennost*
('departmentalism') and *mestnichestvo* ('localism') – in other words,
that specific sectors would look after their own interests by block-
ing reforms or diverting and hoarding resources – it was able
to do little about this in practice. The leadership's reforms were
often inconsistent, and plans were both modest and frequently

changed. As one observer put it, 'economically, the Brezhnev era has to be seen as a disaster'.[58]

In terms of science and technology more specifically, there was sustained disagreement among the leadership, bureaucracy and economy about how to advance innovation. Some, especially scientists, advocated an infusion of Western science and technology to accelerate Soviet progress. But this met considerable resistance not only from manufacturers, but also from the politburo and from within the military. The leadership's decision to develop indigenous innovation was also stymied: the Brezhnev administration found it impossible to make scientific and industrial institutions more innovative without either rooting out bureaucratic resistance or imposing reform towards more research and development competition. Yet the leadership was unable or unwilling to do either. Instead, favouritism led to stalemates and further waste as decisions were taken to produce everything.[59]

The burden of military expenditure may have weighed heavily on the economy, but the armed forces were affected by these conditions in the economy and scientific and technological innovation. If Danilevich pointed to the consequences of leadership 'redirections', 'blunders', 'stupidities' and 'voluntaristic errors', Gareev noted that 'in our country, everyone is for decisive and radical reforms until some issue touches on his department'.[60] The practical effects were that during the 1960s and early 1970s, the Soviet economy was able to produce quantity rather than quality, so it could sustain the large build-up of conventional forces. But during the 1970s, the diminishing economic and technical vitality of the system could not sustain the conversion to implementing Ogarkov's vision. As Ogarkov himself noted, the new weapons and technology that his approach required were insufficiently available to initiate the new force development that he sought.[61]

Gorbachev and the reorientation to the 'defensive defence'

Ogarkov's thinking was certainly ambitious. Yet it was controversial among the military, and ahead of what the Soviet economy could deliver. Perhaps more importantly, it was also ahead of what the political leadership wanted to attempt. Rather than implement the wider socio-economic reforms that would have created the conditions to propel modernisation, Moscow instead sought to initiate civilian economic growth, postponing the military development that Ogarkov advocated. Indeed, Ogarkov himself was suddenly moved from CGS to commander of the western theatre of war in September 1984, replaced by Sergey Akhromeev.

Actually, there was at that time significant change among both the military and the state leadership. In December 1984 Ustinov died, and Sergei Sokolov, who had commanded the ground forces in the Soviet invasion of Afghanistan in 1979, replaced him as Defence Minister. And the deaths first of Yuri Andropov in June 1984 and then Konstantin Chernenko in March 1985 were followed by the emergence as General Secretary of Mikhail Gorbachev, who oversaw a substantial revision in thinking over the next five years that deeply influenced thinking about strategy and war. In 1985 other senior, long-serving officers also retired, including Gorshkov and Vladimir Tolbuko, who had commanded the strategic rocket forces since 1972.

Gorbachev recognised the 'urgent necessity' of reforms at home, pointing to the need to revitalise the civilian economy:

inefficient production, with poor quality and increasingly expensive resources were imposing a brake on economic growth. He saw Soviet society as beset by the erosion of moral and ideological values: disrespect for law and the growth of crime and social ills such as alcoholism and divorce, and the emergence of mediocrity and formalism. He thus instigated and pursued both *perestroika* (restructuring) and *glasnost* (transparency) to reform and reinvigorate Soviet society.[62]

Against the backdrop of this inauspicious domestic context, Gorbachev also recognised the curtailment of détente with the US, the reality of the arms race, and the growing threat of war. He initiated the Soviet disengagement and withdrawal from Afghanistan, and argued that humankind had 'lost its immortality' with the advent of nuclear weapons. War, he stated, was 'irrational', and there was a need to disregard the traditional notions of war and peace. For Gorbachev, Clausewitz's dictum about war as a continuation of policy by different means was out of date: security could no longer be achieved by military means, by perfecting the sword and shield. Instead, political decisions and peaceful means were the only ways to settle international crises.[63]

This approach was confirmed at the 27th Party Congress in early 1986: war was no longer deemed inevitable. The Party's leading role in shaping defence was underlined, and the concept of reasonable sufficiency (*razumnaya dostatochnost*) adopted. These decisions would have significant ramifications for the military through the next five years. Military spending was substantially cut. A process of *konversiya* was imposed on the military industrial complex, shaping it towards supporting the civilian economy. And the military itself underwent far-reaching changes through a major restructuring that included the reorganisation of military districts, a reduction in the number of armies and the redeployment of forces.[64]

Nevertheless, the military adopted the shift in approach towards perestroika. Senior officers emphasised that security could only be achieved by political means and the prevention of war. They echoed Gorbachev's view that nuclear war could not achieve political, economic, ideological or other aims, and that war was thus both 'outdated' and 'irrational'. Soviet doctrine, therefore, they argued, espoused the principle of 'reasonable sufficiency', and that, in line with perestroika, was now oriented towards only the USSR's defensive requirements. Accepting both the new political mentality and the 'binding' nature of Party and government documents, senior officers stated that Soviet doctrine would henceforth be directed towards 'precluding war' and only 'repelling aggression'. Moscow's doctrine and armed forces were reoriented towards an 'especially defensive character' (*sugubo oboronitelny kharakter*). This was confirmed with the signing into legislation of the document 'On the war doctrine of the states-members of the Warsaw Pact' on 29 May 1987.[65]

Gorbachev was no Khrushchev: he had neither the same wartime experience nor the same long-built network among the armed forces on which to rely. But he oversaw the political shaping of this state and military strategy, and, at least at the outset, appeared to have the support of influential civilians and of Akhromeev and others in the defence establishment.[66] Indeed, the official shift to a 'defensive defence' in 1986 appears to have reflected what had been a longer-term debate both at the level of the Defence Council and among the military: Akhromeev suggested that it resulted from what had been a two-year discussion.[67]

Senior officers emphasised that a defensive posture was not synonymous with a passive one that would allow the enemy to seize and retain the initiative. Mikhail Moiseev, Chief of the General Staff from 1988 to 1991, and who oversaw the withdrawal from Afghanistan, asserted that if the enemy attacked, he would not simply be halted in his tracks, but 'brought to his senses'.[68] But this was a different approach to that which Ogarkov had advocated, and it spurred considerable debate and critique from within different parts of the Soviet system. *Konversiya*, for instance, was criticised for being costly and inefficient, and for undermining mobilisation preparedness; by 1989, detractors were calling it *konvulsiya* (convulsion).[69] It also prompted debate about the theory and practice of war among senior military officers, including Ogarkov and Stanislav Postnikov, his successor as commander of the western theatre, and civilian analysts, over reconsidering the idea that only the offensive would bring victory, and what a 'defensive defence' should mean in practice.[70]

Two particular contributors to these debates stood out. Makhmut Gareev, a decorated veteran of the Great Fatherland War and Manchurian campaign, had graduated from the General Staff's War Academy in 1959, and then held command at divisional and military district levels. In 1974 he was appointed to lead the military scientific directorate of the General Staff, responsible for overseeing the development of war science. In 1984 he was promoted to Deputy Chief of General Staff for scientific work and planning, a post he held until 1989, when he became Chief Armed Forces Advisor in Afghanistan. As we shall see in the next chapter, he went on to have a long career as the doyen of Russian war science in the post-Cold War era, serving on the Security Council and as the first (and long-term) president of the Russian Academy of War Sciences until his death in 2019.

The other contributor was Andrei Kokoshin. A civilian analyst, he worked closely with senior officers in the General Staff's main operational directorate, including General Valentin Larionov, who had been part of Sokolovsky's team that wrote *Voennaya strategiya*. As we will see in the next chapter, he would go on to hold senior positions in post-Soviet Russia, including serving as First Deputy Defence Minister from 1992 to 1997, and then in the Security Council in 1998. He continues to serve as the deputy president of the Russian Academy of Sciences, and remains one of the most prominent and substantive writers on war, strategy, forecasting, deterrence and strategic stability.

The debate about modern war, Soviet strategy and 'defensive defence' was still held on familiar intellectual terrain, though with some subtle changes. It again reflected the persistent tension between a short war, throw-down strategy and a strategy of exhaustion and the need to prepare for a long war.[71] Officers sought to draw on the theoretical legacies of the past: among others, the works of Tukhachevsky, Frunze and Svechin were republished and re-examined, and there was extended discussion about the applicability of past experience, especially that of the Great Fatherland War, in outlining plans for the future.[72] Indeed, the experience of that war was extensively mined for source material, with attention now shifting to the first years of the war as officers sought to emphasise the significance of the initial period, the importance of an organised state-level defence, and the commitment of the state's resources to war.

On the one hand, senior officers and civilian analysts voiced a number of criticisms of the Soviet leadership. In many ways, these echoed the discussion of the early-to-mid 1960s and late

1970s. The leadership was (again) criticised for inadequately reviewing the forms and means of strategic defence before the war, an inaccurate assessment of the changing character of the initial period of war, and especially Stalin's incorrect assessments of German intentions and the Stavka's 'hesitation' (*kolebanie*) over adopting a strategic defence after the German assault.[73] The posthumous publication of Rokossovsky's memoirs spoke to the Red Army's lack of preparation before Operation Barbarossa – including a lack of prepared fortifications and the absence of an overall plan – and also poor information and coordination when Germany invaded. He described the tragic difficulties of the initial retreat: a lack of command and control, confusion, apathy and defeatism, including at the divisional command and commissar levels, nonsensical orders from senior officers leading to the constant loss of lives, such as commanding tanks to attack without infantry support, and units being thrown into hopeless situations. This was driven home by Ogarkov, who (again) pointed to the miscalculations in anticipating Operation Barbarossa, and highlighted the catastrophic effects of the 'unfounded' repressions in the mid-1930s.[74]

On the other hand, there was a focus on 'active defence' as the optimal combination of manoeuvre and positional forms of defence to seek the effective destruction of the enemy by fire and with counter-strikes and counter-attacks. The defensive should be resilient and active, both holding up the adversary as best as possible, preventing them from penetrating to strategic depths and disrupting mobilisation capacity, and 'maximally weakening the enemy's forces' to create conditions to counter-attack. Thus, active defence reflected the need to see the offensive and defensive in their 'dialectic unity' as interactive features of strategic activity. For these officers and civilians, the war showed that to achieve a successful counter-offensive it was first necessary to achieve superiority over the adversary, and then suddenness in the delivery of the counterstroke; deception in the shape of both *maskirovka* and *khitrost* was an essential ingredient. The activeness of the strategic defence lay in conducting hard defensive struggle in one place, while in others conducting offensive operations with limited tasks.[75]

In this way, the battle of Kursk became the focal analytical example of prepared and 'organised' strategic defence providing the conditions for the shift to the counter-offensive with strategic results. Although much had changed in the intervening years, it still offered an example of how the defensive offered a more economic means of waging war and an 'essential example in the history of war and the art of war in terms of the dialectic between the offensive and the defensive'. History might not give ready-made recipes, but it could teach much and 'become a source for new thinking'.[76] In this way, the likes of Gareev and Kokoshin drew on the work of Frunze and especially Svechin to make their case.

The changing character of the initial period was, therefore, widely considered to be potentially crucial in terms of the need for the correct assessment of evolving threats and the deployment of forces and mobilisation before the initiation of war. But for many in the military, it was the ability to sustain and wage a long war that was most important. There was much criticism of the 'bankruptcy' and 'adventurism' of the German Blitzkrieg of 1941: the 'one-blow' style dash to Moscow and to occupy the Donbass and the attempt to destroy the Soviet armed forces quickly failed to cut the link between the defence and its mobilisation potential. Berlin's strategy not only underestimated Soviet strength but served to divorce its military plans from Germany's economic and moral-political capabilities. The German leadership had tried to fit reality to its own theoretical views. Moscow's victory had resulted from its ability to fight a long war – to adopt a strategy of exhaustion, creating the conditions for a successful counter-offensive.[77]

The second half of the 1980s, therefore, reflected a reorientation of Moscow's thinking at the state level about strategy and war towards the 'defensive defensive', and thus state guidance of doctrine and strategy. Changes were less pronounced at the military level, representing more of a longer-term evolution in thinking than dramatic change. Not everyone agreed with the shifts: Danilevich later observed that the General Staff disagreed with Gorbachev's view that war was not the continuation of policy by other means. He wryly noted that whereas previously the General Staff had pursued a policy of deterrence, but a strategy of destruction (*sokrushenia*), under Gorbachev this changed to a policy of deterrence, but a strategy of 'capitulation'. Consequently, he said, the General Staff did not change the military aspects of doctrine, only the political aspects.[78]

This reorientation took some six years to effect, driven and buffeted by an inauspicious blend of domestic and international conditions. The 1980s were a time of tumultuous change for Moscow's strategy making. Gorbachev's leadership contributed to a rapid change in the international context, including the easing of relations with the West. The combination of competitive elections in eastern and central Europe and the fall of the Berlin Wall with the easing of relations with the US through arms control agreements and summits led to Bush and Gorbachev hailing the end of the Cold War in December 1989. Equally, Moscow's armed forces were attempting simultaneously to restructure and to reconsider the implications of large-scale modern war, while also waging and then disengaging from a counter-insurgency campaign in Afghanistan,[79] all while perestroika and glasnost were taking shape and the economic context deteriorated.

If the idea of war was now rejected at a state level, doctrine and strategy settled on what was essentially a strategy of exhaustion, reflected in the idea of active defence. Indeed, the reorientation was at the state level and in the political aspect of doctrine, rather than in its military-technical aspects. The military dimensions represented the ebb and flow of a longer-term evolution. As this complex evolution was finally taking practical shape, however, Iraq invaded Kuwait on 2 August 1990, overwhelming it in two days.

5

War in the information age

Gorbachev and Bush might have announced the end of the Cold War in 1989, but the US-led response to Saddam Hussein's conquest of Kuwait in 1991 revealed the Soviet military's ongoing concerns about Washington's intent and capability and Soviet unpreparedness to deal with it. Akhromeev interpreted the deployment and build-up of coalition forces in Saudi Arabia in preparation for a campaign to evict Iraqi forces as a potential threat to the USSR, not least because of the possibility that the war might spread. Others reflected on previous examples of how the US and its allies had conducted amphibious landings, including Inchon in 1950 during the Korean war, the Suez crisis of 1956 and the 1982 Falklands war.[1]

When it finally came, the allied campaign against Iraq – beginning in January 1991 with an extended aerial and naval bombardment, followed by a ground assault – delivered a swift and unequivocal victory. The Gulf War appeared to deliver what theory had foretold in the 1980s – an information-led war in which international diplomacy and sanctions had secured an advantageous situation, followed by the decisive use of long-range precision firepower and modern armed forces: the speed and weight of the blow had disorganised and disoriented the Iraqi forces. The campaign appeared to offer, therefore, an intelligent form of modern manoeuvre warfare, a strategy of destruction delivering a knockout blow quickly to achieve political goals.[2] This campaign, on the 50th anniversary of Operation Barbarossa, also had echoes of the Soviet Manchurian campaign: study of 'August Storm' inspired and provided guidance for Western military planners.[3]

Through the spring and summer of 1991 the Soviet political and military leadership engaged in a heated discussion about the campaign's implications. Amid the debate about the roles of aviation and maritime power, and the successes and failures of both sides, including the apparent obsolescence of Iraq's Soviet-supplied equipment, two questions stood out. Was this the last of the 'old wars' or the first of a 'new' kind of war? And did it reflect a major change in the global balance of power?

Gorbachev argued that the implications of the war did not pose a threat to the USSR, and Moiseev that the war should not be used as a pretext for doctrinal changes. But other senior officers disagreed. Vladimir Lobov, First Deputy Chief of the General Staff, argued that the war was not simply an episode, but reflected something new in warfare. And Gareev argued that the war was a blow against ideas of passive defence and the pacifist approach to international affairs.[4]

The Soviet leadership also had other concerns. In January that year, Moscow had used its armed forces to quell anti-Soviet independence demonstrations in the Baltic states and Azerbaijan. In the latter, Gorbachev declared a state of emergency, and deployed the armed forces: once special forces had cut communications, 26,000 troops entered Baku. During the following three days, more than one hundred people lost their lives, and hundreds more were wounded. These demonstrations were one symptom of a wider malaise spreading through the USSR, and by the summer of 1991 Moscow was facing a severe political and economic crisis. Rather than rejuvenating the Soviet state, Gorbachev's reforms had deprived the state of resources and enabled separatist tendencies. At the same time that Moscow was on a path to state bankruptcy, with currency and grain crises, it faced a series of secession movements. In summer 1991 the Warsaw Pact dissolved.

In August the brewing sense of political crisis resulted in a coup attempt by the so-called State Committee on the State of Emergency, which tried to remove Gorbachev and reverse his reforms. The attempt collapsed within two days, not least because parts of the armed forces refused to support it. But it had significant ramifications for the defence and security leadership, since some high-placed officers supported the attempt: Defence Minister Dmitry Yazov and Chief of the General Staff Moiseev were dismissed, and Akhromeev, an advisor to Gorbachev, died by suicide on 24 August. The coup drained what remained of the Communist Party's legitimacy and power; by the end of the year Gorbachev had dissolved the Soviet Union and resigned.

As 1992 began, therefore, with US strategic power on full display, Moscow's own strategic position had undergone a serious deterioration. On the international stage, the double dissolution of the Warsaw Pact and the USSR had returned Moscow's strategic horizon to one that had last pertained in the eighteenth century. Domestically, the political and economic ramifications of the collapse of Soviet ideology meant the pronounced and prolonged disarray of state power across Russia and widespread socio-economic crisis. The armed forces and defence industry were unavoidably and deeply entangled in this unfolding dislocation.

The consequence was the almost complete disaggregation of the facets of Russian strategy making, with confusion and dilemmas in state policy and war doctrine, and gaps emerging between state goals and available resources, between war theory and the ability to implement it in practice, and between Russian visions of future war and actual experience. These challenges characterised the next fifteen years of Moscow's strategy making and thinking about war, a period of change, to be sure, but also of important threads of continuity in terms of thinking about a 'way in war'.

A new, 'Russian' war doctrine?

In February 1992 the Soviet armed forces ceased to exist, being divided among the Commonwealth of Independent States. Russia's withdrawal from Eastern Europe meant that Moscow lost access to a great deal of infrastructure, including access to ports and shipbuilding facilities, and early warning and air defence capabilities. As Russian forces withdrew, they left much equipment in the newly independent states.

When they were established in May 1992, therefore, the newly independent Russian Federation's armed forces were officially described as not representing a 'coherent organism'.[5] One senior officer was more forthright, describing it as 'complete disorder' (*polnaya nerazberykha*).[6] If the intent was to preserve the Soviet structure of the armed forces, the result was rather different: more than ten different state bodies emerged that were created to fulfil defence and security-related tasks: alongside the armed forces, there were, in parallel, border troops, interior troops, civil defence forces and railway forces, among other formations and bodies, each with their own separate legislative base, and each subordinated to different authorities.

Among the armed forces and party circles, it was thought that Colonel-General Dmitry Volkogonov would be appointed Defence Minister.[7] Instead, Russian president Boris Yeltsin appointed Pavel Grachev, a highly decorated officer but one with limited experience of managing an army or military district. Viktor Dubynin, appointed Chief of General Staff in June, died of cancer in November, and was replaced by another armoured warfare officer, Mikhail Kolesnikov.

At the same time, the General Staff produced a draft war doctrine document. Though it acknowledged the decline in the threat of world war and an invasion of Russia, the doctrine indicated that the sources of danger remained much the same. Hinting at the US and NATO, it suggested that some states remained focused on world domination and the resolution of disputes through the use of armed force.[8]

Despite the 'complete disorder' and changes in leadership, therefore, there were some threads of continuity connecting the late Soviet armed forces with those of the early Russian Federation, both in terms of personnel and concept. Grachev, Dubynin and Kolesnikov had all held senior positions across the armed forces in the late 1980s and early 1990s. Grachev had commanded the airborne forces since 1990, been First Deputy Defence Minister since late 1991, and had supported Yeltsin in opposing the August coup. Initially, at least, they became personally close: Yeltsin later called him a 'real army General', the 'best' Minister of Defence.[9] Dubynin commanded the 40th Army in Afghanistan before going on to command the Northern Group of Forces in Poland, overseeing their withdrawal from the

Warsaw Pact. Kolesnikov had risen through senior command posts to become deputy commander of the ground forces by 1990, then Deputy Chief of General Staff, heading the main directorate for organisation and mobilisation in 1991.

Reflecting the uncertain circumstances and the quickly evolving domestic political situation, this initial draft war doctrine was almost immediately revised, and a new one formally adopted in November 1993.[10] This new version was more closely aligned with the foreign policy concept which was also debated and drafted in 1992, and subsequently signed by the president in 1993.[11] This concept underlined that 'military power factors' continued to play a role, especially at the regional and local levels, and so force retained its 'important place' in international affairs. Indeed, the concept emphasised striking a balance between establishing Russia as a democratic, free and economically independent state, while ensuring its 'Great Power' status with sufficient 'war power' (*voennaya moshch*) to terminate armed clashes and conflicts around Russia, preventing their irruption on to Russian territory to ensure territorial integrity and unity.[12]

For its part, the updated war doctrine framed a 'transitional period' through to 2000, covering the establishment of a new Russian state, the instigation of democratic reforms and the shaping of a new system of international affairs. The doctrine set an initial series of targets to create groups of forces, to improve branch structure, to complete the withdrawal to the Russian Federation of remaining forces, to switch to a mixed system (contract/conscription) and reduce personnel to an establishment level of 1.5 million by 1996, and to complete the restructuring of the armed forces by 2000.

Moreover, this new version both acknowledged that doctrine was only one part of broader national security, and swung the emphasis towards a more varied range of dangers and threats. The new doctrine underlined the shift from a Cold War outlook in two ways. First, it acknowledged internal sources of (armed) danger, such as organised crime and violent nationalist and separatist threats to constitutional order. Second, it indicated that the main military danger was posed by local wars and armed conflicts, especially near Russia's borders, and that the likelihood of these was rising. The task of the armed forces, according to the doctrine, was, if necessary, to confine these local wars or armed conflicts and terminate military operations at the earliest possible stage. According to the doctrine, mobile forces could quickly deploy to seize the initiative. The use of peacetime groupings of forces stationed in the conflict region could achieve this without further mobilisation, if necessary reinforced by partial deployment of other groupings. Such military activities would be waged at the operational and tactical levels.

Nonetheless, older concerns were not forgotten. The doctrine underlined the concern that local wars and armed conflicts could be used by states as an excuse to intervene and thus escalate into large-scale war. This would require mobilisation. Other official military publications indicated the ongoing importance of the need to prepare for protracted wars, even when they did not appear to be likely.[13] Rather than a revolutionary conceptual change, therefore, official doctrine reflected a shift of emphasis, one that indicated the ongoing tension in thinking about war and operations. The definition of war did not change: it was still seen in Clausewitzian terms as the resolution of policy disputes through the use of armed force. Doctrine, too, was intended to fulfil much the same function; indeed, officially, doctrine was defined as showing 'uninterrupted' evolution.[14]

As we saw in the previous chapters, particularly since Great Fatherland War, the main focus on thinking about strategy was on large-scale world war, with local wars a secondary concern. This was now inverted. Local wars and armed conflicts represented a form of war fighting that could be waged with a strategy of destruction – a decisive deployment to achieve unequivocal political results. But this was hedged by the need to retain a capacity to cope with a large-scale, protracted war, one that would require the material and spiritual resources of the state.

These documents represented little more than paper being blown in the wind of dramatic political and economic change. Nevertheless, they reflected initial attempts to face three new, interrelated strategic dilemmas that in different forms would continue for years. Given the new conditions both internationally and within Russia, the first dilemma was reflected in the need for a two-tier approach to reform. At one level, there was a need to overhaul, modernise and reform the armed forces, to oversee their downsizing and transition to a post-Cold War force. This involved debates over the need to restructure the armed forces, such as changing the principal structure from a conscription basis to a contract/volunteer one, and establishing mobile forces organised under centralised joint command.

At another level, though, given the changed state structure, there was a need for broader reform, addressing the whole state's war-making capacity. This was imperative: from the dissolution of the USSR, Moscow inherited a system of defence and security control in disarray, exacerbated by the establishment and expansion of a range of security and military forces and agencies. These new forces and agencies dislocated the centralised command, given their different bureaucratic loyalties, and they absorbed significant resources, simultaneously diluting the impact of the state's investment in security and defence and reducing the resources available for the armed forces. By the middle of the decade, for instance, the troops of the Interior Ministry numbered some 264,000, with access to armour, artillery and aircraft.

This level of reform would address core political and socio-economic questions relating to the raising, training, organisation and equipping of the armed forces and their deployment as an element of national power. This wider reform touched on the very structure of strategy making – whether strategy was the responsibility of the General Staff, or the collective political, economic and military leadership. The way some senior figures drew on the Soviet theoretical inheritance, including, as we shall see below, the work of those such as Svechin, hinted at an underlying sense of continuity, even as the new state took shape.

The second dilemma concerned indecision about relations with the new neighbours and what this meant for Russia's armed forces: should Russia's defence commitments be 'national', or should they be focused at the regional level? This dilemma partly related to infrastructure, and partly to uncertain relations with Moscow's new neighbours. Some in the Russian leadership proposed that, given the additional expense of building new border defences for Russia, Moscow should protect the borders of the whole CIS, including forward positioning of forces and establishing collective CIS peacekeeping forces.[15]

Connected to this, the third dilemma hinted at continuity in Moscow's approach to strategy and a traditional Russian way in war: given the declining likelihood of world war, and conflict 'hotspots' in its neighbourhood, what kind of threats should Russian forces prepare to face and deal with? This reflected the tension between those who advocated the maintenance of a national mobilisation capability and those who argued for the shift to a more professionalised, combat-ready force.[16] This in turn echoed the long-lasting debate about the lessons of the past for future war, and war's potential scope and scale: the ongoing tension between the need to prepare for a longer war of exhaustion and the development of a capacity to fight a decisive short war. Although disagreements with the US had eased, and the main concern was about potential local hotspots, the persistent focus of much thinking about war remained on the lessons of the Great Fatherland War, and the implications of US technical modernisation and superiority as a potential threat.

Russia's befuddlement and the disaggregation of strategy

The practical reality remained, however, that in the early 1990s the Russian state faced continuing political and socio-economic crisis. To make the leap from a command economy to a market one, the Russian leadership introduced shock therapy, liberalising all prices and introducing privatisation. This accelerated social dislocation, poverty and mortality, and it entrenched a deep and prolonged recession. Soaring inflation was in dramatic counterpoint to the drop in output. Tax evasion became a national sport; the black market thrived, with senior officials acknowledging that between 25 per cent and 50 per cent of Russian GDP was hidden from the government.[17]

Yeltsin's foreign policy, initially seen by many as too pro-Western, together with the results of economic shock therapy generated political opposition within the Russian parliament. Yeltsin narrowly overcame an attempt to impeach him in April

1993, and declared a state of emergency in October that year, even ordering an assault on the White House. In December he introduced a new constitution to consolidate and extend presidential power, and offered a more assertive advocacy of Russian foreign policy interests. Even so, his popularity remained low, and the threat that he would be evicted at elections in 1996 by a political alliance between the Communist Party and nationalists seemed real. Yeltsin later suggested that in 1995 Russia was 'infected by a new disease' of 'total negativity', and even a 'dislike' of itself.[18] He survived the electoral test, but had his first major heart attack that June, indicative of what would become the prolonged and pronounced decline in his health and ability to command Russian politics.

The reality of these political and economic conditions was a sharp contraction in the resources available to the armed forces. Indeed, this had begun before the dissolution of the USSR. Where the budgetary process for 1991 had foreseen a reduction of 14 per cent compared to 1989, it was actually approximately 17 per cent, further exacerbated by inflation and increasing civilian costs.[19] Then, in 1991–92, Yegor Gaidar, architect of the shock therapy approach, imposed swingeing budgetary cuts from nearly 30 billion roubles to some 11 billion.[20] These cuts set the context for the next decade – spending on the armed forces would not really recover until the early 2000s.

The fallout from the cuts landed on both the defence industrial complex and the armed forces, and revealed what one prominent Russian defence economist called a 'complete loss of touch with reality', caused largely by the near total absence of competent military economists in government, parliament and the military.[21] It also disaggregated the pieces of Russian war strategy making.

On the one hand, while severely reducing the resources available, the government was tasking the armed forces with more, and more complex, operations. As we will see below, without an increase in spending, the leadership not only sought to increase the armed forces, but even sent them into combat. On the other, it aggravated the already difficult relationship between the armed forces and the defence industrial complex. The armed forces already harboured grievances against the defence industry, which they accused of imposing unnecessary and unreliable equipment. By the mid-1990s the MoD was refusing to pay the defence industry, citing a lack of government funding, and the defence industry was turning down orders from the MoD.

The defence industry had inherited a large part of the Soviet defence industrial base, but suffered the same dramatic, systemic transformation as the economy as a whole. For the first half of the 1990s, there was no coherent policy for restructuring. By 1994, 400 defence enterprises had stopped all production, and nearly four times that number were working part time. By 1995 the labour force had shrunk by more than a quarter from its 1990 level. Output declined yet more sharply: by 1995 the defence industry was producing barely 20 per cent of its 1990 total output. Given these conditions, the defence industry as a whole showed remarkable resilience. This was partly due to the new international conditions – Russian defence enterprises had greater access to Western technology. They also benefited from the continued focus on thinking about high-technology war, as measures were introduced to protect the technological base and the ability to develop new weapons and dual-use technologies, and an attempt to increase arms exports. Indeed, the defence industry was able to produce some new and modernised equipment, including the T-90 tank, variants on the Su-25 jet and the Ka-52 helicopter.

In many ways, this resilience was due to the ingenuity shown by the directors of enterprises and the way that the defence industry had been established during the Soviet era. The defence industry had been built in a way that would enable it both to produce large numbers of weapons and to function autonomously for long periods in the case of war, until the economy as a whole could be moved to a total mobilisation effort. In consequence, this meant that the main resources were not spent on producing weapons, but instead on creating 'gigantic capacities' in raw materials industries. Furthermore, it meant that decentralised defence plants were provided with stockpiles of materials to continue to produce weapons during war. This was supplemented by the way the defence industry worked during the Soviet era: in an economy ruled by plans and deficits, managers retained hidden assets and accumulated all kinds of reserves.[22]

This mobilisation reserve reflected poor Soviet understanding of Western defence policies and mobilisation capacities and Moscow's concern that it would not be able to outproduce the West in case of war. This militarised economy – in which the defence industry was the heart and core of the economy, rather than part of a wider civilian economy – proved difficult to dismantle after the USSR's dissolution. Continuing macro-economic militarisation meant that a cut in defence expenditure did not result in greater efficiency in the economy as a whole. But with restrictions on its use and even export lifted, the mobilisation reserve served as 'hidden wealth' on which to draw until policy became more coherent and defence spending stabilised. Despite the sharp drop in defence expenditure and the structural disorganisation, the defence industry was more or less capable of equipping the armed forces with weapons.[23]

The effects of the cuts on the armed forces, however, were more severe, with a dual impact. The first effect was felt in the service conditions: the dire economic situation translated into sharp socio-military problems. As one Russian observer put it, conditions for conscripts were similar to life in prison, if not 'incorporated slavery'. Conscripts were put to work in factories and on farms to earn enough money to feed regiments; conditions were so poor that draft dodging and desertion acquired the 'character of an epidemic'.[24] Those who either could not or did not escape service endured poor accommodation, diet and hygiene and a culture of severe bullying (*dedovshchina*). 'Strictly speaking', one Russian soldier turned reporter wrote, 'there is no *dedovshchina*.' Equally, he described an unofficial code of rules, and bullying that 'exceeded all imaginable bounds'. A soldier could be beaten for anything at all: 'beatings were just the norm'. 'Everyone beats everyone', everyone 'gets stinking drunk and hammers the ones below them': 'colonels beat the majors, majors beat the lieutenants, all beat the privates'. The Russian armed forces suffered some 3,000–5,000 non-combat-related deaths each year in the early 1990s.[25]

Conditions were hardly better for officers, who were 'addled with impoverishment and hopelessness'.[26] The sharp loss of prestige and authority of the officer corps was one thing, conditions in day-to-day life another. Officers went unpaid for months; housing shortages meant that many lived in tents, tank sheds and other makeshift lodgings. Conditions were so poor that some officers, unable to support their families, died by suicide.[27] Officer recruitment and retention plummeted: in the early 1990s, official plans envisaged the departure of some 71,000 officers; in reality, some 155,000 left the service.[28]

The scars and ramifications of this would be felt for many years. Noting the 'catastrophic' conditions of the 1990s, and the consequent departure of so many officers and specialists, Viktor Murakhovsky, a retired colonel turned editor of *Arsenal otechestva* magazine, suggested that even in 2021 the Russian armed forces still faced the problem of the gap in generations of officers caused by the 1990s. The 'middle generation of the 1990s and early 2000s was largely washed out as the result of processes in the state and the army', and so 'generals continued to serve beyond their term because they need to pass their experience on to the younger generation'.[29]

Given the conditions, crime, misappropriation of funds, equipment and weapons, and deception undermined cohesion, discipline and reform. Colonel Baratyanov, a General Staff inspector, stated that 'deception compensates for the absence of reform': reform efforts were covered by the 'dirt of immorality'; 'wherever you poke your fingers, you see lies, hypocrisy, deception and the powerlessness of our higher military leadership'.[30] Senior officers were accused of accepting bribes;[31] Defence Minister Grachev was nicknamed 'Pasha Mercedes' for allegedly embezzling luxury cars, misuse of funds and asset stripping during the withdrawal of Russian forces from Germany. The case included the murder of journalist Dmitry Kholodov who had reported on the allegations – Kholodov's editors accused the military of ordering his murder. The corruption allegations were not tested in court; four officers were acquitted of Kholodov's murder in 2000 and again in 2002.[32]

And this leads to the second effect of the state's sharp reduction of material support for the armed forces: cuts and inertia stifled reforms. The armed forces were designed to wage large-scale war against a high-tech adversary. But the state did not provide the resources to build a scaled-down version of the Soviet armed forces, nor was there sufficient investment to pursue what would have been a complex and costly process of root-and-branch reform. While there was debate over the dilemmas noted above, in practice the structure of the armed forces began to rot away for lack of money for spare parts, maintenance and training; as reforms withered and died on the vine, officers left, and large numbers of soldiers deserted or dodged the draft.

The lack of resources provoked sharp disputes about the roles of the services and branches. There was, for instance, renewed debate about the role of the navy. While some, such as Kokoshin, argued for sustaining an ocean-going navy, given the nature of Western maritime power, others, including Gareev, argued for a reduced navy, more attuned to theatre support of the flanks of the army and continental power. The reality was that the navy consumed vast resources and capital investment, and so the reduction in defence spending had direct, practical results: cuts to the navy were immediate and deep. According to Felix Gromov, then the navy's commander in chief, the navy received just half of the funding it required. Consequently, the global horizon of Gorshkov's navy withered: in terms of numbers of ships, it shrank by nearly 50 per cent. If it received an average of 15 new ships each year from 1992 to 1995, it simultaneously lost an average of 174 each year. Many of the ships that remained in service were past the time of their mid-term repair. Naval aircraft were reduced in numbers by some 60 per cent, and manning of combat and support forces was at approximately 60 per cent.[33] The navy, then, entered a period of deep and complex crisis – underfunding meant non-payment of wages and bills and understaffing that led to widespread problems of health and discipline, accidents and losses. The loss of the *Kursk* submarine with all hands in 2000 crystallised the navy's parlous condition.

As Lobov put it, Russia did not lack concepts for reform: what it lacked was effective leadership and economic resources.[34] And when the armed forces were put to the test of having to fight, they were found wanting. As one Russian specialist said, in Russia, 'only war can demonstrate to the Kremlin the real condition of the armed forces and the necessity of their reform'. When Yeltsin decided to deploy force in Chechnya, it soon became clear that the armed forces 'had no units capable of going into battle'.[35] The consequence was a disastrous episode in Russian military history, one of such a scale that Yeltsin would subsequently admit that the country parted with the 'exceptionally dear and dangerous illusion about the might of its army, its degree of training, its combat readiness and ability to prevail'.[36]

The Chechen campaign

Yeltsin would later write that during the first years of Russian independence, from 1990 to 1996, the 'shadow of a time of troubles, a civil war, hung over Russia'. Even so, he admitted that Moscow had 'overlooked the little national disaster brewing in Chechnya: the scale of violence that swept across the republic in the first years of Dzhokhar Dudaev's rule was simply incredible'. Chechnya had declared independence in 1991, refusing to acknowledge federal rule. Indeed, Russian forces had withdrawn from Chechen territory in 1992, leaving a considerable arsenal of equipment behind.

By the summer of 1994, however, as far as Moscow was concerned, Chechnya had become a black hole of banditry, with soaring murder and kidnapping rates and widespread armed violence. Dudaev was seeking to create a single Transcaucasian republic, including parts of Russia and Ukraine, and threatening terrorist attacks on nuclear power plants and military bases across Russia.[37]

Yeltsin's initial idea was to 'create a respected alternative political group' in Chechnya, introducing anti-Dudaev sentiments and 'encourage the people themselves' to remove him, deploying peacekeeping forces 'if necessary'. When the attempt to ensure that this opposition to Dudaev held military superiority failed (including a costly repulse of this 'opposition force' from Grozny in November 1994), Moscow's position was, according to Yeltsin, 'unanimous': they could not stand idly by while a piece of Russia 'breaks off, initiating the collapse of the country'. So, the leadership decided to restore constitutional law and order on the territory of the Chechen Republic by launching a 'lightning' operation.[38]

A special grouping was established to direct operations to stabilise the situation and destroy armed bandit groups. The operational planning was conducted with the experience of the Great Fatherland War in mind. The main structure was organised by the General Staff, with the details taken care of by a joint federal force group. The whole operation would take one month, from the creation of force groupings in late November 1994 to the armed forces handing over responsibility to the Interior Ministry in late December, having re-established stability. Active operations, characterised by a lightning advance on the Chechen capital Grozny from six directions to blockade it, then seizing the presidential palace and other government and communications buildings, followed by the implementation of control over lowland Chechnya, would be over within a week in early December.

For some, this decision to dispatch troops to resolve a political problem and 'restore constitutional order' was little more than a repetition of the same 'fatal mistake' that Brezhnev had made in Afghanistan and Gorbachev in Azerbaijan. What was meant to be a quick campaign – a 'lightning' campaign, a 'cakewalk' – turned into a decade of bitter and costly fighting.[39] The decision to deploy forces to Chechnya highlighted and then amplified the almost complete disaggregation of Moscow's strategy.

The plan almost immediately fell apart. The assault on Grozny began late, because one of the units of the forces was not ready. When it did begin, having already lost the element of surprise and with parts of the forces blocked by unforeseen opposition, only one of the six groups attacking along separate routes was able to maintain the schedule demanded by the plan. The decision to attack the capital was then taken, though the blockade was not in place. By the end of December none of the groupings had attained their goals, and it took another two months of heavy fighting to take Grozny.

After five months of campaigning, Russian forces finally occupied most of the lowland area of Chechnya. But the highlands remained beyond control and Chechen forces mounted major attacks, including on the Russian town of Budennovsk in 1995. While some senior Russian officers claimed to be on the verge of victory in summer 1996, Chechen forces launched a major attack that retook Grozny, and Moscow was obliged to seek a negotiated peace.

Yeltsin later stated that the poor performance of the Russian armed forces and the subsequent chaos of the fighting demonstrated the army's 'monstrous lack of grip' and the 'complete disarray in the actions of the power ministries'. The campaign was 'horribly bloody', with many 'violations and victims'.[40] But the extent of the brutality and appalling destruction and loss of life and limb, combined with poor communications and command and control, and poor logistics and a shortage of supplies among Russian forces, were more vividly depicted by the film *Chistilishche* ('Purgatory') as an 'unforeseeable shitshow' (*nepredskazuemoe govno*).[41]

General Anatoly Kulikov, appointed in early 1995 to command the joint group of federal forces, later described three interlocking structural problems. The first and one of the most significant was the difficulty encountered in the attempt to organise a single unified command for the range of Russian forces deployed, which included the armed forces, troops of the Interior Ministry, the Federal Counterintelligence Service (reorganised in 1995 into the Federal Security Service, FSB), the Border Guards and other intelligence and emergency services. Second, not only did these different forces represent competing command structures, but the equipment used by them was often incompatible: the leadership found it difficult to create a single system and this impeded operations. Third, because of a lack of combat-ready units, troops that were deployed were largely composite forces 'cobbled together' from different parts of the Russian armed forces as a whole. Units had little, if any, time to meet, let alone train before being committed to action.[42]

Problems cascaded throughout the system, from the strategic leadership to the combat units, and from the preparation of the plan to its implementation. The planners may have had the Great Fatherland War in mind, but the context was very different: Moscow did not even declare a state of emergency, let alone war, and did not substantially increase resources for the armed forces. There was no mobilisation: the operation was intended to be just that, a 'peace operation' to 'disarm illegal formations and restore constitutional order'.

And if they had the Great Fatherland War in mind, in practice it was redolent not of the organised, massive campaigns of 1944 and 1945, but instead of the hasty planning and consequent miscalculations, the lack of preparatory intelligence and reconnaissance, even of maps, and the lack of coordination that characterised Moscow's costly counter-assaults of first two years of that war. This composite force was committed to action with little notice and little clarity of purpose: commanders were surprised by the order to attack, soldiers did not expect to have to fight.[43]

The assault on Grozny in 1994 may have immediately revealed the disaggregation of Russian strategy. But the subsequent decade of bitter campaigning caused a cascade of other effects and implications for Moscow's strategy and way in war which would simultaneously ripple out, albeit at somewhat different speeds, into the mid-2000s. The first set of effects were that it led to (some) shifts and changes within the Russian defence and security landscape as a whole, as the defence ministry and armed forces leadership was replaced.

In the campaigning for Russia's presidential elections in summer 1996, Alexander Lebed, a popular general who had retired in 1995 and won a seat in parliament, campaigned on ending the war. Lebed came third, but Yeltsin fired Pavel Grachev and his deputies, appointing Igor Rodionov Defence Minister in his stead, and then appointed Lebed secretary of the Security Council. Yeltsin then tasked the Security Council with taking strategic leadership for the 'entire complex of Chechen problems', which meant ending the war.[44] Lebed negotiated the Khasavyurt accords with the Chechen leadership, which enshrined the withdrawal of Russian forces and a joint Russia–Chechen interim governing commission. But while they also established Russia–Chechen relations, the accords postponed the question of Chechnya's status until 2001.

The accords resolved, albeit temporarily, the Chechen problem. But the internal disputes within the Russian state and military leadership continued. Although popular within the armed forces and with the public, Lebed quickly fell out with almost everyone else in the strategy-making landscape, including the head of the Defence Council Yuri Baturin, Yeltsin's Chief of Staff Anatoliy Chubais, Prime Minister Viktor Chernomyrdin and Interior Minister Anatoliy Kulikov. Suspected of plotting a coup, Yeltsin fired him in October 1996.[45]

Thus began another round of changes among the defence leadership. Viktor Samsonov replaced Mikhail Kolesnikov as Chief of General Staff in October that year. Rodionov, too, having pursued an active public campaign to highlight the plight of the armed forces and insisted on proposing defence budgets well above what the government would tolerate, had fallen out with Baturin, and was replaced in May 1997 by Igor Sergeyev. Samsonov was also replaced in May by Anatoly Kvashnin.

At the same time, Yeltsin issued a degree on urgent measures to reform the armed forces and improve their structure. While Sergeyev and Kvashnin may have had better relations with Yeltsin, they had their own disputes. Inter-service rivalry characterised the lack of consensus about reforms to the armed forces; Sergeyev, formerly strategic rocket forces commander, abolished the main command of the ground forces. The air force and air defence were again to be formed into a single service. Indeed, the changes among the defence leadership continued, with Yeltsin merging the Defence Council into the Security Council in spring 1998, appointing Andrei Kokoshin secretary.

While the defence budgets of 1996 and 1997 reflected the state's parlous financial position and the political leadership's priorities, they imposed very real constraints on what the armed forces could achieve in reforms, which were also intended to cut costs further: reducing the size of the armed forces from 1.5 to 1.2 million and decentralising the administrative apparatus of the MoD. Social costs, salaries, pensions and housing absorbed most of the budget; the money allocated to procurement went on paying debts to the defence industry.[46] The armed forces also had to compete for the budget: a large share of spending on defence and security went on the Interior Ministry's troops.

This situation accelerated in 1998 when Russia went into severe financial crisis. The stock market collapsed, Central Bank interest rates increased to 150 per cent and tax revenue collapsed. The state devalued the rouble and defaulted on domestic debt. Political crisis ensued, with widespread strikes; Yeltsin fired the Prime Minister, but the opposition blocked his preferred candidate. Under such conditions, the disaggregation of Moscow's war strategy was again apparent: the system remained designed to fight a large-scale war against the West, but the government was unable and unwilling to fund such a military, even to basic requirements. In a context of severe economic hardship and political and military indecision, reform stalled, equipment was neither procured nor maintained and conditions remained poor: officer pay fell still further, and large numbers of officers still had no housing.

And then, in 1999, the Chechen war resumed. In fact, according to Yeltsin, preparations had been underway since Khasavyurt, since the high command had not admitted defeat. In March 1999 Deputy Interior Minister Gennady Shpigun was kidnapped and killed in Chechnya; in August Chechen groups launched an armed assault into Dagestan. In September there followed a series of bombings of apartment buildings across Russia, and the newly appointed Prime Minister, Vladimir Putin, requested the 'absolute power needed to conduct the military operation and coordinate all the power structures'. Within weeks, Yeltsin noted, Putin had transformed the situation in our power ministries into 'one united fist'.[47] For his part, Putin stated that his first task was to resolve 'ministerial disconnection' (*vedomstvenuyu razobshchennost*): the army did 'not understand what the Interior Ministry was doing, and the FSB was criticising everybody, but itself not taking responsibility'. Only acting as a 'unified organism' would bring success. The army would 'do its business and then return to barracks'.[48]

Moscow presented the second campaign – in many ways a continuation campaign – as a fight against an international aggressor, a 'well equipped and trained army of killers', including mercenaries from Afghanistan and the Arab world. Putin asserted that Chechnya was being used as a 'launching pad for further attacks' on Russia, that Moscow faced the 'Yugoslavisation' of the Russian Federation, and that the resumption of the Russian campaign was a 'war operation' (*voennaya operatsiya*) and a 'counter-terrorist operation' to destroy extremism and terrorism. Without this, he argued, the whole Caucasus would have been lost, with disintegration spreading up the Volga river to Bashkortostan and Tatarstan. The disintegration (*disintegratsiya*) of Russia would have been a 'global catastrophe'; Russia would not have had sufficient armed forces if the conflict had so spread, and so Moscow would have had to mobilise, and a 'large-scale war' (*krupno-masshtabnaya voina*) would have begun.[49]

The renewed campaign revealed many of the same problems encountered in the first. Although the reforms had promised the establishment of combat-ready forces as a main priority, when Chechen forces invaded Dagestan in 1999 the dispatch of Russian troops took one month. Moreover, the response force had again to be drawn from across Russia. As Putin later recalled, when the need arose to counter a large-scale attack by international terrorists, the problems in the armed forces became painfully evident. To repel the assault, he stated,

> we needed a group of at least 65,000 troops, but the combat-ready army came to only 55,000 men, and they were scattered throughout the entire country. Our armed forces came to a total of 1.4 million men, but there weren't enough men to fight. This is how children who had never seen combat before were sent to fight.[50]

If there were some improvements in command and control, and some new equipment, such as the BMP-3 tank and tactical reconnaissance drones, many of the same problems remained. Coordination between air and ground forces was poor, leading to 'friendly fire' incidents. Assaults on Grozny were again ruthless and costly; the reliance on firepower by the Russian armed forces inflicted extensive destruction and casualties, civilian and military. As in the first campaign, Russian forces suffered heavy casualties, among them numerous senior officers. On occasion, whole units of Russian forces were lost: in early 2000, shortly after Sergeyev had assured Moscow that the campaign had been successful, a Chechen force ambushed and trapped a group of Russian airborne forces on Hill 776. The military initially tried to cover up the losses;[51] subsequently, films such as *Proryv* and

Grozovye vorota sought to portray the heroism of Russian soldiers against overwhelming odds.

After three months of heavy fighting, Russian forces finally took Grozny (again), and, in May 2000, Moscow announced the reimposition of its direct control. Separatists continued to wage an insurgency campaign, characterised by suicide and terrorist attacks, even killing Akhmad Kadyrov, Moscow's appointed leader of the Chechen government, in 2004. But Moscow achieved sufficient military success to be able first to hand operational control from the military to the security services and Interior Ministry in 2003, and then announce the end of the operation in 2009.

The protracted struggle in Chechnya was brutal. The costs for Russian society and the armed forces were very high. The way that the armed forces campaigned, and the conduct of Moscow's Chechen allies, gave rise to widespread accusations of human rights abuses. And the way Moscow conducted the war served to drive a wedge between Moscow and the Euro-Atlantic community. Indeed, the causes and conduct of the war in Chechnya became one of the initial and then most serious disputes in relations. Moscow refuted in the strongest terms Western criticism of Russian operations, accusing the West not only of double standards but of supporting the separatists. Nevertheless, Moscow achieved its overall goal – territorial integrity and sovereignty over the Chechen Republic.

If tomorrow there's war: the influence of geopolitics

If poor material conditions offer one reason why Moscow's armed forces performed as they did in Chechnya, another was that Russian war science did not equip the armed forces with the tools to conduct a counter-insurgency campaign. The focus remained very much on conducting large-scale war against a technologically advanced opponent. Actually, the combination of the experience in Chechnya and NATO's Kosovo operation in 1999 confirmed the dispute between Moscow and the Euro-Atlantic community, and entrenched views among the Russian armed forces and other parts of the Russian state that, yes, Russia did need conventional forces to wage high-tech, large-scale, theatre-wide war within the foreseeable future. As one senior Russian observer put it, 'today – Yugoslavia, tomorrow – Russia' was a 'deeply held consensus'. Especially among the armed forces, opposition to, and concern about, NATO, and particularly the US, remained strong.[52]

Russian war science faced the same context as the defence sector as a whole: the 1990s were a period of sustained scarcity. The political and military leadership simply had other priorities, leading to severe resource constraints, a shifting organisational structure and the departure of many specialists. This all contributed to what some referred to as a broader de-professionalisation, not to say crisis, of war science.[53] Nonetheless, some important individuals and structures remained from the Soviet era and continued to lead and shape war science. As in the late Soviet period, this reflected a wider blend of influences, both civilian and military. Among the civilians was Andrei Kokoshin, who, as we saw above, became one of the most prominent MoD civil servants. Others, such as Alexei Arbatov and Sergei Karaganov, were involved in the Council for Foreign and Defence Policy, which was established in 1992, and immediately began to contribute to the formulation of national defence and security debate and policy.[54]

Within the armed forces, the Centre for War Strategic Research, established in 1985 as a structural division of the General Staff under the influence of Akhromeev and Gareev to raise the level of scientific research on war strategy and develop the theoretical and practical formulation of defence policy, continued its activities under General-Lieutenant Sergei Bogdanov. The Centre's focus remained on the question of large-scale war: the lessons of the Gulf War and the development of proposals regarding the maintenance of strategic parity and 'to counter the enemy in the event of a threat of war'.[55] Gareev himself remained very active, and established the Academy of War Sciences in 1995. This provided a platform for a number of prominent retired officers such as Andrian Danilevich to contribute to the shaping of defence policy. And the General Staff also established in 1991 a section for the multidisciplinary study of geopolitics and security; and, in 1993, under the direction of Rear Admiral Vladimir Pirumov, a scientific council to support the Security Council.

This sense of continuity of those who shaped the debate masked and mitigated what would otherwise have been a complete, radical change in Moscow's strategy: the shift from a communist, class-based character of thinking about strategy and war to one that befitted a democratic state. As the establishment of the geopolitical section in 1991 and the scientific council indicated, Moscow's thinking about strategy and war was characterised by a shift from a class approach to a geopolitical one. As Pirumov put it, the priorities of the state's geopolitical factors became the 'basis for working out its national interests and goals and the objective assessment of available resources'.[56]

Many of those in Moscow who were thinking about national security thought in geopolitical terms: the control of space (*prostranstva*) and resources in a longer-term trajectory from the past into the future. Geopolitics provided the method for thinking about the future character of war, and served as the intellectual basis for a focus on the potential for large-scale war between Great Powers. Connected to this, for a state that faced chronic shortages and restricted spending on defence and science and technology, it provided context for thinking about the changing character of war. If technological development was driving a 'revolution in military affairs' and an acceleration of Western technological superiority, the geopolitical approach reorganised the strategic basis: rather than military-technical change, the point of focus should be the possible sources and causes of wars in future. The political condition formed the context in which the revolution in military affairs should occur, and guided the contours of war.

Together, this meant that the Russian strategic discussion, especially among the military leadership, concentrated on the most dangerous threat, even if not the most likely – Western superiority in a high-tech future war, but also US power and NATO enlargement. For Gareev, the end of the Cold War had neither 'terminated the actual geopolitical positions of different nations', nor the objective contradictions between them. War was still the continuation of politics by other, violent means. At its root, international politics would be shaped by the struggle for territory and natural resources. Consequently, while Great Powers should ensure the readiness of their armed forces for participating in local wars and conflicts, the foundations of national defence must be laid with a view to ensuring readiness to rebuff aggression and participate in large-scale warfare with mobilisation. Simply, regardless of technological development, wars between Great Powers could not be short because those states had vast resources. It would be necessary, according to Gareev, 'to prepare for rather long, persistent and fierce armed struggles'. This negated the advantages of small, professional armies because wars would be fought by nations. Indeed, even local wars sometimes demanded large forces, because attempts to resolve problems using small armed forces often led to unexpected resistance, the expansion of the conflict and the prolongation of military actions. Gareev pointed to Malinovsky's view that local wars inevitably developed into world war, and therefore the primary emphasis must be on that.[57]

Indeed, in these terms, Gareev's 1995 book *If War Comes Tomorrow?* – echoing the 1938 Soviet film and song – set a long-lasting foundation for Moscow's debate about strategy and future war. This was characterised by two threads. The first was the persistence of long-running debates referencing Moscow's strategic inheritance: Clausewitz, Liddell Hart, Tukhachevsky and Frunze, among others, all implicitly and explicitly featured. But it was Svechin's work that provided the main conceptual reference point for Kokoshin, Lobov, Gareev and many others. Svechin was referred to as 'our prominent contemporary' and 'our Clausewitz', and as especially relevant for shaping contemporary doctrine.[58]

These senior figures invoked Svechin to frame strategy making in conditions of comparative economic and technical weakness, especially when compared to the West, and to assert the need for integration between politics, economics and the military when preparing national defence. The relationship between war and politics was the pre-eminent consideration – and the whole of the state's capacity must be brought to bear, rather than just the armed forces, which thought in terms of operational art, rather than war. The emphasis was clear: it was an attempt to reassert strategy over operations. A strategy of destruction enthroned operational art, which reduced the political-economic content of strategy. Instead, given Russia's circumstances, a strategy of exhaustion was necessary, one that wove together all of the state's resources.[59]

In this context, influential thinkers repeatedly referred to Moscow's persistent difficulties in aligning political and military leadership and the transition to war. For Gareev, close coordination between political, economic and military leadership was in short supply, leading to serious miscalculations in the Winter War, Afghanistan, Chechnya and, of course, 1941. The work of these different parts of the state was too often carried out in isolation from the others, and if there was excessive self-confidence and thoughtlessness, especially among politicians, the military too often were too deferential, leading to tragic mistakes.[60]

And with this in mind, the primary focus of thinking about future war was about the initial period of war. For Gareev and others, the relationship between war science and the future was explicit: the task of war science and forecasting (*prognozirovanie*) was to establish possible changes in political and military affairs to determine how the next war might erupt. The link between the experience of the past and future war was also explicit. As Gareev asserted, any radical forecasts that emphasise only change and revolution will miss profound continuities in strategy and war. The content of war and its conduct evolved – rather than radical leaps, the question would be of old forms of war taking on new content; technique would guide technology in a dialectical as opposed to a technical determinist approach.[61]

These foundations conditioned the second, contrapuntal thread that emerged in the early 1990s, and that would ensure that the tension between strategies of destruction and strategies of exhaustion continued to characterise Russian thinking about and preparation for war. Although it reflected the longer-term short war thesis, this phase of the strategy of destruction debate emerged in the early 1990s with the Gulf War and the revolution in military affairs. The debate focused on new conceptions of modern war, particularly 'network-centric war' (*setetsentrichnaya voina*) and 'non-contact war' (*bezkontaktnaya voina*), which reflected the automation and intellectualisation of war that promised short, attrition-free wars. Variations on this theme continued into the mid-2000s as officers reflected on the 'lightning wars of a new generation'.[62]

The most prominent advocate of this approach was Vladimir Slipchenko, a retired officer of the post-war generation who questioned Soviet-era approaches to war. In a series of publications in the late 1990s and early 2000s about the future of war, he argued that Russia needed a completely different structure of armed forces: instead of infantry and tanks rolling across Russia's borders in future, Moscow would face a massive airborne attack against its economy from any strategic direction. Slipchenko argued that what the combat in the Falklands and the Bekaa valley in the early 1980s had foretold, the Gulf war had underlined, and NATO's Yugoslavia operation in 1999 had confirmed: the US and some other Western states had moved to a 'new generation' of war. In such a war, superiority in long-range precision weapons, command, control and communications and logistics meant that smaller forces could quickly defeat larger ones. Victory consisted of defeating an adversary's military on its own territory, destroying economic potential and replacing the political system. This Western 'new generation' represented a sixth generation in war fighting, and had defeated Iraq in 38 days; Russia, he argued, as Iraq had been during the Gulf War, was still in the fourth generation.

To move beyond the fourth generation and meet this challenge, Slipchenko was clear: the navy must become Russia's main strike component, offering range and mobility, an arsenal and a launch pad. Indeed, without a powerful navy, Russia would lose its economic potential because it would not have the capability of reaching its opponent. Actually, Russia's defence capability needed a complete overhaul, with the reorganisation and modernisation of the military-industrial complex and the reorganisation of the armed forces into 'strategic strike' and 'strategic defence' forces.[63]

Slipchenko's views are often cited in the Western debate about Russian military thought, more often referred to, perhaps, than actually read. But they did not reflect a consensus in Russia. For all those who advocated the idea of 'non-contact' war, there was a like number who asserted that 'contact' war was inescapable, with combined arms operations, assaults and Zhukov-style firestorms. For those who advocated network-centric and information war, there were those who challenged these concepts. Indeed, Russia's then internal conflicts in the Caucasus, budgetary limitations, and entrenched parochial interests all inveighed against Slipchenko, especially regarding the navy, in the view of many a costly folly.[64]

Most prominent among those who disagreed, however, was Slipchenko's boss, the president of the Academy of War Sciences. Some of Gareev's positions have been outlined above. But the way he reiterated them through the mid-2000s reflected the military leadership's views and where the balance lay in Russian strategy. Gareev underlined his view that a discussion of modern and future war should be about not military matters, but the nation's defence. He acknowledged that war would involve a struggle in the aerospace and information domains, the value of suddenness and the 'extreme disadvantage of passive, defensive actions'. But he rejected the 'neologisms' – network-centric, non-contact, information and the like. All these elements will be part of a war, he argued, but none will individually characterise the appearance of war as a whole: there can be no 'non-contact' war, because sooner or later non-contact operations must be followed by contact actions. War will not be conducted in a vacuum, and concepts such as battle and operations will not disappear, he argued. While military reform was an important theme, therefore, the primary point for Gareev was the improvement of the entire military organisation of the country.[65]

Reviving the state?

While this discussion was underway among the armed forces, the Russian political leadership was also changing and attempting to reinvigorate the state's power. When Putin became acting president on 31 December 1999, Russian strategy was deeply dysfunctional. The state was characterised by executive weakness, even, as Putin phrased it, 'disintegration', and a shrunken and anaemic economy that lacked competition and innovation. Russia's armed forces were simultaneously in structural crisis and waging a devastating counter-terrorist campaign in Chechnya, while conceptually focused instead on the potential for a major war with the Euro-Atlantic community. Defence Minister Sergeyev and Chief of General Staff Kvashnin were at loggerheads over the use of resources and the appropriate structure of the armed forces.

Putin's intention was to overcome the protracted crisis by pursuing a long-term strategy of national revival and prosperity

through reasserting central executive control and creating conditions for fast and stable socio-economic improvement. Putin
sought to achieve macro-economic stability through tax reform
and the reassertion of the state's role in the economy. This
achieved important short-term results – tax revenues grew, Russia
achieved a budget surplus in 2001 for the first time, and inflation
fell from 85 per cent in 1999 to 15 per cent in 2002. This was
followed by the paying down of state external debt, and the
establishment of both a stabilisation fund and state corporations.
Over time, however, this would have more mixed effects – the
growing role of the state began to suppress competition, in turn
diluting the need to restructure and dampening innovation and
efficiency.[66]

One of the priorities of Putin's strategic agenda was the
reform and modernisation of the armed forces.[67] In 2000, with
the Kosovo campaign fresh in the mind and campaigning in
Chechnya still underway, Moscow published updated versions
of the national security concept and war doctrine. The former
depicted a world that was becoming more multipolar, but also
one fraught with concerns for Russia, notably about attempts
by the US-led West to assert its domination and resolve problems
through the use of armed force. While the concept pointed to
a range of challenges, it also framed NATO's eastward enlargement as a threat, along with the possibility of the appearance
of foreign military bases near Russia's borders and the eruption
and escalation of conflicts near Russia.[68]

The doctrine broadly aligned with the concept, noting the
existence of armed conflict near Russia's borders, the expansion
of military blocs to the detriment of Russia's security, and the
introduction of foreign military bases and capabilities on to
the territory of states that neighboured Russia. The doctrine

acknowledged the decline in the threat of the unleashing of a large-scale war, but at the same time emphasised that Russia should maintain readiness to wage war and take part in armed conflicts. Moreover, it underlined the spread of local wars and armed conflicts and that large-scale war might result from the escalation of one of these conflicts. Such a large-scale war would require the total mobilisation of all the material and spiritual resources of the states involved, and the conduct of strategic operations. Modern war, the doctrine suggested, would be coalition in nature and have an impact on all spheres of human activity. It would be characterised by the extensive use of indirect, long-range weapons to seek to disrupt the adversary's state and military command and control, with attacks being made against armed forces and their logistical support, as well as the economic and communications infrastructure throughout the territory of each warring party. There would be a high likelihood of new states being drawn into the war, with a corresponding escalation and expansion of scale and range of means employed.[69]

With this horizon, Putin embarked on attempting to reform and modernise the armed forces – their organisation, equipment and force structure, a 'new type' of army, one that would be 'mobile and compact' (*mobylnoi i kompaktnoi*). Putin replaced Sergeyev with Sergei Ivanov, a long-term ally, former deputy director of the security services, and, since 1999, secretary of the Security Council. This was a significant and symbolic moment: Sergeyev was (to date) the last armed forces officer to be defence minister; Ivanov represented the security services.

Putin re-established the ground forces high command, and sought to drive a transition to a professional army, with improved service conditions and a reformed defence industry. 'In accordance with the plans we have agreed', he stated, we will 'continue to move towards a professional army, air force and navy', a process that would be completed in 2007.[70]

In 2003 the strategic leadership instigated the elaboration of a concept for the further improvement of the armed forces in a draft doctrinal document entitled the 'Vital Tasks of the Development of the Russian Federation Armed Forces'. This was intended to shape the priorities for development based on how Moscow saw Russia's place in international affairs and national security requirements. While strategic deterrence forces would be maintained, this implied major changes for the conventional armed forces, including increasing the number of permanent readiness units and integrating them into groups of forces with unified control capable of fulfilling their combat missions *in their peacetime composition*. The reforms envisaged, therefore, combat missions in both peacetime and wartime *without additional mobilisation*. Furthermore, Moscow sought to increase contract-based recruitment and move the armed forces on to a professional basis.[71]

While these moves were underway, the international environment was rapidly changing. Following the terrorist attacks on the US on 9 September 2001, Putin stated that 'many people realised that the "Cold War" was over' and that another war was underway, one with international terrorism. This 'fully applies to Russia'.[72] Nevertheless, tensions in Russia's relationship with the Euro-Atlantic community, so vividly illustrated by the Kosovo crisis in 1999, continued to ensure that significant parts of the Russian policy community, including in the armed forces, still considered the main challenge to be a US-led NATO. In the early 2000s these tensions were highlighted by Russian campaigning in Chechnya, another round of NATO enlargement, the

US withdrawal from the anti-ballistic missile treaty and the US-led invasion of Iraq. At the same time, there were a series of what Moscow called 'colour revolutions', including in Georgia (2003) and Ukraine (2004), leading to the emergence of more Western-leaning governments in those states.

In early 2004 Sergei Ivanov stated that such developments were motivating Russia's political and military leadership to 'amend its view' concerning the role and place of military policy and assets. Military force, he observed, was increasingly being used to defend economic interests; the range of threats that Moscow faced included interference in Russia's internal affairs, instability in Russia's immediate neighbourhood and NATO's 'offensive military doctrine'. To meet these challenges, Russia needed 'radically' to reform its armed forces to be able to fulfil tasks simultaneously in two armed conflicts '*of any type*', the ability to ensure 'strategic deployment and check the escalation of an aggravated situation by means of strategic forces and permanent readiness units'. In wartime, Russia should be able to 'rebuff an aerospace attack and, upon full-scale strategic deployment, to perform tasks simultaneously in two local wars'.[73] That said, Ivanov asserted that the Russian military had overcome its period of crisis. Facing a new and more favourable situation, the General Staff now needed to focus less on the current situation and more on the prospects for its development and the war of the future. To do this, Putin promoted Colonel-General Yuri Baluyevsky to replace Kvashnin as Chief of General Staff. Baluyevsky had extensive experience in the Soviet and then Russian main operations directorate, including during NATO's Kosovo campaign, during which he oversaw preparations for the intervention of Russian airborne forces to Pristina airport.

Since 2001 he had served as First Deputy Chief of General Staff.[74]

Like Ivanov, Baluyevsky pointed to Moscow's concerns about growing US geopolitical and geo-economic interests in the Eurasian region and the growing role of military force in resolving conflicts on Russia's borders. That said, he acknowledged Russia's state and conventional weakness and the need to trim strategic ambitions. Threats, he argued, called for the presence of a 'small number of permanent readiness units that could quickly and effectively influence local conflicts'.[75]

Given these changes and new conditions, in 2005 the Security Council decided to update the war doctrine, and in 2006 Putin reiterated the strategic importance of modernising the armed forces to ensure combat readiness. Russia needed armed forces that were 'professional and mobile', he said: 'we should not go after quantity and simply throw money to the wind'. To this end, defence spending was increasing year-on-year. Priorities included long-range aviation and rebuilding the navy.[76] The complexity and practicalities of strategy, however, ensured that progress in implementing reforms was slow. Under Prime Minister Kasyanov, in 2003 the government did not sign off the Defence Ministry's requests for more funding. The defence industry resisted the leadership's efforts to consolidate it, and output grew only slowly; even by the end of the decade the delivery of military supplies was barely half of the 1991 level.[77] The shift to a contract-based, professional armed force was slow, and conscription was not abandoned. This had important knock-on effects: the failure of the federal programme to replace conscripts with professional soldiers affected the ability to establish regional commands, resulting in a decision to postpone their creation.[78] And service conditions in the armed forces remained poor: large numbers of officers were still without permanent accommodation, and abuse, beatings and suicides continued among private soldiers and officers alike.[79]

There were also practical ramifications of fifteen years of neglect: the sharp decline in investment in equipment meant a regression in capabilities. Limited equipment, poor training and insufficient officers meant inadequate preparation, development and implementation of essential elements of war strategy, especially deception and leadership. The conceptual development of *maskirovka* and *khitrost* was curtailed and characterised by cliché and formalism, and it was applied incorrectly in practice.[80]

And although the Security Council had commissioned an update of doctrine in 2005, rather than a decision, this only led to a period of protracted debate at the highest levels of the armed forces about what that doctrine should look like. This reflected the problems of assessing the probable character of wars in the foreseeable future, and what this meant for the structure of the armed forces. As the head of the General Staff Academy's strategy department suggested, although the essence of war remained much the same – the attainment of political aims by the resort to armed force – the concept of war was being 'filled with new meaning' because of changing international conditions, the actions of other powers and technological development.[81] Gareev noted that it was impossible for armed forces structured only for operating in small conflicts to quickly reshape for 'serious' war.[82] Although Moscow was attempting to reshape and modernise the armed forces, therefore, strategy was still stymied by indecision over whether those armed forces should be designed for waging short, professional wars with strategic operations, or for waging longer wars of attrition.

6

A twenty-first-century blitzkrieg

By the mid-2000s, therefore, the leadership was attempting to inject impetus into its strategy, a stimulus that would lead to a sustained drive to invest in and modernise the armed forces, finally to shift them beyond their Soviet inheritance and shape them towards 2030. This was partly because Moscow's strategic capacity was regenerating – during the early-to-mid 2000s, the economy showed average yearly GDP growth of 7 per cent– and partly because of an intensifying dissonance with the West, widely described as a 'return to the Cold War'.[1]

Putin's speech at the Munich Security Conference in February 2007, during which he described NATO's enlargement as a 'serious provocation' and pointed to 'serious international tensions', crystallised Moscow's positions. A US-led unipolar world was 'unacceptable', he asserted, and 'unilateral and frequently illegitimate actions' were leading to 'new tragedies and centres of tension'. 'Wars, as well as local and regional conflicts have not diminished', he stated; indeed, 'today we are witnessing an almost uncontained hyper use of force – military force – in international relations, force that is plunging the world into an abyss of permanent conflicts'.[2]

This posed a problem for Moscow. Economic growth was one thing, but the leadership still faced many sociopolitical problems, including a high degree of dysfunctionality in state power. Observers pointed to bureaucratic 'de-professionalisation'. Officials acknowledged the waste of resources, with the budget being executed in a chaotic and uneven manner, and the tardy (or non-)implementation of plans and instructions. State plans were affected by *vedomstvennost* as ministerial rivalries and empire building delayed and diluted policy making; handpicked officials proved unable to prevent passive resistance to, or even the quiet sabotage of, the leadership's instructions.[3]

Moscow thus sought to generate grand strategy by overhauling the legislative and policy-making architecture. In 2006 the State Council initiated legislation to establish the legal basis for the preparation, development and function of the system of strategic planning. The Security Council began to take on a greater role in the formulation and then oversight of implementation of strategic plans. In 2006 it formed an inter-agency commission dedicated to strategic planning; the Council would subsequently emerge over the next ten years as the main body for pooling ministerial resources and authority. For Kokoshin, this application of strategic planning 'means a significantly higher level of governance', and was 'justified' as one of the mechanisms for shaping Russia's development; 'advancing this kind of strategy has a political-mobilisation function'.[4]

This overhaul was intended to modernise all aspects of state function, and would take shape over the next decade in various forms as 'Strategy 2020'. Parts of this agenda advocated socio-economic and technical modernisation, with investment in technology, infrastructure and innovation.[5] And among a plethora of other strategic articles, plans, concepts and doctrines, Moscow published updated versions of the foreign policy concept (2008), national security strategy (2009) and – finally – the war doctrine (2010). These documents painted Russia as a Great Power in a time of growing international tension.

While the national security strategy emphasised geo-economic security and energy diplomacy, Moscow's war doctrine pointed to a complex and dynamic threat environment. Ideological confrontation might be weakening, but it pointed to the rising influence of states seeking all-embracing domination and the tendency towards the violent resolution of local conflicts. Nikolai Patrushev, who became secretary of the Security Council in 2008, acknowledged the lessening of the possibility of a large-scale war against Russia, but stated that 'in a number of directions' the military dangers to Russia were growing, due to NATO expansion as a primary challenge, especially when it positioned the US and NATO on Russia's periphery.[6]

The Putin–Serdyukov–Makarov 'new look' reforms: towards high readiness for short war

Defence and security were a central feature of this grand strategy, and the first step was a change in defence leadership. Putin appointed Anatoliy Serdyukov, head of the federal tax service, Defence Minister in February 2007, making him Russia's first civilian defence minister. With ever larger sums of money being allocated to defence modernisation, Putin tasked him with improving the management of the political-military machinery and answering the Kremlin's questions about where all the money was going. The armed forces initially dismissed Serdyukov as a civilian with no military experience: he was known as 'Marshal Taburetkin' ('Marshal Stool'),[7] due to his earlier experience as a furniture salesman. But other observers suggested that he quickly became the 'CEO of the MoD', and 'the most able and effective manager to assume the helm of the Russian military since Stalin's commissars'.[8] Bringing with him more than thirty colleagues from the tax service, Serdyukov moved immediately to audit the armed forces and to control the defence budget, implementing severe anti-corruption investigations and seeking to address acute problems in procurement. Well-informed observers indicated that inspections were thus 'conducted by people who have neither slept on armour, nor toasted to friend-ship' with those they were auditing, and that senior generals attended defence board meetings 'as to the scaffold'. The process led to the dismissal of numerous senior officers.[9]

One senior officer to depart was Baluyevsky. Following a sustained dispute when Serdyukov's civilian colleagues began to go beyond financial matters to interfere in military-strategic questions while showing their disregard for the views of the military,[10] Baluyevsky resigned in protest in June 2008, moving to become deputy secretary of the Security Council overseeing military-political forecasting. Nikolai Makarov, who had previously commanded the 2nd Guards Tank Army, and then the Moscow and Siberian military districts, before working with Serdyukov since 2007 as chief of armaments, replaced him as Chief of the General Staff and First Deputy Defence Minister.

Together, Serdyukov and Makarov began to implement fundamental changes in Russia's conventional forces. Often known as the 'Serdyukov/Makarov' or 'new look' (*novy oblik*) reforms, for some well-placed observers they were not only the most far-reaching of the post-Soviet era, but since Trotsky; for his part, Shlykov called them 'Serdyukov's blitzkrieg'.[11] Even so, we should remember that they were part of a wider state effort – and so were more accurately *Putin's* 'new look' reforms.

The Russo-Georgia war

As events would have it, the timeliness and necessity of these reforms were revealed by the confrontation between Moscow and Tbilisi that resulted in a short campaign in August 2008. As discussed in Chapter 1, although colloquially known as the 'five-day war', the Russian leadership interpreted this clash of arms as a 'coercion to peace' (*prinuzhdenie k miru*). It is 'difficult to call it a war by modern standards', Ivanov stated, since active operations only lasted three days, Moscow used only a portion of its conventional forces, and did not conduct a mobilisation. According to Shlykov, the fighting was 'low intensity': there were no real battles, and only a limited air campaign.[12]

Moscow's short campaign might have achieved success, followed by the recognition of South Ossetia and Abkhazia and the establishment of military bases there, but Russian officials and observers alike point to the events revealing 'absurdities'.[13] The first such absurdity was reflected in how the war began. Relations between Moscow and Tbilisi had been deteriorating already for several years. The Russian General Staff had shaped plans for a potential conflict with Georgia in 2006 and 2007, and exercised accordingly. According to Vladimir Boldyrev, then commander of the Russian ground forces, this plan was for a 'victory-bringing, lightning war' (*pobedonosnaya, molnienosnaya voina*).[14] Yet when Georgian forces began their assault on the separatist regions of South Ossetia and Abkhazia in early August, the Russian leadership was taken by surprise. President Medvedev was on holiday. Prime Minister Putin was in China. The Defence

Minister was on holiday, and allegedly could not be reached by phone for ten hours. According to Baluyevsky, therefore, Russia lost the first day of the war due to political indecision (*nereshitelnost*) at the highest levels.[15] This surprise led senior Russian political figures such as Boris Gryzlov to compare the initial Georgian attack with the blitzkrieg of Operation Barbarossa. In a similar vein, Grachev and Gareev criticised Russian military intelligence for their failures to 'uncover' Tbilisi's plans and concentrations prior to the attack.[16]

The second 'absurdity' lay in confused command and control. Baluyevsky, as noted above, had lost his job just weeks beforehand, as had Alexander Rukshin, head of the General Staff's main operational directorate. The latter was rumoured to have refused requests from senior MoD officials to return to office until Putin himself telephoned to 'make the request'.[17] In the meantime, three different headquarters were controlling operations – the General Staff, the North Caucasus Military District and the 58th Army – meaning that orders took too long to reach units. This was compounded because when the war started, the officers in the main operations directorate were on leave because their offices were being moved to a different building. Furthermore, the air force was subordinate to neither the North Caucasus Military District nor the 58th Army, and was allegedly run by the air force commander-in-chief, Alexander Zelin, by mobile phone from his office. In practice, therefore, the Russian armed forces were also taken by surprise by the way the war started; with command and control in a 'dire state', the ground forces and air force began by waging two separate campaigns.[18]

With the war underway, Moscow's forces suffered from poor reconnaissance and orientation. Partly, this was because Russian forces did not use their GLONASS receivers: commanders were afraid to distribute such expensive equipment to troops for fear of it being stolen or lost.[19] This led to the ambush of a column of the 58th Army and, according to Troshev, the failure to suppress Georgian air defences, leading to the loss of several aircraft.[20] Indeed, the short campaign was marked by a number of casualties among senior Russian officers, including the commander of the 58th Army, Anatoliy Khrulyov, who was wounded, and several air force officers.

Despite overall victory, widespread discussion emerged about the problems faced by the Russian armed forces, including logistical support (there were many vehicle breakdowns) and squalid service conditions.[21] Others pointed to both the 'organisational conclusions' (*orgvyvody* – effectively, dismissals) after the war, and the obvious separation between theory and practice. Some suggested, indeed, that the campaign had shown that war science was 'secondary, paper-based and essentially nothing'. Intelligent officers 'should study theory', leaving practice to those 'who can swear, pound their fists, determine what will bring material benefits, and, most importantly, know how correctly to enter high offices'.[22]

Makarov, too, was clear that the campaign had (again) shown the gap between theory and practice, that there was a mismatch between words and reality. Indeed, according to him, the armed forces had not been properly reformed since the 1960s: it was time to stop preparing for the wars of the past and instead to prepare for wars of the future that would appear quickly and develop rapidly and end with the task being achieved, without time to perform full mobilisation measures. Such reforms to establish permanent readiness forces were not only necessary,

Makarov indicated, but were fully in line with general international trends.[23]

For its part, the state leadership was able to use the military's performance in the Russo-Georgia war to overcome internal opposition to reforms. As Medvedev later put it, the campaign experience showed the strengths and weaknesses of Russian military power and gave a 'powerful incentive to rethink the entire military strategy to a certain extent'.[24]

Shortly after the foreign policy concept was published in 2008, therefore, a document began to circulate entitled the 'new look of the armed forces: being a concept of the development of the military force structure to 2030'. The document suggested that Russia faced a new era of acute crises, one in which the USA was both superior in terms of military technology and sought to retain its dominance of the international system through global deployments and intervention in the domestic affairs of sovereign states. Consequently, it proposed that the armed forces should undergo a structural shift from the Soviet era mobilisation model to a more flexible, high-readiness force capable of conducting network-centric operations.[25]

The reforms envisaged a reduction of the armed forces to a strength of 1 million, with extensive cuts to the officer corps, more than halving it in number over three years. Likewise, the number of units in ground forces, air force and navy was to be substantially cut, eliminating the cadre and reduced strength units that represented the mobilisation system built for waging large-scale, protracted wars. Further cuts were imposed to reduce central Defence Ministry personnel and the number of military education institutions from 65 to 10 over six years. On the basis of these cuts, a major procurement programme would be implemented, along with a reorganisation of command and control to provide a new structure with a single information and communications space. Divisions were disbanded and new brigade structures established.[26]

The end of the Putin–Serdyukov–Makarov reforms and the shift back towards mobilisation

The 'new look' reforms were the subject of sustained and vigorous debate among politicians, government policy makers and public media alike. Some asserted that they destroyed the armed forces and undermined Russia's strategic potential and the ability of the state to defend itself.[27] Others were fully supportive. That dynamic reforms were necessary appeared obvious: in 2008, only 17 per cent of the armed forces were combat-ready, equipment was obsolete and increased financial support from the state had not led to practical improvements.[28]

Equally, the reforms were beset over time by a number of conceptual and practical problems. Conceptually, although the reforms were initiated by the senior leadership amid an overhaul of the state's strategic planning, as one observer pointed out, they appeared to be so disconnected from the 2010 doctrinal update that it 'defied logic'. The scale of the reforms meant that Russia's armed forces were 'not adequate' to the tasks set out in the war doctrine: there was a shortage of junior officers and inadequate mobilisation capacity. While conflicts might unfold quickly, conflict settlement could take years – for which Russia would likely need a substantial number of troops. The armed forces were too small to be able to cope with potential local conflicts, let alone the prospect of a large-scale war which the armed forces appeared to anticipate.[29]

Practically, the implementation of the reforms suffered from missed deadlines and shifting goalposts. Exercises revealed that the fighting capacity of the new force was still low, and that the abolition of layers of command had weakened command and control – leading to the reinstatement of command layers and further structural reorganisations.[30] Long-standing problems continued. During the wildfires of 2010, Medvedev fired senior officers for their failure to prevent damage to a base near Moscow. The military had initially denied the damage; 'despite the fact that we asked the MoD to help extinguish fires to help the civilian population, in the majority of cases the ministry cannot (even) protect itself', Medvedev said.[31]

Indeed, if the Putin–Serdyukov–Makarov reforms had proceeded despite internal opposition from conservative elements of the armed forces, in 2012 they were hoist by their own petard. Theft from the defence budget remained a significant problem. In 2011 Chief Military Prosecutor Sergei Fridinsky said that approximately 20 per cent of the budget was stolen: 'every year more and more money is set aside for defence but the successes are not great … the sums of money stolen are shocking'. Finally, an anti-corruption investigation in the Defence Ministry revealed extensive embezzlement, but also that Serdyukov was having an affair with a subordinate.[32]

Putin dismissed Serdyukov and Makarov in November 2012, appointing Sergei Shoigu and Valeriy Gerasimov respectively in their steads. Shoigu had occupied prominent positions since the early 1990s, both in politics and as Emergencies Minister since 1994. The militarised character of Russian civil defence and emergency services meant that Shoigu was highly decorated (Hero of Russia) and had held the rank of army general since 2003; his ministry was one of the most powerful force structures in Russia. He was in many ways a civilian, therefore, but one with a reputation in the power ministries; not a general of the army in terms of professional experience perhaps, but an army general by rank. For his part, Gerasimov had served as first deputy commander of the 1st Guards Tank Army and then the 58th Combined Arms Army, commanding the latter during the second Chechen war, before going on to military district command and then becoming Makarov's deputy in 2010.[33]

The command change offered the Russian leadership an opportunity to alter trajectory in shaping its military tool; Putin indicated that specific corrections and adjustments were already underway.[34] Partly, this was because of Moscow's growing pessimism about the trajectory of international affairs; the debate about modern war continued in the light of the so-called Arab Spring that began in 2011. Partly, it was because Moscow sought to give another impulse to its development of grand strategy with the president's 2012 May Decrees. Putin stated that the 'dynamics of the geopolitical situation require us to take well-considered and rapid actions'. Russia's armed forces had to 'reach a fundamentally new level of capabilities in the next three to five years'.[35] Together, this shifted the emphasis back towards mobilisation preparation.

Moscow's assumptions and 'modern war'

Moscow still faced a difficult situation. Domestically, the global financial crisis of 2008 had inflicted protracted socio-economic problems: the economy shrank by some 8 per cent that year, and Russia was driven into deep recession with high inflation. Rather than build a new economy, the government was obliged to conduct a major fiscal expansion to support the population.

These policies may have demonstrated economic resilience, but as the economy began to grow again, it entrenched the role of the state in the economy as a whole.[36] By 2011 and 2012 the leadership was still asserting the need for economic modernisation, even as it managed some social unrest as various groups protested Putin's return to the presidency.

Internationally, the horizon was no brighter. In early 2012 Putin suggested that the world faced a serious systemic crisis, that international affairs were entering a 'long and painful' 'zone of turbulence'. He repeatedly returned to this theme: he noted in 2014, for instance, that he saw a sharp increase in the likelihood of a set of violent conflicts with the direct or indirect participation of the world's major powers. Indeed, he suggested that 'history's lessons' showed that 'changes in the world order – and what we are seeing today are events on this scale – have usually been accompanied by if not global war and conflict, then by chains of intensive local-level conflicts'.[37] At the time, there was a wide-ranging discussion of what modern 'war' looked like among the public, security policy and armed forces professionals. In 2011 novelist Viktor Pelevin had published the science fiction novel *S.N.U.F.F*, describing post-apocalyptic 'wars' as a form of high-tech entertainment: the media filmed armed forces using drones and conducting bombing campaigns against essentially defenceless opponents.[38]

The political and security policy debate emphasised a 'Cold War 2.0' and the struggle for resources, even whether World War III was unavoidable, and called for mobilisation preparation. In the context of the Arab Spring, policy makers and commentators alike emphasised the political and socio-economic aspects of 'colour revolutions': they represented a modern form of war, waged through strategies of 'controlled chaos' to reformat geopolitical space. These indirect strategies sought to undermine a state's sovereignty, weakening it from within so as to change the government.[39]

The professional military discussion chimed with this broader discussion, but in ways that couched it in a longer-term context. Observers referred to Leer, Liddell Hart and Svechin, examined the lessons of 1941 and 1991, and reflected on network-centric war and the influence of science and technology. Officers critiqued the strategic connections between the state and the armed forces, officer training, and combat readiness and organisation. Officers also critiqued the condition of war science, underlining the need for the further assessment of how to address traditional problems of managing space and time, mobility and suddenness. Perhaps most significant, though, was the continued discussion about the evolving nature of the initial period of war and the balance between strategies of destruction and of exhaustion, with some noting that the former were becoming obsolete and a shift to the latter.

These points were reflected in the early speeches of the new Defence Minister and Chief of General Staff. Gerasimov echoed Makarov's views that geo-economic competition for resources would lead to a significant increase in military threats to Russia through the 2020s, together with the US's technological superiority and the global reach this afforded Washington. Explicitly posing the question 'what is modern war?', Gerasimov pointed to the widespread use of political, economic and information tools of strategy, noting that they were followed by the open use of armed force to achieve final success. The consequences of such measures, he suggested, were that, as the Arab Spring demonstrated, a hitherto prosperous state could be turned into an arena of fierce struggle within days, leading to its collapse.[40]

Gerasimov also highlighted the dynamism of modern military operations and the evolving nature of the threatening and initial periods of war, referring to Isserson when discussing how mobilisation took place prior to war's eruption. Likewise, Shoigu, who had for years been an active participant in the discussion about the Great Fatherland War, emphasised the increase in military dangers and the dynamism of modern conflict. He instructed the General Staff to consider the threat posed by US prompt global strikes and to resolve problems in, and to develop the basis of, mobilisation preparation.[41]

Such discussions characterised the debate throughout the mid-2010s, with the emphasis on emergent signs of a large-scale war and the need to learn the lessons of 1941 – to prepare in advance and ensure the swift and smooth transition of the state to wartime command. Gareev stated that humanity was going through perhaps the 'most dramatic turning point in its history'. War was 'very close', he observed, and the leadership must enhance the internal strength and unity of the country while also implementing a return to mobilisation training and preparation. Gerasimov stressed similar messages, and the updated versions of the war doctrine (2014) and national security strategy (2015) again noted the tendency to resolve conflicts through the use of armed force.[42]

This conversation, however, took place against a background of continuing problems in the armed forces. These ranged from poor service conditions and rife alcohol abuse among servicemen, to problems in reporting up the chain of command, financial irregularities in the state budget and even combat power. In early 2013 Putin himself pointed to the delayed or 'improper' fulfilment of the defence order, the need to learn how to maintain, repair and store new equipment, and the ongoing need to provide officers with permanent accommodation: 'there are still many military families on the waiting list', he stated. Furthermore, because of 'irresponsibility and carelessness' (*bezotvetstvennost, bezalabernost*), towns faced winter fuel and heating shortages.[43]

This meant initiating three sets of measures. The first was to accelerate a series of state-wide measures to improve the effectiveness of the state system. These included rotations of senior personnel, with some long-standing senior officials being relieved of duty. Additionally, it meant shifts in the policy-making landscape, including enhanced roles for both supra-institutional bodies to improve coordination between state bodies, and movements such as the All-Russian Popular Front to oversee implementation of the leadership's instructions.

The second set of measures related to the defence industry in the continued effort to modernise the armed forces and implement the extensive procurement plan set out under Serdyukov and Makarov in 2010. The leadership continued to invest heavily in defence, despite the fluctuations between recession and slow growth that characterised the wider economy for most of the decade. Measuring Russian defence spending is not straightforward, given the way the budget is framed – it includes not only the 'national defence' chapter of the budget, but also MoD spending under other chapters and additional instruments to finance military spending, such as state-guaranteed credits. Taking all three of these aspects together, Moscow's spending on defence rose from nearly 4 per cent of GDP to above 5 per cent from 2014 to 2016; the national defence chapter alone rose from nearly 3 per cent to nearly 4 per cent over the same period. Moreover, such spending is best interpreted by recognising purchasing power parity: in 2010, this meant expenditure of $125 billion, growing to $150 billion in 2013 and over $200 billion in 2016, before declining (somewhat) to \$160 billion in 2020.[44] In 2015 Putin underlined both the importance of this work to 'make up for lost time' in the 1990s when the armed forces and defence industry were 'chronically underfunded', and the need to resolve persistent interruptions and delays in implementing the state defence order. He returned to these themes again the following year, emphasising that the main topic on the agenda was increasing mobilisation readiness – the general ability of the defence industry and the economy as a whole to fulfil the state defence order, and the ability of enterprises rapidly to organise, or increase the production of necessary goods and ensure the supply of required volumes of arms, equipment and spare parts.[45]

The third set of measures applied to the armed forces and defence planning. In part, this meant a sustained drive to increase the combat capabilities of the armed forces and a return to scale. This involved the reintroduction of larger units, including the re-establishment of some divisions and the 1st Guards Tank Army (2014), and the reversal of the Serdyukov-era decision to scrap thousands of Soviet-era armoured vehicles, and instead to modernise them.[46] At the same time, this meant reorganising the armed forces – including the merger of the air force and aerospace defence forces (again) in 2015, the establishment of the Arctic joint strategic command and the (re-)introduction of military-political commissars – and seeking to integrate a coherent state command. To this end, in 2013 the leadership had begun to shape the Defence Plan, a complex of interconnected strategic and operational plans to forecast developments in the political-military situation and to formulate a unified national defence policy. This unified understanding of the defence concept included military, economic, informational and other aspects, the 'main tasks for strategic containment and prevention of military conflicts, as well as for solving the main mobilisation issues'. Putin stated that 'in the near future, we must fully complete the creation of an integrated system of strategic planning in the military sphere', and asked the MoD to submit for approval a new version of the regulation on military planning.[47]

This plan envisaged new powers for the General Staff to coordinate the activities of all federal bodies to ensure defence and security; Gerasimov stated that these planning documents were intended to prepare the country in advance for the transition to wartime conditions and ensure nationwide coordination of measures across federal executive bodies. This would serve 'maximally to reduce' the state's response time in the transition from political and diplomatic measures to the use of force.[48] This reflected the continuing focus on what the transition from a threatening period of war to the initial period might look like.

These, then, were the answers to the 'lessons of 1941' that Gareev and Gerasimov repeatedly asserted. The Defence Plan had two practical consequences. The first was the establishment of the National Defence Management Centre (NDMC), opened in 2014, intended as a permanent body of control over the state's armed forces under the supreme commander (the president). Again, this embodied Moscow's discussion about the lessons of the Great Fatherland War: as Mikhail Mizintsev, the NDMC's first commander, put it, the closest analogy in terms of the Centre's intended functions was the Commander-in-Chief's Headquarters during the Great Fatherland War, which 'centralised all controls of the military machine and economy of the nation in the interests of the war'.[49]

The second was the attempt to integrate large-scale exercises across the state to test the capacity to wage war. These exercises

– such as Tsentr 2015 and Kavkaz 2016 – tested not only territorial defence, but mobilisation readiness – and included government ministries and major banks alongside civilian regional and municipal authorities. For Shoigu and Gerasimov, these exercises revealed the insufficient alignment of the organs of state power, and they repeatedly asked Putin to instruct regional governors and other civilian authorities to undertake mobilisation preparation courses at the General Staff Academy.[50]

Moscow's deployment of force: Crimea and Syria

By the time of these exercises, Moscow had deployed force twice. The first was against Ukraine in February 2014, in an operation to take over the Crimean peninsula, which in many ways echoed 1968's Operation Danube. The critical phase of the operation lasted one week. Moscow airlifted special forces to bolster troops already in place, used the Black Sea Fleet to establish a blockade, and then deployed other forces by sea to confine Ukrainian forces in Crimea. Having seized the initiative, Moscow distracted and deterred Kyiv by deploying more substantial forces to the Ukrainian border and seized full control of the peninsula within the month.[51]

Moscow waged a second, less successful campaign in eastern Ukraine, beginning in March 2014, characterised by political agitation and more-or-less covert support for separatist paramilitaries in Donetsk and Luhansk, including weapons and volunteers. After some initial success by the separatist paramilitaries, Ukrainian forces were able to muster superiority in numbers and firepower, and inflicted a number of defeats and setbacks on them. Indeed, by August that year the separatist campaign was failing, and Moscow directly intervened with conventional forces, defeating the Ukrainian armed forces in battle first at Ilovaisk in August 2014, and then at Debaltseve in February 2015, leading to the Minsk II treaty.

Later that year, Moscow deployed its armed forces to Syria to assist Bashar al-Assad's government in the civil war that had erupted in 2011. Framing it as a limited intervention, even as a 'special operation of a complex structure' (*spetsalnaya operatsiya, kotoraya imela slozhnuyu strukturu*), the Russian leadership was more explicit about the deployment as a 'comprehensive application of force' to ensure the 'fire defeat of the enemy' and 'qualitatively to change the situation' in Syria.[52]

The campaign was conducted in three phases. The first, from September 2015 through to January 2016, was to deploy, stabilise and degrade the adversary with offensive operations. The second, through December 2016, was to continue offensive operations to secure key territory. The third and final phase, through 2017, was to conduct decisive campaigns to clear Islamic State forces from west of the Euphrates and to create the conditions for a political resolution. The campaign in Syria was the first attempt, therefore, to conduct expeditionary operations since the Soviet intervention in Afghanistan, and the Russian armed forces again showed improvement. Russian forces suffered some reconnaissance failures, tactical setbacks and inter-service rivalry. Nevertheless, they conducted large-scale, long-range strikes with precision guided weapons for the first time, achieved better alignment between air and ground forces, and improvements in logistics. The Russian military also successfully coordinated operations with allied armed forces, particularly the Syrian 5th Assault Corps.

Gerasimov pointed to improvements in command and control, partly through the coordinating role of the NDMC, but also due to greater initiative among senior officers. He suggested that campaigning in Syria had demanded creative thinking on the part of leaders in the spirit of Suvorov and Zhukov: initiative, non-standard thinking and purposefulness in solving assigned tasks. All told, Gerasimov suggested that the armed forces had shown skill in conducting 'new type' warfare, characterised by the need to master multiple capabilities and state tools, as well as high-intensity combat with constant fire on the enemy.[53]

In different ways, these campaigns reflected the use of suddenness (*vnezapnost*) and mobility to seize the initiative, and the emphasis on the use of heavy firepower to seek decisive battlefield success. The campaign exposed some of the limits of indirect measures such as the use of proxies, and the continued cost of conventional power: Russian forces suffered comparatively substantial casualties during the short second campaign in Ukraine, and Moscow has officially acknowledged over one hundred casualties in Syria, including a number of senior officers: Lieutenant General Valery Asapov, two major generals and a number of colonels were among those killed in operations. But it also revealed the improvement in Moscow's military capabilities, including in discipline, equipment, command and logistics.

For one prominent Russian military observer, these campaigns showed not just the 'refurbishment' (*remont*), but the 'resuscitation' (*reanimatsiya*) of the armed forces by Shoigu and Gerasimov after the 'destruction' of the Putin–Serdyukov–Makarov reforms. As far as Murakhovsky was concerned, it represented a 'major success': 'we have demonstrated the ability to deploy our troops to a remote theatre of military operations, thousands of kilometres from Russia, in the shortest possible time'.[54]

Even so, two broader points stood out. First, although the campaign led to the Minsk process in Ukraine and to Putin's claim of success in Syria in 2017, neither conflict has (yet) been resolved in Moscow's favour. Indeed, a rapid rebel advance forced the collapse of the Assad regime in late 2024, leaving Moscow's position uncertain at the time of writing. At best, therefore, the operations represented qualified and essentially temporary successes in the use of armed force as a political tool. Furthermore, they exacerbated the growing dissonance between Russia and the Euro-Atlantic community. Relations significantly worsened following Moscow's annexation of Crimea: diplomatic relations were much reduced and (mutual) sanctions imposed; talk on both sides of a new Cold War – and then a Great Power competition – intensified. Each side accused the other of waging a 'hybrid war' against them; in Moscow, senior officials explicitly connected the conflicts in Yugoslavia, Iraq and Syria with the Chechen, Georgia and Ukraine wars as 'links in the same chain'.[55]

Second, senior officers have noted that although the campaigns offered extensive combat experience for a large part of the armed forces, they also pointed to the need to 'generalise' the experience and to learn lessons. Gerasimov suggested that the armed forces were 'resolving tasks through practical experience, without having the opportunity to draw upon the recommendations of military science', and that missions that were new to the troops were often resolved 'on the spot, taking into account experience that had been acquired and expedience'. Military scholarship, he indicated, had not given the necessary attention to the problems of conducting combat operations in contemporary conditions.[56]

Defining war and rethinking war strategy

With these deployments still underway, in 2016 the General Staff and Security Council held a series of discussions about the essence of war. This debate continued along essentially familiar lines: Gerasimov acknowledged that there were scholars and specialists who supported classical interpretations and also those who advocated a fundamental review of the content of modern war because armed conflict is not its only defining attribute. Gerasimov himself was clear that an obvious evolution had taken place – wars of the early twenty-first century differed from those of the late twentieth century in terms of participants, weaponry used and the blend of methods of confrontation. Nevertheless, the 'main foundation of wars today and for the foreseeable future remains as before. And their main characteristic is the fact of armed struggle.' Prominent observers agreed, suggesting that to change the interpretation of war would be 'premature' (*prezhdevremenno*). Moreover, officially, the definition remained unchanged: war was a sociopolitical phenomenon, defined at the national, state level, and a form of solution for interstate or internal state contradictions using military force.[57]

While the debate on the essence of war rolled on, the focus of the discussion shifted towards the development of war strategy in modern conditions. This was stimulated partly by the realisation that Russia's campaigning experience showed that practice was ahead of war science and theory.[58] Equally, it was because the Russian leadership considered the US and its allies to be refining their own strategies for fighting wars and their capabilities for doing so.

This meant three things. First, Moscow invested considerable effort in attempting to 'sanctions-proof' its economy. Broadly, this was because the post-Cold War era was characterised more generally by much greater use of sanctions – the use, especially by the Euro-Atlantic community, of economic strength as a tool of statecraft, as a form of interstate conflict.[59] After 2014 this became a priority for the Russian leadership when the Euro-Atlantic community imposed what would become a rolling series of sanctions on Russia, initially in response to Moscow's annexation of Crimea and associated actions, then in response to other actions, such as interference in Western elections. These sanctions initially caused a surge in inflation, depreciation of the rouble, and an increase in both interest rates and the budget deficit. They additionally impinged on the Russian energy and defence sectors, reducing access to finance, components and technology.

The state coped by implementing a series of adaptive measures, including import-substitution measures and the Russification of technology and capital in the sectors targeted by sanctions. More importantly, Moscow treated the sanctions as a national security threat, and so securitised policy in the targeted sectors. If economic measures were part of modern conflict, then Moscow adapted to protect the strategically important heights of the economy, and to cushion them against sanctions. This meant an acceleration of a 'Kalashnikov economy': seeking to make the economy durable in political terms, albeit unsophisticated when measured by economic efficiency.[60]

Second, linked to the effort to build sanctions resilience, Moscow invested heavily in developing its maritime power. This was because of Russia's recognition of the growing role of the sea in international affairs and the extensive investment by many nations, from the US and UK to Japan, China and Australia, in modernising their navies. It was also for geo-economic reasons and the Russian leadership's view of evolving international affairs, especially the shift of global power to the east. Moscow's interests lay in exporting commodities, and, as noted above, therefore in access to transit routes and markets. For Moscow, this meant an emphasis on developing the northern sea route. With the imposition of sanctions by the Euro-Atlantic community, Russian trade became ever more dependent on the sea – imports from Asia increased significantly after 2014; exports to the Middle East and North Africa, South East Asia and the Pacific region likewise grew.[61]

The practical consequence of this meant sustained investment in port and shipbuilding infrastructure. The navy particularly benefited from the combination of defence modernisation and the shift in attention to the maritime domain, receiving some 25 per cent of the total state defence order in the 2010s. Spending on the navy echoed defence spending more broadly, peaking at over $40 billion in PPP terms in 2015, and although spending declined, it remained above $30 billion by the end of the decade. In PPP terms, Russian naval spending was the third or fourth highest in the world.[62]

Numerous practical problems remained – not least the low base from which improvements had to begin and the thin spread of spending across the navy but also other maritime forces – but this level of investment resulted in considerably renewed maritime capacity. New ships were commissioned, and the Russian navy was able to begin to conduct larger and more complex exercises, and to deploy to the high seas. In 2017 Gerasimov noted that the navy had conducted 672 missions and 650 port visits;[63] in 2019 the navy conducted its first circumnavigation since the nineteenth century.

The third point was reflected in war strategy. Gerasimov pointed to the US categorisation of 'hybrid war', though he suggested that as far as Russian war science was concerned, it was 'too early' to add this categorisation to the Russian strategic lexicon. Instead, he pointed to the development by the US of a 'twenty-first-century blitzkrieg'. The

> US has developed ... the concept of a prompt global strike. The US military is counting on achieving the ability to inflict damage on enemy troops and targets anywhere in the world within a few hours. It is planned to introduce a promising form of warfare – globally integrated operations. It involves the creation in the shortest possible time in any region of inter-service force groupings capable of defeating the enemy by joint actions in various operational environments. As conceived by the developers, this should become a kind of blitzkrieg of the twenty-first century.[64]

And in 2019 he embellished this by adding that the Pentagon had begun to develop a 'fundamentally new strategy for conducting military operations': a 'Trojan Horse' strategy. This involved using the protest potential of a fifth column to destabilise a state using sabotage, while simultaneously inflicting long-range precision strikes on it. The US posed, therefore, a multi-dimensional challenge to Russia: technologically superior, Washington 'did not hide' its intention to achieve its goals in the course of local conflicts with limited objectives, but was also preparing to conduct wars with a 'high-tech enemy, using precision weapons from the air, sea and space with active information confrontation'. 'Under modern conditions, the principle of warfare based on the coordinated use of military and non-military measures, with the decisive role of the armed forces has been developed', he continued, and the principles of advanced preparation of the state for defence are 'ensured by constant high combat and mobilisation readiness', and the creation and maintenance of strategic reserves. The principles of suddenness, decisiveness and uninterrupted strategic action remained relevant, but Gerasimov stated that all required significant scientific study.[65]

In 2019 the armed forces held a series of conferences convening the military leadership with the General Staff Academy and other scientific research organisations to debate the theory of the art of war and the development of war strategy. Indeed, war strategy in contemporary conditions was the central theme of the Academy of War Sciences' annual conference.[66] This debate referred frequently to a roll call of the classics of military thought – Clausewitz, Frunze, Tukhachevsky, Sokolovsky and Ogarkov, and foreigners including Liddell Hart. Those who paid careful attention could spot references to Semyon Ivanov and Andrian Danilevich. Gareev's work was, of course, prominent, promoting the lessons both of the Manchurian campaign as a 'geopolitical operation' and the Great Fatherland War, particularly foresight about the war and the organisational transition towards it. Nevertheless, the most prominent of these classics, the most consistently referred to, including by Gerasimov, was Svechin, indicating the broader bent towards a focus on strategies of exhaustion, and the importance of resilience and the socio-economic aspects of war.[67] Indeed, in the broader context of Moscow's shift towards mobilisation preparation, it was Svechin's thinking that received official countenance: the MoD explicitly defines his strategy of attrition (*strategiya izmora*) as 'a method of conducting military operations that involves achieving war aims through methodical manoeuvring in the theatre of military operations and influencing the enemy's communications and supply bases'. Proponents of such a strategy, it notes, are Lloyd, Corbett and Svechin. (The more Tukhachevsky-esque *strategiya sokrusheniya* did not merit official mention.)[68]

Seeking to shape the debate, Gerasimov reiterated themes addressed in previous speeches, again noting new spheres of confrontation in modern conflicts. While non-military means were important, he confirmed that the main content of strategy continued to be the preparation for war and its conduct in the first instance by the armed forces; actually, the role of the armed forces was only increasing. The priority of war strategy, he emphasised, remained the study of the means of increasing Russia's combat power: the size and quality of the armed forces, their staffing and technical equipment, their moral and psychological condition, and their level of preparation and combat readiness. War strategy, he stated, encompassed two directions: the theoretical, in terms of understanding the changing character of war; and the practical, in terms of preparing to deter an aggressor and, if necessary, waging war. It represented the search for rational strategies for waging war with various adversaries, and in this context, he named three particular features of Russia's strategy.[69]

Given the operations in Syria, one feature of this related to expeditionary campaigning. Gerasimov pointed to the fulfilment of tasks for the 'protection and promotion' of Russia's national interests beyond its territorial boundaries in the framework of a 'strategy of limited actions' (*strategiya ogranichennykh deistvii*). This included the creation of self-sufficient groupings of forces based on the formation of one service – in Syria, this was the air force – to ensure flexibility and high mobility.

The second feature was one that he had emphasised since 2013: a strategy for territorial defence during an escalating threat in a crisis situation. He reiterated the need for an enhanced system of territorial defence against attempts to destabilise Russia's internal security. This emphasised the state-level approach, since it would include coordinating the actions of all federal executive bodies to protect critical infrastructure against terrorism and sabotage.

The third feature was an 'active defence strategy' (*strategiya aktivnoi oborony*), which, in 'accordance with the defensive character of Russia's war doctrine, envisages a complex of measures for the pre-emptive neutralization of threats to state security'. Such a strategy should capture and retain the strategic initiative by coordinating military and non-military measures (albeit with the armed forces retaining the decisive role) to wear down and bleed large enemy forces. Again, this emphasised the role of the state as a whole, including socio-economic and industrial dimensions, in addition to requiring high combat-readiness from the armed forces.

The principal points remained suddenness, decisiveness and uninterruptedness of actions. A strategy of active defence meant the persistent engagement of the enemy throughout the theatre of operations, and the conduct of strategic operations to affect the enemy's ability or will to sustain the struggle. On the battlefield, this would be defined by fire strikes to degrade the enemy: territory was of secondary importance. Instead, the intent would be to inflict a degree of disruption and disorganisation on the enemy, to shape their political calculus through long-range strikes against critical infrastructure. All told, the primary intent of such a strategy would be to prevent the adversary from achieving decisive advantage (or victory) in the initial period of war and to force a conflict of exhaustion.

Amid these discussions, senior officers emphasised the search for innovative approaches. This meant the use of new technology and different types of units, as well as addressing the question of shifts in the composition of command groups and encouraging officers to depart from standard templates. It also meant finding a balance between respecting the unity of command (centralisation) and delegating greater rights to headquarters to solve issues and coordinate among themselves, as well as encouraging *khitrost* and *initsiativa* among junior officers.[70]

If the armed forces were showing growth in capacity, then, the leadership also sought to experiment and look to the future. Gerasimov announced in 2017 that five years of efforts had resulted in the development of the general purpose forces, the establishment of autonomous groupings of forces in strategic directions, and an emphasis on the modernisation of equipment. These improvements made it possible to extend Russia's military presence in strategic areas of the world and to pursue technological development. In 2019 he again hailed progress, pointing to the development of 'fundamentally new types of weapons', particularly in hypersonic missile technology, such that Russia was 'confidently leading in comparison with the technologically developed countries of the world'. This echoed Putin's 2018 speech to the Federal Assembly, when he asserted Russia's 'breakthrough' in developing weapons – 'highly effective, but modestly priced systems' – and its embarkation on the development of the 'next generation of missiles'. These, Putin stated, were based on the 'cutting edge, unique achievements of our scientists, designers and engineers'.[71]

Much of this modernisation effort appears to have been guided towards preparing Russia to fight a large-scale war, including the renewed development of a mobilisation reserve capacity. As Murakhovsky put it, during this time mobilisation preparation was a mandatory element of yearly exercises: checking mobilisation and combat-readiness, and the processes involved, from the call-up of military personnel from the reserve, the deployment of relevant units, checking the readiness of the federal agency for state reserves, and civilian bodies (from transport to the treasuries of the Central Bank) being able to work in wartime conditions.[72]

Strategic culture and the condition of Russian war theory

Even so, the inheritances – or hangovers – of the past weighed heavily on the leadership's efforts to invigorate war strategy. The first of these related to ongoing problems in organisational structure. Although Moscow sought to restructure the policy-making landscape, this posed its own problems, including imbalances and inconsistencies, especially in funding.

On the one hand, in seeking to enhance internal security, the state established the National Guard, which absorbed considerable resources. On the other, reforms to the armed forces were not always fully seen through. The establishment of the aerospace forces in 2015 is a good example, not only because it underlines the backwards-and-forwards nature of reform, but because it created a 'complex branch', born in an atmosphere of 'fierce arguments' and 'compromise'. Conse-quently, by the late 2010s, as an organisation it remained 'far from perfection' and effective combat performance.[73]

The shifts in the landscape could not mask the practical problems of strategy making. Dysfunction remained an important characteristic of the organisation and chain of command. In 2016 Shoigu dismissed the Baltic Sea Fleet command for serious lapses in service, including omissions in the organisation of combat training, failure to improve the conditions of service, a 'lack of concern for subordinates as well as distortions in reports about the real state of affairs'.[74] And in 2021, even after efforts to re-establish and modernise mobilisation preparation, Shoigu was displeased to discover that a military commissariat office in the Moscow region had no computers to contact other commissariats. Indeed, the military commissariat service was burdened by heavy bureaucracy, poorly motivated staff and obsolete technology: the General Staff acknowledged that 70 per cent of commissariat offices were not equipped with modern automated mobilisation deployment systems, and 30 per cent of offices had no access to the internet through the ministry's confidential channels.[75]

A second hangover from the 1990s and the Putin–Serdyukov–Makarov reforms was the condition of the officer corps. Murakhovsky asserted that by 2020 the Russian armed forces had a problem with a gap between the older and younger generations. The middle generation that should have formed during the 1990s and 2000s had largely been 'removed' (*vymyto*). Consequently, there was a shortage of officers with sufficient authority for the top leadership positions. Moreover, the older generation of generals continued to serve beyond their term, to 'pass on experience' to the younger generation.[76]

Indeed, although large numbers of officers rotated through the Ukraine and Syrian campaigns, the command problem appears to have run deep. To be sure, some cultural inheritances remained: 'all our traditions in military affairs', Kokoshin noted, 'can lead to a fettering of initiative' and 'strengthen fear in junior officers in the face of senior officers', leading to attempts to shift responsibility up the chain of command.[77] But if some old traditions retained their force, they were intensified by new problems in education. These were as much to do with officer training as with punitive traditions; the fact was, senior Russian officers argued, that the development of practical skills in command and control lagged behind modern requirements. For Murakhovsky, this meant teaching officers their trade: tank officers, he argued, needed less personnel management training and instead more basic engineering.[78] For Gareev, military education was no longer preparing the infantryman or the commander. Rather than preparing officers to organise a battle, education was 'at best' training staff officers how to stamp documents. Such a 'formal-bureaucratic method' (*formalno-byurokratichniy metod*) was 'emasculating' and 'deadening' the command and control process. Greater initiative and independence at all levels was essential, he asserted, but to achieve this, modern officers should look carefully at how Zhukov and Rokossovsky acted in a situation, understand it and *then move on*.[79]

Indeed, if Murakhovsky and Gareev were critical of officer preparation, this was just part of the wider problems in war science. For all the references to Ogarkov and Svechin, serious problems remained in Russian war theory. Gerasimov's speeches throughout the 2010s read as a sustained jeremiad about the condition of Russian war science, and the need to restore its prestige and ensure that it made a practically effective contribution to doctrine and strategy. It is impossible to accept a situation in which scientific projects are carried out and problems remain unresolved, he stated: the 'main result of work is not plump reports but new ideas and well-founded proposals'.[80]

Gerasimov and Gareev may have pointed, therefore, to the establishment of numerous research organisations and scientific companies, and the need to boost the Academy of War Sciences in search of a nationally unified system of research in the interests of defence.[81] But this ran in the face of deep structural problems in two key ingredients of war science: history and science and technology.

If the leadership has established a number of organisations for historical research, the wider context of the study of history in Russia and the narrower context of the history of war are hobbled. Consequently, the contribution of history to war science is less propitious than a first glance might suggest. Official efforts to guide and shape the historical debate took shape in the late 2000s with the establishment of a department of the history of war to combat what Moscow saw as the falsification of history, and have continued through to the publication in 2023 of an official state history textbook. This official history does not go uncontested in Russia – Putin initially gave an order for a state textbook in 2013, one he had to repeat in 2014. That then Culture Minister Vladimir Medinsky had to oversee it himself after a lengthy pause might suggest that the Russian historical establishment was not fully supportive of the project. There is also vocal criticism of the 'falsification and mythologisation' of history, which gives it a dead-end, 'narrowly utilitarian value for an even narrower group of people'.[82]

Criticising the state narrative, however, can have retributive consequences. In 2016 the long-standing head of the state archive, Sergei Mironenko, was unexpectedly dismissed having debunked a Soviet-era myth about the defence of Moscow in 1941 as a 'falsification' and publishing associated historical documents. 'The task of history', he stated, 'is the search for truth.' Medinsky, Culture Minister at the time, replied that the 'leadership of the Russian state archives' should 'stick to their profession and not give their own assessments of archival documents', and that if Mironenko wished to 'change professions', then he would understand.[83] Others who have challenged the state narrative have also found themselves dismissed: Valery Garbuzov, director of the US and Canada Studies Institute, lost his job in 2023 as the result of publishing articles critical of 'utopian ideas' and 'myths', and how the debate about relations with the US had evolved.[84]

Similar problems are also to be found more specifically in the study of history of war. Specialists underline the importance of historical study in educating those in military service, but critique the inaccurate interpretations and incorrect assessments of campaigns, even the lack of desire to study them.[85] Indeed, quite heated debates have emerged about the quality of the history of war in Russia. Mikhail Khodaryonok, a retired colonel and prominent commentator, has often criticised both the quality of professional war history and its usefulness in shaping contemporary strategy. The history of war, he argued, is not properly taught: battles and operations are not studied, nor is the experience of war; assertions are often 'vague' or inaccurate. Some 95 per cent of domestic films about war should be 'banned', since they suggest that 'any fool could command at the front'; the number of war history books that are of practical use for commanders is 'negligible', and memoirs, both Soviet and Russian, offer only false narratives.

Indeed, as far as Khodoryonok was concerned, no sensible Russian-authored textbook on strategy has emerged since Svechin's *Strategiya*, all recent attempts being written in 'unspeakably boring language', such that the only effect is as a 'sleeping pill'. Furthermore, they are written by those with no experience or idea of command, with the result that they offer little more than 'an exceptional level of dilettantism' in analysing front operations, 'silly advice' and banalities. Consequently, in his view, no serving senior Russian officers would pass a state exam on the 'Suvorov' questions of the history of war, likening such a scene to the film *Chapayev*. Almost any war, he argued, begins with at least two things – a personnel disaster and complete ignorance of the lessons of history. In writing thus, Khodaryonok was taking on not only the Academy of War Sciences but Gareev personally.[86]

The academy and Gareev both responded to this criticism, defending the value of Soviet-era memoirs and studies such as those by Zhukov, Shaposhnikov and Zhilin. But while rejecting some of Khodaryonok's specific points, they concurred about the thrust of his argument. According to some of the teaching staff, the study of the history of war at the academy had been halved in favour of physical education and foreign languages. A particular problem was the shortage of trained specialists able to teach these subjects. Since the reforms of 2008, the academy's work had endured a 'difficult time', and a lack of continuity in military education took many years to rebuild. Moreover, they agreed that most films should be banned, since they were becoming 'weapons of information warfare', though *Brestskaya krepost* was 'worthwhile', and *Osvobozhdenie* 'relatively correctly shows the work of commanders of different levels … with a high degree of objectivity'.[87] For his part, referring to Isserson's experience, Gareev also acknowledged that good new ideas were sometimes not noticed or not accepted, and that a wider 'intellectual front' was necessary, with ideas for reform being discussed across the armed forces as a whole.[88]

If anything, conditions in scientific research were more problematic than in historical research. Partly, this was because of the wider economic conditions in Russia. The sanctions regime imposed by the Euro-Atlantic community from 2014 had a series of cascading effects. As noted above, the state invested and adapted to weather the sanctions. But the implications were further growth in the state's role in the economy and the deepening of a contradiction between the state's persistent commitment to strengthening Russia's military and industrial base and developing technology on the one hand, and the reduction of competition and efficiency caused by the growing state role.[89] In other words, in the 'Kalashnikov economy', the state seeks not economic efficiency but security – this might cushion it against sanctions or 'economic statecraft', but it imposes constraints on the innovation needed to drive science and technological development.

Partly, though, the issue was due to problems more specifically in science and research. Here, there were deep 'contradictions': while the state set ambitious development targets, those same targets were rendered unrealistic by growing centralisation, layers of bureaucracy and structural reorganisations; limited funds were distributed in an uneven manner and with unsatisfactory effects on scientific research. The Russian Academy of Sciences appears to have been insufficiently consulted in these reorganisations; a drop in standards resulted as scientists sought to achieve the unrealistic targets, which were not met in any case. Indeed, the state's targets do not appear to be sustained by the allocation of resources. Official figures suggest that spending on research and development, having risen during the 2010s, is approximately 1 per cent of GDP, comparable with spending in 2000. Likewise, the number of researchers has declined by some 20 per cent since 2000, while their average age has increased.[90]

Perhaps more important is the increasing role of security in science, in terms of legislation and oversight. Since 2012 legislation has imposed restrictions on receiving support for research from abroad and on cooperation with foreign scientists, prohibiting joint projects, conferences and publications without state authorisation. The practical effects of this legislation are the opening of Federal Security Service (FSB) offices on research campuses and the role of the FSB in approving or rejecting scientific research projects.

These effects are also visible in the surveillance, arrest and imprisonment of scientists. The FSB has arrested numerous scientists on charges of espionage and treason: since 2018 more than 12 scientists connected with hypersonic research have been arrested for treason; some have died in custody. The situation has become such that leading scientists have signed an open letter to the presidential administration asserting that the persecution of researchers in aviation science was now 'systemic'. This, they asserted, was having a negative impact on the morale of the 'entire scientific community, not only of their institute, but of the country as well', leading to an 'unprecedented outflow of young scientists from the field and a decrease in motivation to conduct scientific research'. Such a trend, they stated, could only contribute to the 'decrease in quality of scientific research and development'.[91]

There are many reasons for the various challenges that the Russian defence industry faced during the 2010s as it sought to modernise the armed forces, from the weight imposed by bureaucracy, to the waste, squandering and theft of funds and the impact of sanctions in terms of access to technology and disruption of supply chains. These partly explain the tardy development of shipbuilding, drone technology and the T-14 tank. Even the modernisation of existing equipment has proved problematic. Specialists deemed that after extensive modernisation, older equipment remained of limited combat capability; because of its weak armour and poor protection against modern anti-tank systems, the infantry nicknamed the BMP-1 armoured personnel carrier the 'infantry battle grave' (*boevaya mogila pekhoty*).[92] But there would seem to be a connection between the arrests of scientists involved in hypersonic missile development and the continued serious problems faced in new missile technology. Although officially it is combat operational, the Sarmat missile has failed at least four test attempts.

From 'special war operation' to 'large-scale war by proxy'?

This, then, was the condition of Moscow's strategy entering the 2020s. The Russian leadership's view of the trajectory of international affairs was pessimistic, with an emphasis on lasting geo-economic competition and the growing likelihood of conflict, even major war. Of particular concern was the active role of the US and NATO in causing increasing strategic instability, and the growing potential for a global strike, a 'twenty-first-century blitzkrieg'. Relations with the Euro-Atlantic community were characterised as part of a global power competition, one shaped by comprehensive policy and value disagreements across the agenda.[93]

Moscow's view of how wars were fought and won or lost had evolved through the 2010s, with the Russian emphasis shifting from a focus on short, limited war to re-establishing mobilisation capacity and 'active defence'. While there was extended discussion of non-military struggle as part of war, the official emphasis remained very much on war being a state-level activity *defined by the use of armed force*. This debate about security reflected a sense of evolving continuity: the importance of the lessons of the Great Fatherland War and a renewed concern about a modernised form of blitzkrieg. This was a protracted reflection, therefore, on the blurring of the lines between the threatening period of war and the initial period, about the potential for a 'mobilisation gap', and about establishing resilience for a major, Great Power war either as the result of a local conflict that escalated or as the consequence of a direct attack.

A sustained effort to modernise Russia's armed forces certainly produced some improvements. But this led to what might be termed an 'archipelago' armed force: islands of new capacity amid a wider context of unresolved problems. These included structural organisation, officer numbers and their training and the chain of command, and the ongoing obsolescence of infrastructure and equipment. The armed forces were hamstrung between those needed for short wars and limited mobilisation capacity.

This, too, was the context in which Moscow began to build up its forces around Ukraine during 2021 and into 2022. The leadership appeared to have a degree of confidence in the utility of force to resolve political problems, and in the ability of the modernised armed forces to deliver operational success. But this confidence was by no means universal. As tension rose between Moscow and Kyiv, well-connected and prominent military observers argued that if some representatives of the Russian political class claimed that Russia could inflict a crushing, knockout blow to Ukraine within hours, this was 'unbridled optimism' and it would be no 'easy walk'. Among others, Khodaryonok argued that the Russian armed forces lacked sufficient firepower to defeat Ukrainian forces, whom the West would support with extensive material resources, including weapons. There would be 'no Ukrainian blitzkrieg'; instead the likelihood was of a protracted war, including extended urban combat.[94] The persistent tension in Russian strategic thought between short, decisive campaigning and long war could hardly be clearer.

Nevertheless, when Putin launched the 'special war operation' on 24 February 2022, he couched it in terms of Chechnya, Iraq, Libya, the Ukraine campaign in 2014 and Syria, and even 1941.[95] And, in many ways, the 'SVO' was a direct echo of Moscow's previous use of force: what might be called a 'fifth generation' special operation akin to Operation Danube, the assault on Kabul in 1979, the assault on Crimea in 2014 and in Syria in 2015. It was an attempt to deliver a decisive lightning strike to achieve policy goals, using suddenness and speed to achieve a *pobedonosnaya, molnienosnaya operatsiya*.

The challenges of such an operation quickly became apparent, and were in many ways equally familiar, including the combination of an underestimation of the adversary and an overly ambitious timetable for a complex offensive. To this might be added many of the characteristics described above with other operations – politicians giving the military a complex and difficult task, excessive secrecy in internal preparation, poor planning assumptions and so on. The lightning attack achieved some initial success in the east and south, but was dislocated when the airborne assault on Hostomel airport was stalled by Ukrainian resistance, and the offensives along different axes fell behind schedule. The security required to achieve deception and thus suddenness had resulted in a widespread lack of clarity of purpose, not to say bewilderment, across the attacking forces, parts of which appear to have been surprised to encounter combat.

Furthermore, the number of different offensive axes resulted in confused command and control and pressure on logistical support, creating a compounding set of problems as the offensive not only fell further behind a demanding schedule, but became exposed to resilient Ukrainian defence. This, in turn, exposed and exacerbated two problems. The first was the unfavourable force ratio as Ukraine was able to mobilise: the balance of forces, already in Ukraine's favour, quickly accelerated away from Russia. The second was the effect of incompetence, waste, corruption and squander that had diluted the modernisation of the armed forces and thus the weight of blow Moscow could deliver.[96]

The result was a campaign that has, to date, evolved into three phases. The failure of the 'Danube' or '2014' style operation in March 2022 led to Moscow's withdrawal of its forces from the Kyiv region, and the conversion of the operation into a focus on Donbas, relying on firepower advantage and Ukrainian exhaustion. This second phase through the spring and summer included the capture of the cities of Rubezhnoe, Severodonetsk and Lisichansk, but ran out of steam by the autumn. The third phase, beginning in October 2022, represented Moscow's shift to a more positional approach and a shift to a graded war footing with a partial mobilisation draft.[97]

If Moscow continued to call the offensive a 'special war operation', these three phases reflected an escalating slide towards war. Baluyevsky has argued that the scale of the forces involved, the level of means used and the intensity of the hostilities mean that it has gone beyond the scope of a limited armed conflict. Pointing to tactical and technological change, he considers it to pose an unprecedented test, with a new face of war emerging. The infantry is undergoing a renaissance and artillery has returned to its place as the God of War – though Russia lags in artillery and missile systems, he thinks, which should be a priority for development.[98]

Others agree. The designation of the campaign as an SVO was clearly political and appears to reflect, once again, the gap between state political intent and doctrine as espoused by the armed forces. If the state leadership are less constrained by doctrinal definitions, the armed forces have nevertheless begun to debate what the category of 'special war operation' means. Some suggest that it indicates a new category of military conflict: the special actions of troops, with tasks carried out according to a single plan to achieve specific goals: effectively, a single combined arms operation to achieve a strategic success. This, Viktor Litvinenko suggests, makes it closer to the MoD's definition of 'armed operation' than to its definition of 'war': it is more limited in scope. (Equally, it must be said, it sounds very much like the kind of adventurism of which Soviet officers were highly critical, more akin to 'blitzkrieg' than *molnienosnaya voina*.) Nevertheless, he is clear that the operation has now evolved into something else. Others point to the 'new normal' of war: it was not intended as such, but it has become militarily attritional and a 'protracted war', and the state has begun to adapt to these conditions.[99]

This poses an important question, though: what kind of 'war' is it for Moscow? If it is 'attritional', it must also be noted that the Russian economy, while becoming more militarised through 2023 and 2024, is not, at the time of writing in January 2025, mobilised, nor is Russian society. Moscow is still pursuing its other major socio-economic strategic plans, such as housing development and infrastructure, and committing to a (very expensive) development strategy for the northern sea route to 2035. In this sense, therefore, it remains *militarily* attritional (this poses different challenges for Kyiv, of course) rather than socio-economically attritional at the state level.

Although the combat remains limited to the territory of Russia and Ukraine, the conditions – as defined in Chapter 1 – indicate a 'regional war by proxy', or even a 'large-scale war by proxy'. As far as Moscow is concerned, given NATO's assistance to Kyiv, multiple states are involved in seeking significant political changes, and combat involves air, land and sea operations, with strikes against critical infrastructure. Given the support of Iran, North Korea and China for Moscow, the struggle involves more than one region, which implies a 'large-scale war by proxy' – though Moscow has not mobilised all the material and spiritual resources of the state to wage it, and strategic weapons are not being deployed.

These definitions of 'regional' and 'large-scale' war can be cross-referenced with Moscow's thinking regarding an escalation ladder. In 2021 Kokoshin and Baluyevsky co-authored a short book with Viktor Esin, a former deputy head of Russia's strategic rocket forces, and Aleksander Shliakhturov, the retired head of the main intelligence directorate, on escalation. The authors indicate a ladder of 17 rungs which chart the escalation through armed conflict, and local, regional and large-scale war.

'Local, conventional' war is at the sixth rung, with limited political aims and the limited use of armed force in terms of time and place. 'Regional' war begins at the seventh rung, including, as noted above, major political change and strikes on critical infrastructure with wider global implications for the disruption of supply chains. Conventional regional war becomes conventional large-scale war through rungs nine to eleven, with intensifying attacks on critical infrastructure and including the greater use of cyber attacks, particularly targeting state function and large urban centres.

A twenty-first-century blitzkrieg

If the current situation between Russia and Ukraine appears to be somewhere between the seventh and ninth rungs, 'nuclear conflict' first appears as a means of political-military pressure at the twelfth rung. It escalates through the fourteenth with a demonstrative use not targeting civilian, military or economic centres to the seventeenth rung, involving massive nuclear exchanges. The authors do not evince confidence that limited nuclear war is possible; rather they suggest that the introduction of nuclear weapons would generate a situation that would lead to the massive exchange of nuclear assaults with catastrophic consequences for humanity.[100]

Conclusion: Russian way(s) in war

In this book, I set out to examine Moscow's theory and practice of strategy and war, particularly to explore whether there are patterns in Russian thinking about war so that we can speak of a recognisably Russian 'way in war'. This would reflect a broadly coherent rationale or philosophy based on digested experience, one that underpins and shapes Moscow's strategy making as it seeks to advance its agenda and address challenges and dilemmas: a trajectory of ideas formulated and revisited through generations, evolving, debated and adjusted. This could give some useful context and guidance for thinking about the future, helping to add nuance to assessments of capability and intent.

The stakes are high. In early 2025 Moscow continued to describe the campaign in Ukraine as a 'special war operation' and sought to pursue other state activities in as close to a 'normal' manner as possible.[1] But Moscow's level of effort in its campaign against Ukraine, combined with the active support for both sides from other states, and increasingly explicit references to Russia being in a struggle with the 'collective West', suggested that Moscow saw Russia as being in a bigger struggle. Indeed, given NATO support for Ukraine and the roles of states beyond the European region in supporting Russia – China, Iran and North Korea among them – this may even be defined as a 'large-scale war by proxy'. This points to an unstable and potentially escalatory condition, and coincides with Moscow's long-held views of global contest lasting throughout the 2020s. It may be that the Russian leadership considers itself to be in a 'threatening period/period of direct threat', with all this entails for the initial period of war.

Given how Russian war strategy acknowledges that a local war can spiral quickly into regional or large-scale war, this should be a point of focused attention for the Euro-Atlantic community in interpreting escalatory possibilities. A shift to these different levels of war would provide the context for Moscow's escalation to a fuller mobilisation, including the move to a full war economy, the use of non-strategic and strategic capabilities, and any potential widening of the theatre of war.

Despite the obvious and explicit contest and heightened tension, however, Moscow is *not* currently waging war against the Euro-Atlantic community. Nor is such a war inevitable. But given the unresolved and potentially escalatory situation in Ukraine, and the wide range of entrenched policy disputes between Moscow and the Euro-Atlantic capitals, it is an essential question, especially if war is understood to be the resolution of policy disputes through the use of armed force. So, as Euro-Atlantic states plan for the future and shape deterrence and defence, how to interpret Russian strategy and thinking about war?

Russian and Western ways in war

The starting point, even as we recognise Moscow's adversarial, antithetical policies, is to note that Russian strategic thought asserts that national ways in war exist. If war science is generally applicable, war doctrines are national, specific to the unique circumstances of each state. As we have seen, senior figures including Sokolovsky, Gorshkov, Ogarkov and others have asserted Moscow's own distinctive national approach, and that of others – Western, US, British, and so on.

Even so, Moscow's thinking about strategy and war is defined by deep and prolonged interaction with Euro-Atlantic strategic thought, both drawing on and arguing against it. Clausewitz and Liddell Hart are in the Russian pantheon of strategic theorists alongside Russia's own. While Russia follows its own path and style, therefore, this cannot be seen in isolation and cannot be understood without the parallel study of the general foundations of war strategy.[2]

Liddell Hart's lens of a 'way in war' is a useful means of interpreting Moscow's strategic approach and culture – how strategy is shaped, and the priorities and problems that the Russian leadership faces. There are many recognisable European 'family ties' in influences and debates over the central questions about strategy and war, whether in terms of the continental/maritime dilemma or direct or indirect strategies. Despite some obvious differences, there are notable similarities in thinking about strategy and war, and with these more clearly understood, we can more accurately interpret what is distinct.

For Moscow, 'war' is a sociopolitical phenomenon: it is the resort to armed force to resolve a policy clash. State strategy informs and shapes strategy in war: use of the armed forces is a policy tool. In this sense, Russian definitions of war have changed little. While the character of war is always under debate, official, doctrinal definitions of war have remained consistent: the use of armed force is what defines it.

Conclusion

War is therefore envisaged and waged at the strategic level: it means a large-scale, mobilisation-style confrontation, one overwhelmingly defined in Moscow throughout the period covered by this book as potentially being with the West. Local confrontations, even armed ones, are not defined in the same way. This offers insight into the levels of state effort in the pursuit of its goals, including the diplomatic and socio-economic efforts and capacities of the state. The battlefield is certainly important to Moscow: the use of armed force in war is intended to be decisive, to conclude the policy clash by destroying the enemy's armed forces and capacity to resist; it should be *pobedonosnaya*: victory-bringing. But in war, the battlefield is only part of a larger whole-of-state effort, both in terms of attempting to ensure domestic socio-economic and political resilience, and in conducting strikes to undermine the resilience and war-making potential of the enemy.

That said, the character and content of war is constantly evolving, given scientific and technological development and changing socio-economic conditions. Moscow's thinking about how to wage war has therefore evolved considerably within a dialectical tension between strategies of lightning, *molnienosnaya*, destruction and protracted attrition and exhaustion, *izmor*. These debates echo those taking place in Western militaries, even if the periods of their fashion or taboo do not necessarily coincide. Western capitals were more prepared to use force in the 1990s and 2000s, with success in the first Gulf War, Kosovo and Sierra Leone. But this faded after the allied interventions in Afghanistan and Iraq, and a growing reluctance was evident in the decision not to intervene in Syria in 2013. A similar shift over time was also reflected in debates about the possibility of victory in short war, even in the idea of 'victory' at all.[3]

This dialectical tension has shaped theoretical development and reforms to force structure, though Moscow's experience has not always reflected harmony between theory and practice when it has used force. This has led to the widespread view that Russian war theory is sophisticated, but its practice is flawed. We can take this further.

We should be aware of the difference in the Russian debate between officially accepted doctrine and authorised concepts on the one hand, and, on the other, the ongoing debate. There is much to be gained from careful reading of Russian professional military analysis, but not all writers carry equal weight in shaping the debate. Furthermore, although there is indeed some very sophisticated and innovative theory, some caution is warranted. As Gareev and Slipchenko, among many others, have observed, innovative theory is not always read or accepted, let alone transmitted into practical reform. Moreover, theory has often languished, given both the broader sociopolitical and economic context, stifling intellectual conditions, and conditions of state (dys)functionality. The result, as Gareev and Gerasimov repeatedly pointed out through the 2010s, is that Russian practice has often been conducted ahead of theory, and in this sense, military strategy making is often tantamount to anti-dysfunction or retaking control measures (*protivo-bardachnie mery*).

Moscow and its armed forces have gained significant experience in Syria and Ukraine, and have observed other conflicts in the Caucasus and the Middle East. The second half of the 2010s was often framed as a period of experimentation and learning. It may be that the various armed forces research organisations, including those reorganised and established during the 2010s, will distil valuable conclusions from this. But, as discussed in Chapter 6, whether the intellectual context for historical and scientific development is fertile is open to question.

So, it is not immediately clear that a new strategic theorist of the capacity of Frunze, Svechin, Gorshkov or Ogarkov is yet emerging from the current armed forces. Gareev died in late 2019, Baluyevsky is in his late 70s; Gerasimov, in many ways Gareev's intellectual disciple, is simultaneously overseeing the campaign in Ukraine, running the armed forces and acting as president of the Academy of War Sciences. We must wait to see who forms the new generation of Danileviches and Gareevs advising behind the scenes and shaping strategy.

This raises the question of 'cultures' in Russia's strategy: Russia's way in war is state-led, and there are multiple cultures within that. If we can discern specific cultures within the armed forces – broadly sketched as those of the ground forces, navy and strategic rocket forces – we must also recognise other powerful cultures across the state, particularly in the internal and security forces, and in the military industrial complex. That Sergeyev was the last military officer to be Defence Minister, and that he was succeeded first by Sergei Ivanov, and then Serdyukov, reflects this evolution.

The primary actors in shaping thinking about strategy and war today – and probably for the immediate future – are in the state leadership and the economic-industrial sectors. The senior echelons of the armed forces appear to be focusing, at least in public, on operational and particularly tactical level questions. The appointments in May 2024 of Patrushev and Andrei Belousov to oversee maritime affairs (and shipbuilding) and as Defence Minister respectively emphasise the state's desire for a firmer state and industrial hand in defence matters to prepare a strategy of exhaustion. Furthermore, much is made of how defence industry specialists have accompanied equipment to the front in both Syria and Ukraine so as to test it. Perhaps innovative approaches to war will transpire from the combination of these sectors.

Continuity and change

The examination of strategy reveals not just concepts and traditions, priorities and problems, but also persistent assumptions and evolving fashions and taboos that characterise Russian strategic and military thought. The result is a reflection on the tension between continuity and change in the Russian way in war – and some pointers about what does and does not cause change, and over what timescale that change takes place.

The first point to observe is considerable structural continuity. Strategic and doctrinal references and debates consistently return to core themes of speed, mass, surprise, longevity, firepower and comparatively high spending on defence, even during times when the national economy was in the doldrums. It is worth remarking, too, that the problems that Moscow's strategists have faced have proved equally enduring.

The persistence of these central themes in Russian thinking about war, based on the ongoing debate between strategies of the short war, the lightning blow, and those of exhaustion and a longer war, went hand-in-hand with a remarkable sense of longevity in Soviet and Russian political and military leadership. As we have seen, they evolved over decades. Despite repeated repressions from the 1920s through to the 1950s, and political revolution and military success or failure, there have been long periods in which there was considerable continuity of political and military command.

Conclusion

Within this broader context, there was of course continual change, though at variable pace and scale. Persistent reforms, force structure alterations and reinstatements, combined with technological development and domestic socio-economic and intellectual conditions, the international environment and threat perceptions, have all shaped or influenced strategy to varying degrees. Real strategic and doctrinal change, however, is not aligned with victory or defeat in war, let alone on the battlefield, or even necessarily state-level political change. The real points of substantive change in Moscow's strategy and war came in four stages. The first was in the late 1920s/early 1930s with the combination of theoretical development and economic resources provided by the Five-Year Plan. The second was in 1960, when Khrushchev introduced his nuclear and missile doctrine. The third was in 1986–87, when Gorbachev instigated 'defensive defence'. The fourth took shape from the early-to-mid 2010s, with the shift back to mobilisation for a new era of national security and geo-economic competition.

From this, three broad points emerge. The first is that the driving influences behind changes in Russian war strategy are the shaping of state (grand) strategy and shifts in war doctrine (i.e. the philosophical interpretation of the changing character of war and future war). The state leadership's assessments of strategic conditions, international relationships and perceived or real strategic threats drive the structure and resourcing of the armed forces, as well as technological development. State strategy also sets the prevailing intellectual conditions which shape debate about war doctrine, both in terms of its richness and limits, and its ability to change war science, doctrine and strategy.

The second is that, in the Russian experience, theory is hard, and putting it into practice still harder. Moscow often commits the Russian armed forces to delivering blows in difficult circumstances, often amid a reform cycle and regardless of doctrinal preparation. On occasion, the state and the armed forces have not been satisfactorily aligned, and within the military community more specifically, the tension between a strategy of throw down and a strategy of exhaustion has rarely been satisfactorily resolved, either theoretically or in practice. The consequence is such that Russian strategists have gone backwards and forwards or hedged between the two. This combination at the strategic and military levels has meant that, especially at the outset of wars and operations, Russia has often incurred the costs of both strategies and the advantages of neither. The resolution of the tension in its ideal forms is the use of a lightning operation to seize the initiative and achieve the political result *without resorting to war* (Operation Danube), or, in effect, a combination of the two – speed, surprise and weight of repeated blows – to win a war outright, as exemplified in Manchuria. This latter is *molnienosnaya voina*, lightning war, which, as we have seen, is different to (Western) forms of 'blitzkrieg'.

The third is that real change, in both war doctrine and strategy, has often proved slow and subject to reversals and mitigation due to internal resource constraints and disagreements among and between politicians and senior officers. Change has proven largely evolutionary rather than revolutionary, and its practical effects become visible usually only some years afterwards. Care should be taken with the idea that military defeat in war, and especially defeat in battle, leads to substantive change in war doctrine or strategy, though it can certainly lead to considerable adaptation at the technical and tactical level. Moreover, even a dramatic change in state leadership would not necessarily change how Moscow thinks about strategy and war. This suggests that although Putin is central to contemporary Russian state strategy, it does not follow that his departure from office would lead to substantial, immediate change in Russia's way in war.

'Russia's war'

This provides a basis from which to consider the present and look to the future regarding what Moscow's war strategy might look like through the remainder of the 2020s and beyond. To read the current debate is to have a sense of a new era: for some Russian observers, the campaign against Ukraine represents a 'milestone', the 'most important military event since 1991', and as such a 'revolutionary event and a new starting point for the military-technical dimension of conflicts'.[4] Shoigu is among those who have indicated that the operation signifies the start of a new era.[5]

And there is much that seems new in the current campaign as both Ukraine and Russia experiment with technology and tactics. In their efforts to adapt to the new conditions, the Russian armed forces are experimenting with ammunition, by importing it from other states such as Iran and China, and in domestic production. This experimentation, especially with glide bombs and unmanned aerial vehicles such as the Lancet and Supercam S350, has led to a number of tactical shifts; a more sophisticated approach to targeting seems to be underway, with more deliberate pre-attack analysis and battle-damage assessment, and increasing coordination between the services to deliver strikes. Tactical experimentation also includes the dispersal of command posts, dismounted assaults and means for evacuating the wounded.

Even so, the value of history and the longer-term trajectory in attempting to interpret Russian thinking about strategy and war is clear. While there is debate about whether the renewed assault on Ukraine is 'Putin's war' or 'Russia's war' in terms of popular support for it, in strategic terms the campaign launched by Moscow in February 2022 fits squarely into the broader Russian experience of campaigning in this 'long century'. Two sets of characteristics stand out.

First, the current situation reflects very persistent threat perceptions in Moscow. This is not simply in the way the leadership portrays Russia as facing the entire 'collective West' and summoning the symbolism of the Great Fatherland War.[6] It is clear in the echoes of how in the 1920s and early 1930s Moscow anticipated 'future war'. As discussed in Chapter 2, Svechin described the threat to Moscow's interests posed by a Western coalition that would strive to use the national question in Ukraine to strike Russia in the south, in the Black Sea and Donetsk basin, and attack the freedom of sea communications.

Furthermore, in the Russian leadership's recent assertions of the need for buffer territory to protect Russian cities from Ukrainian shelling, and exclamations about Ukrainian nationalism being supported by Western powers, we can hear the echoes of Moscow's assertions and concerns throughout this 'long century' which underpinned the leadership's military thinking, strategy and its use of force. These include the assertion in the 1930s that Leningrad could be shelled from Finnish territory, and that the government of Finland was pursuing hostile policies towards Moscow and would put its territory at the disposal of the Soviet Union's enemies.[7] They also include the assertions that Hitler used Ukrainian nationalists as his agents in Ukraine, and that US and British imperialism had many similarities with German fascism: 'Ukrainian nationalists gave us more trouble than anyone else' in 1939–41 and after the war, according to Khrushchev, and it took a 'large-scale military and police operation' to 'break up these rebel forces'. And they include the belief that 'in its desire to encircle us with military bases ... America will throw itself all over a country, appearing to give that country economic aid but actually being much more interested in currying political favours' and having militaristic motives to establish military blocs.[8]

These assertions and accusations will hardly ring true to Euro-Atlantic capitals; they may well appear 'absurd' or 'ridiculous'. They certainly underline that Moscow lives in a different world to the Euro-Atlantic community. Yet it is already long clear that Moscow's reality and Western expectations do not converge, and that Moscow's moves are not designed 'even coincidentally' to chime with Western interests.[9] Putin may have given the order in February 2022, but this more structural, geopolitical view of the war is revealing, particularly since Moscow has explicitly adopted a geostrategic and especially geo-economic view of international affairs which underpins its strategic decision and policy making.

Placing current operations squarely into this Russian experience, such that the campaign against Ukraine is very much 'Russia's war', is not to assert some form of determinism or 'inevitable' continuity, that 'everything remains more or less the same'. Instead, it is to tease out persistent themes that echo through the years and to illuminate change, and what causes it, and therefore the balance between evolution and the extent of change we might expect looking to the future. Familiarity with Russian (war) history and the way that strategy has been shaped and implemented in the past helps to mitigate surprise. It places Moscow's current policies in longer-term context, and provides the means to more effectively shape Western strategies: parsing this longer-term context is essential for shaping deterrence, defence and dialogue today and tomorrow.

The second set of characteristics is that, for all the particularities inherent to each war, in its implementation Moscow's renewed assault on Ukraine is emblematic of how the Russian state has used armed force to resolve a strategic problem. One Russian observer has suggested that despite shifts in tactics and the introduction of new technology, the campaign reflects a return to Soviet approaches in the Great Fatherland War, simply at a new technical level.[10] If this appears reductive to Western audiences, we have seen that senior officers including Gerasimov and Gareev have since the mid-2010s pointed to the lessons of the Great Fatherland War as relevant for today.

At the same time, our attention is drawn to the initial use of surprise and speed in attempting to secure success in a short campaign that echoes the campaigns in Poland (1939), Finland (1940), Manchuria (1945), Czechoslovakia (1968), Afghanistan (1979), Chechnya (1994), Georgia (2008) and Ukraine (2014). And if the assault reflects characteristic efforts, it equally reflects characteristic strengths, difficulties and problems: the political leadership handing the military a difficult task, departmentalitis at scale, underestimation of the adversary and problems in coordinating both command and control and logistics across distance, fighting well-equipped adversaries, and suffering heavy casualties.[11]

The campaign might feature thoroughly modern means, and echo the war depicted in Pelevin's book *S.N.U.F.F.*, but it is also characterised by much that Gareev repeatedly pointed to about the experience of war in the 1990s and 2000s. There are echoes from Afghanistan, Chechnya and even the Great Fatherland

War, too, in terms of defective equipment, insufficient supplies and command incompetence. Gareev's point that the new is in constant tension with the old, therefore, is essential; he might well have had much else to say about the operation and conditions in which Moscow placed the Russian military and matters of a potential transition to what he called 'serious war'.

Force is a blunt tool, though, and, as these examples show, it does not always achieve Moscow's intent. The attempted knockout blow has worked before for Moscow, for instance in Poland, Manchuria and Czechoslovakia. But Moscow's experience is that while in theory it proffers a tempting solution to a policy problem, in practice it is messy and difficult to deliver. More often than not, Moscow has had to escalate its level of state effort and resort to organised, hammer blows of heavy firepower to achieve its goals, adding a large dose of attrition to the strategic mix. Where the initial knockout blow has not worked, the escalation of effort has reaped rewards for Moscow, albeit at appalling cost, against Finland in the Winter War and Chechnya. The failure of the knockout blow in Afghanistan was also followed by an increased effort, including larger deployments of forces and firepower in offensive sweeps, but even over time this was not enough to secure Moscow's objectives, leading to an organised withdrawal in 1988–89, leaving a state structure in place.

The shift to the 'Svechin school' and a strategy of exhaustion

The (long-running) tension between a strategy of lightning throw down and a strategy of exhaustion is clear, and was visible in the years leading up to the assault in 2022. There are valuable questions to be asked about exactly where the balance between 'one blow' and 'exhaustion' lay among Russian strategy makers and planners, both political and military, when preparing the renewed assault. As we have seen, there were visible signs that influential Russian military thinkers recognised the difficulties of such an endeavour. Moreover, the core tenets of Russian war history and conceptual thinking would suggest that beyond public view, there was a wider group, especially in the armed forces, who entertained doubts about the likely success of a knockout blow approach against Ukraine.

Yet there is a sense that the Russian leadership – state and military – had since the mid-2010s been focused on trying to prepare a broader strategy of resilience. The state leadership sought to build sociopolitical and economic resilience against Western economic statecraft and sanctions, and had begun to test and practise systemic mobilisation capacity while conducting a major military modernisation programme. And the military leadership began to debate modern war in a way that emphasised state capacity and active defence. A lightning win – *pobedonosnaya, molnienosnaya* – might remain the theoretical ideal, but a strategy of attrition/exhaustion is where we are for the foreseeable future. It was Svechin's ghost, not Tukhachevsky's, that hovered over this debate; Gareev and Gerasimov frequently referred to Svechin as they tried to assess the changing character of modern strategy and war.

As Gareev said, there is no need to idealise Svechin; much has changed since his time and the influence of other strategic thinkers can also be discerned. Nevertheless, identifying a 'Svechin school' of strategy is a means of providing cultural context for interpreting Russia's strategy and way in war, continuity and change, and a basis for looking ahead, including for the 'progressive development of the armed forces' in the second half of the decade. Rather than simply referring to select works and citing specific quotes, though, this offers a more holistic analytical approach, distilling three overarching points of reference. The Svechin school emphasises, first, that Russian strategy in war is guided by state strategy – without a grasp of Moscow's strategy, war strategy cannot be interpreted. Second, the Svechin school emphasises that wars are waged at the strategic (not tactical) level, that war strategy must be seen in the context of the state's wider effort to coordinate its socio-economic resources in support of military action. Third, the Svechin school frames a war strategy that balances defence and (counter-)offensive blows in a longer struggle, one based on a strategy of exhaustion.

Indeed, within the context of a broader state approach towards sanction-proofing the economy and mobilisation practice, the state appears to have set the foundations for a strategy of exhaustion from the early-to-mid 2010s: while pointing to the acceleration of the speed of operations, the MoD appeared to renew a focus on scale by reversing earlier decisions to cut back Soviet equipment stocks, beginning to reintroduce division-scale units and to introduce organisations such as Yunarmiya (a military-patriotic youth movement) and the military-political commissars. The failure to achieve a lightning knockout of Ukraine in 2022 has surely confirmed this approach: the military has adopted more attritional campaigning methods, and the state has implemented a further range of measures to coordinate its efforts and to enhance socio-economic support for the armed forces and campaigning.

A twenty-first-century Svechin school of strategy, one focused on state resilience and capacity for exhaustion, provides the context for questions that deserve further examination as more evidence becomes available, not least because they will shed additional light on the level of state effort and how Moscow sees the trajectory of the combat with Ukraine and the contest with the Euro-Atlantic community. It clarifies the chronology of the contest, the war and the 'special war operation', thereby also helping to estimate how Moscow interprets the escalation ladder.

And again, these points help us to consider the Russian experience in a broader context, and provide the basis for interpreting Russian strategy and war. Some structural changes to the armed forces are already visible, with the (re-)creation of the Moscow and Leningrad military districts and adaptations to conscription legislation. Other commands and formations are also being created, such as the Northern Group of Forces, specialised assault units,[12] and the (re-)introduction of many more divisional-scale units. Some of these are not necessarily 'new' in that versions have existed at different times in the Soviet and Russian armed forces. But they give an indication of how Moscow sees warfare evolving in future: scale and firepower are to the forefront.

Of particular note, though, and again suggestive of a modern interpretation of the 'Svechin school of strategy', is the attempt to produce better coordination between the state and the armed forces through the establishment of the Government Coordination Council and the adaptation of the state's effort to what might be called a more 'public–private partnership' or 'socio-commercial' approach. This includes the very visible aspect of new roles for a number of private military companies and contracting large numbers of soldiers. But it also includes a greater role for civilian support for the armed forces through regional political and social structures and businesses. The increasing commercial involvement supporting the armed forces includes research and development and crowd funding for equipment and supplies, from medical equipment to vehicles and communications; it is visible in terms of UAVs produced by the Sudoplatov Project and 'Ghoul'.[13]

To understand this development means exploring the roles of movements such as the People's Front in 'Everything for the Front' and 'We are Together' campaigns, but also the establishment of public associations such as the Defenders of the Fatherland Foundation and the Committee of Warriors of Fatherland Families. While regional governors have a role to play in coordinating and delivering equipment as part of the 'partial' mobilisation process, volunteer organisations and businesses have become more adept at acquiring considerable financial resources and sophisticated equipment and delivering it to units.[14] At the strategic level, in terms of how the state wages war, we might ask what the implications of the socio-commercial aspect of the current campaign are, and about the implications for Moscow's ability to sustain its campaign and regenerate its armed forces.

These arrangements have their problems, not least in terms of coordination with the state: the MoD initially sought to maintain full control over the process, and customs and border control also impinged upon it, since the process often involved importing goods. But since summer 2023 measures have become more effective and more formalised, including with the MoD. This is now framed as the 'people's military industrial complex', with Shoigu and Putin asserting its role in the repair and production of tanks, artillery ammunition and UAVs.[15] Civil–military cooperation in the form of voluntary participation and start-up companies have added a more modern, dynamic and flexible contribution to the supply of the armed forces, facilitating adaptation to a quickly changing battlefield, adding both financial and intellectual resources to the campaign effort. It again underlines the extent to which this is 'Russia's war', and the significance of Russian state resilience and escalatory capability.

We might also ask what the combined effects of modern technology and enhanced network coordination mean for both leadership and command in terms of organisation, deployment and the striving for 'suddenness'. In other words, how might the initial period of war evolve? And what might decisive operations begin to look like in the current context of a long war? This should guide questions about Russian theory and innovation, especially in suddenness (*vnezapnost*) and its constituent features in reintroducing decisive offensive operations. What lessons have the Russian armed forces learned from campaigning in Ukraine, and what will future *maskirovka* and *obman* look like? A vital element of Russian war strategy, as discussed, it is already recognised by the Russian military to be resource-intensive, complex and difficult. But what are the technical and organisational features and changes that would enable Russian forces to implement it and to scale it to different levels of campaigning?

Equally important, though, to achieving *obman* and *vnezapnost* will be leadership and command – the art of war and *voennaya khitrost*. One of the central features of the Euro-Atlantic analysis of Russian campaigning against Ukraine has been a critique of Russian (military) leadership. With some exceptions, this has primarily focused on the implications of more authoritarian aspects of Russian political culture, especially the rigidly centralised nature of decision making and concomitant lack of 'mission command', initiative and 'reasonable challenge' within the chain of command. This will not be surprising for those familiar with Russian history, since problems in command have characterised Russian campaigning throughout the modern era. While Russian observers acknowledge problems with initiative, they also highlight officer training and education. As we have seen, they point to personnel and staff education that has failed to prepare officers who can organise battles. Indeed, Gerasimov and other senior officers explicitly attempted to inculcate initiative in the Russian armed forces during the 2010s.

Given recent Russian experience, and the emergence of a new generation of combat-experienced officers and men, many of whom will have been promoted quickly through the ranks,[16] Western observers should be attuned to nuances and evolving command styles across the Russian armed forces. This will include careful assessment of how Russian forms of 'mission command' and 'division command' take shape, given the architecture of the Russian armed forces, the traditions of command, and the lessons of the experiences of Syria and Ukraine, and with a patriotic education born from participation in organisations such as Yunarmiya.

Familiarity with the complexity of strategy and command allows us to delve deeper into the nature of Russian leadership and strategy making in the Russian way in war. It should draw us beyond a one-dimensional assessment of Russian strategy and command as a simple reflection of authoritarian centralisation. Actually, there are a number of Russian traditions of leadership: if the punitive and brute force version is best-known, other traditions include the 'father figure' (with such historical models as Alexander Suvorov and Mikhail Kutuzov) and the 'inspirational figure' (Stepan Makarov, Vasiliy Chapayev, Semyon Budyonny). How do the current generation fit such categories?

What other categories are useful? How might they compare to Western command types?

Such an investigation will facilitate a more sophisticated assessment of the changes underway in the armed forces, such as the attempts to overcome stove-piping and enhance networking and reconnaissance fire and strike systems, and also to interpret leadership as the Russian armed forces move towards more divisional-level command. This will provide the context in which a new Chief of General Staff will be appointed, and more importantly, what that individual and his leadership team will seek to implement. More broadly, experience in Ukraine and Syria will shape the officer corps for the coming generation.

The future of Russian war strategy

What does this mean for our understanding of Russian strategy and war as we look to the future? As noted, the two primary points are Moscow's grand strategy and war doctrine. Without major change in either of these, there will not be substantial change in Russian war strategy. To what extent, therefore, should we anticipate change in Moscow's grand strategy as a result of the experience in and against Ukraine? Certainly, senior officials and observers in the Euro-Atlantic community consider Russian actions to be a costly strategic mistake and expect this to cause change. Yet despite the costs and the necessity to increase its level of state effort, there is little indication that the Russian leadership sees the situation in the same way. Indeed, the Russian leadership appears to see its foresight thinking – such as its Strategic Foresight to 2035 – being proven accurate. There is no course change in Moscow's strategy; instead there is attempted acceleration.[17]

Conclusion

As we saw in Chapter 6, Moscow has long sought to generate strategy to cope with what it saw as a highly competitive
international environment, one characterised by the increasing
use of armed force. Since the mid-2000s Moscow has anticipated
the 2020s as being a decade of intense global competition for
economic leadership. This geo-economic competition over access
to resources, transit routes and markets is understood to be global
in horizon and to be leading to a redistribution of global power
and a consequent structural shift in the international architecture.
During this period, Putin has repeatedly pointed out that such
competition and structural change has in the past often led to
war and conflict; such views are reflected also in much scenario
thinking and strategic planning through into the 2030s.

Since 2022 such thinking has continued to guide Moscow's
actions. Senior officials, including Putin, have reiterated their
view that a global struggle for dominance is underway, and that
the United States and its allies are seeking to impose a strategic
defeat on Russia. These views are formalised in Russian strategic
documents. The foreign policy concept, 'refreshed' in 2023, notes
that 'humanity is going through revolutionary changes': 'conflict
areas are expanding in a number of strategically important
regions', with the build-up of offensive military capabilities and
the destruction of the arms control treaty system. The concept
points to the escalation of protracted armed conflicts in a number
of regions, increasing the risk of a collision between major
states and the possibility of conflicts 'escalating and growing into
local, regional or large-scale war'. According to the concept, the
'Western policy' of attempting to weaken Russia by 'limiting
its sovereignty' in foreign and domestic policy and 'violating its
territorial integrity' is 'enshrined at the doctrinal level and has
become comprehensive'.[18]

This is the context in which any regeneration of Russia's armed forces will take shape: a world characterised by contest, conflict and war throughout the 2020s. Consequently, Putin underlines the need to 'expedite the resolution of social, demographic, infrastructural and other problems' and 'simultaneously' advance the quality of the army and the navy. This latter point, he stated, is primarily about improving general purpose forces, refining the principles of their organisation, and 'shoring up forces in the Western strategic theatre'. The volume of purchases and repairs of weapons and equipment will be 'significantly increased', given the additional budget allocations necessary to create the foundation for the future of the army and navy.[19]

On the one hand, therefore, this regeneration will be about seeking to defend Russian interests against perceived threats from the US and its allies. Alongside the 'shoring up of forces in the Western strategic theatre', this will emphasise the role of strategic deterrence. It will highlight the significance of socio-economic coordination and resilience, with an emphasis on mobilisational aspects and organisations, such as the Popular Front, Yunarmiya and the Russian Orthodox Church. The rotation of personnel in the wake of Putin's inauguration in 2024 suggests that this is underway. Shoigu was appointed secretary of the Security Council, and there were promotions and appointments in the economic and industrial sector: Denis Manturov, an experienced and prominent figure in industry and trade, was promoted to First Deputy Prime Minister, and Andrei Belousov, an industrialist who emphasises government control over the economy, was appointed Defence Minister.

On the other hand, however, this regeneration reflects the leadership's view that a new 'post-West' era is emerging, and that

Moscow's strategy will continue to be guided towards promoting and asserting Russian interests across the world. This will include competition for the global commons, seeking to (pre-)position Russian state assets and capabilities and to develop (further) strategic partnerships with states that correspond to Moscow's view of geo-economic competition. An updated strategic foresight document, perhaps looking to 2040, will shed further light on this.

This lends a significant maritime angle to Russian security: the Russian economy is ever more dependent on the sea. As discussed throughout this book, this is not new; it should be seen in the context of Moscow's long-running continental–maritime dilemma, and as an acceleration of state strategy. And although the Black Sea Fleet has played a prominent role in the renewed assault on Ukraine, the Russian navy as a whole is not committed to the campaign. It has not suffered from the same combat attrition that the ground forces have, and has remained active across the world, with exercises and port visits. The navy's strategic role may well become more prominent still, not only as part of Russian strategic deterrence, but through other tasks, including defence engagement through exercises with other states, long-range deployments and conducting research.

The maritime emphasis, too, will shape the regeneration of Russia's armed forces looking ahead. It is noteworthy that among the most prominent points outlined by Gerasimov are threats of a maritime nature, including a potential Western challenge to Russia's ownership of the northern sea route, the development of AUKUS and instability around Taiwan.[20] It is also significant that in the post-inauguration rotation in May 2024, Nikolai Patrushev was appointed to oversee shipbuilding. Indeed, Patrushev's appointment suggests that this is a strategic priority, since, as a graduate of the Leningrad Shipbuilding Institute and a close, long-term Putin ally with extensive experience across the Russian defence and security landscape, he is well positioned for this role. Other developments, such as a major audit of shipbuilding and the establishment of a maritime collegium, also suggest that this is a priority. According to Patrushev, the collegium was established by Putin to 'improve the coordination of the activities of the state authorities in implementing national maritime policy and ensuring the protection of Russia's national interests in the world ocean' and the strategic development of the navy. A new strategic concept for the navy is slated for 2025, and a law on shipbuilding may also emerge.[21]

And what of Moscow's war doctrine? In the context of this grand strategic picture, the 'progressive development' of the Russian armed forces announced in late 2022 and early 2023 provides guidelines for interpreting the evolution of Russian war doctrine and strategy for the next three to five years. It suggests that the long-running strategic debate is for the time being settled in favour of what we have called here the Svechin school of strategy. The emphasis is on scale and firepower, with an intent to build towards armed forces 1.5 million strong by 2026, a restructuring of the military landscape and reintroducing division-scale units. The 'progressive development' will probably be able to achieve some of the goals set. Equally, it will face practical problems. Sustaining sufficient recruitment and retention, for instance, could pose a challenge. There has been a spike in recruitment and retention during the campaign against Ukraine, due partly to the restrictive legislative conditions of the 'partial mobilisation' and partly to the extraordinary financial rewards on offer. But the authorities have long struggled to meet recruitment quotas for contract soldiers.

Conclusion

Simply, some things will not change: Moscow will continue to find that strategy making is difficult. A substantial surge in resources to encourage recruitment and to purchase, modernise and repair equipment will not immediately fix problems of command and control, and the practical challenges of logistics across great distances. The Russian leadership has wrestled with these questions throughout the modern era, and is unlikely to resolve them within the next five years; likewise pervasive 'soft' problems such as buck-passing, indecision, negligence and sloppiness.

At one level, it may be that, once the campaign is over, *orgvyvody* or organisational conclusions take place, with some retirements, resignations, dismissals and 'rotations' among the older generation of officers and civil servants. The promotion of a new, younger generation of officers and civil servants who have fulfilled important roles during the campaign is likely, and observers should be attentive not only to the careers and networks of these individuals – some of whom are already visible – but also the tasks they are appointed to fulfil.

It may also be that a new strategic foresight concept is prepared, and a state armaments programme and an updated or 'refreshed' war doctrine published in the short-to-medium term. There was discussion in the Russian professional military media about the latter two documents being under preparation in 2021. Noteworthy structural points to observe would include any official changes to the definitions of what 'war' is – especially the long-standing and central characteristic of it as a sociopolitical phenomenon and the resort to armed force – and the levels of war. Such a document could also shed light on Russian views of challenges such as the nature of 'twenty-first-century blitzkrieg' and the evolving nature of the US challenge, as well as 'mental' or 'informational-psychological' war and economic statecraft.[22]

Debate is underway about lessons from the campaigns in Ukraine, Syria, Nagorno-Karabakh and the Middle East, and about innovation with technology and tactics. Particular care should be taken not to leap to conclusions about the development of a 'new theory of victory' or a 'new generation' of war. Nevertheless, points of note within this debate will be threefold.

The first is that the 'lessons' from the Ukraine campaign may not harmonise with those that Euro-Atlantic officials and observers recognise; regardless, these should be attentively studied.[23] Second, debates about the transition from the threatening and initial periods of war and trying to reintroduce decisive operations should be a point of particular attention, given that Moscow may now see itself as in a 'threatening period'. And third, the extent of incorporation into this debate of lessons of cooperation with Iran, North Korea and China, and what that means both for the evolution of Russia's strategic horizon and technical capacities, should be considered.

Russia's way in war

Thinking in terms of a 'way in war' offers a synthesis of history, strategic theory and international politics. It is a means of shaping a systematic explanation of how a state shaped strategy and waged war as a guide to thinking about the present and the future. In this book, I have sought to examine the roots of Russian war strategy – why and how Moscow goes to war – by reflecting on persistent themes, traditions, priorities and problems.

The sense of longer-term trajectory from the past into the future adds vital context and colour to our understanding of how Moscow views the world today, illustrating how it has interpreted and sought to cope with evolving strategic challenges and dilemmas, and sketching possible developments through the remainder of this decade. Indeed, such a strategy and 'way in war' approach offers valuable lessons regarding Moscow's assumptions about the future, assumptions on which plans are shaped and then implemented. It offers guidelines for examining not just capabilities but also intent, not just priorities but problems.

Western thinking about Russia often anticipates change: Moscow has made a strategic mistake by renewing its assault on Ukraine, operations are very costly with little reward, and numerous weaknesses are highlighted. All told, many believe that this will either encourage or oblige Moscow to correct its policy course; likewise many believe that after Putin, Moscow might seek reconciliation with the Euro-Atlantic community.[24]

Yet radical change takes time and sustained effort. There must be consensus that there is a problem, and about how that problem is to be fixed. But while there is certainly a recognition by senior Russian officials and experts of problems in the way the initial operation was conducted and in how strategy is made more broadly in Russia, there does not appear to be consensus that radical change is what is required. On the contrary, in their public announcements, senior Russian officials are clear: their assumptions about the future are largely being proven correct by events. Moscow appears to be accelerating its strategy, not implementing a course change.

Indeed, Moscow is seeking to position Russia for a long contest. Because conflict and war feature prominently in official and expert scenarios, the leadership is to all intents and purposes converting Russia into a commodity champion and military-patriotic fortress to cope with a geopolitical struggle: resilience

273

at home, with deployable power across a global horizon. The armed forces are growing substantially, combined with an increasing militarisation of the economy, and enhanced efforts to inculcate patriotism across society. These shifts in Russia are not a reversion to Soviet approaches. They are focused on the future, a competitive world of 2030 and beyond.

Note on terms and translations

Tracing Russian strategy and its traditions means traversing the history of Imperial Russia, the Soviet Union and the Russian Federation: all related, but in many ways distinct. I have tried to bridge these different periods in a way that acknowledges their distinctions, including referring where appropriate to 'Soviet' and 'Russian'. But since the focus is on the leadership's strategy making, I have generally used 'Moscow' as a shorthand for the capital and policy making. Also, I have used the names of cities and other place names as they were known at the time.

Translating and transliterating from Russian/Cyrillic also poses challenges. I have generally rendered transliteration in a phonetic way, to try to make it as easy as possible for non-Russian speakers – Russian speakers will be familiar with or able to work out the original for themselves. Some names have acquired a common transliteration into English – Gorbachev and Yeltsin, for instance – and I have retained these.

Unless otherwise stated, the translations from Russian into English are mine. On occasion this brings unfamiliar or unusual translations. One example is my translation of what Euro-Atlantic audiences usually refer to as the Eastern Front in World War

Note on terms and translations

II. The Russian for this is *Velikaya Otechestvennaya Voina*, usually translated into English as the 'Great Patriotic War'. The literal translation of *Velikaya Otechestvennaya Voina* would be, however, the 'Great Fatherland War'. I have used this latter version, because it is worth seeing it in historical tradition: it is framed as the *second* such war, after Napoleon's invasion in 1812, which is known as the *Otechestvennaya Voina*, the 'Fatherland War'.

Another example is in attempting to render the Russian-language word *voina*, which means 'war'. So far, so standard. But the adjectival forms of *voina*, including *voennaya strategiya* and *voennaya doktrina*, for example, are traditionally translated into English as 'military'; thus 'military strategy' and 'military doctrine'. However, I think it is important to keep the essence of the meaning of *voina*, which is more than simply a military phenomenon. So, I have translated these (and related terms) accordingly as 'war strategy', 'war doctrine', *voennaya istoriya* as 'war history', and so on. Distinguishing this from the term *vooruzhennye sily* – armed forces – allows a clearer delineation between 'operations' by the armed forces and 'war' as a state-level, strategic phenomenon.

Abbreviations

CGS	Chief of General Staff
KZ	*Krasnaya Zvezda*
MoD	Ministry of Defence
NATO	North Atlantic Treaty Organisation
NVO	*Nezavisimoe voennoe obozrenie*
NDMC	National Defence Management Centre
PPP	purchasing power parity
SVO	special war operation
UK	United Kingdom
USA	United States of America
USSR	Union of Soviet Socialist Republics
VAVN	*Vestnik akademii voennykh nauk*
VIZh	*Voenno-istoricheskii zhurnal*
VM	*Voennaya mysl*
VPK	*Voenno-promyshlenniy kurier*
WPA	website of the Presidential Administration

Acknowledgements

This book would not have been possible without a great deal of assistance. First, Manchester University Press has provided skilful and patient support in seeing the book through to publication. I greatly benefited from access to the library at the Wilson Center's Kennan Institute, and the John and Ljubica Erickson Collection at the National Library of Scotland. Thanks go to Simon Blundell, as always, and also to Rachel Daniels at the Russian Military Studies Centre, at Cranfield University's Barrington Library. It is such a rich resource.

I would also like to thank Ken Stolworthy, Michael Rouland and others at the Russia Strategic Initiative (RSI) at US European Command for their support as I have explored some of the themes I address in the book.

My thinking has benefited enormously from conversations with a wide range of people in history, war studies and Russia studies. Thanks are due to, among others, Geoffrey Hosking, John Gooding, Roger Markwick, Paul Josephson, Robert Avery, Stephen Fortescue, Steven Main, David Fields, Carl Scott, Beatrice Heuser, Florence Gaub, Hew Strachan, Patrick Porter, Carter Ham, Henry Plater-Zyberk, Andrew Bowen, Dara Massicot,

Acknowledgements

Carl van Dyke, Les Grau, Chuck Bartles and Clint Reach. For several years already, Richard Connolly, Dima Adamsky, Mike Kofman and Mike Petersen have offered encouragement, advice, challenge and friendship, especially wth this research.

I would also like to thank Bobby, Tim, Catherine, Tony, Simon, Alastair, Catherine, Blair, Michelle and Natasha for all their wise words, support, hospitality and friendship; likewise Nick, James and Adam for educating me in other sides of life. Clive Johnstone's always generous support and encouragement is much missed. My thanks also to DYB, SNP and PRN for their support and insight – the work would not be the same without it.

Audiences in Hamburg, Washington, DC, Rome, Castle Cary, Abingdon, Portsmouth and London have all helped me to think through the questions in the book. Particular thanks are also due to an anonymous reader for providing such a constructive review, and, likewise, to Andrew Lambert and Julian Cooper for reading drafts and offering very useful comments. Dov Lynch went beyond the call of duty and reprised the role of supervisor, examining the draft with care and encouragement: thank you! One reviewer took the trouble to spend a whole afternoon dissecting the book's themes with me, gently pointing out the flaws; another did the same over an extended dinner. I will long remember these enjoyable meetings; your friendship means a great deal. The remaining errors are mine alone.

Finally, and most of all, my thanks and my love go to my family, Charles, Dorothy and Yulia, for their patient, unfailing support and encouragement. Without them, the book could not have been written, and so it is to them that the book is dedicated, and to Lara Andreevna, whose happy presence remains eternally felt.

Notes

Preface

1 G. Shapps, 'Defending Britain From a More Dangerous World', website of the British Government, 15 January 2024, www.gov.uk/government/speeches/defending-britain-from-a-more-dangerous-world (accessed 24 February 2025); 'Chief of the General Staff Speech at the RUSI Land Warfare Conference', website of the British Government, 28 June 2022, www.gov.uk/government/speeches/chief-the-general-staff-speech-at-rusi-land-warfare-conference (accessed 24 February 2025).

2 The casualty toll remains unclear: neither side discloses figures. By early December 2024 Western officials estimated that more than three quarters of a million had been killed or wounded on the Russian side alone. 'Putin's Relative Accidentally Reveals Secret Russian Death Toll in Ukraine', *The Telegraph*, 4 December 2024, www.telegraph.co.uk/world-news/2024/12/04/putin-relative-secret-death-toll-russia-ukraine/?WT.mc_id=e_DM468162&WT.tsrc=email&etype=Edi_FAM_New_ES&utmsource=email&utm_medium=Edi_FAM_New_ES20241205&utm_campaign=DM468162 (accessed 24 February 2025). The United Nations suggests that in early 2024 some 6.3 million Ukrainians were refugees. 'Ukraine Refugee Situation', UNHCR website, 4 January 2024, https://data.unhcr.org/en/situations/ukraine (accessed 24 February 2025); 'Ukraine War: 21,000 Alleged War Crimes Being Investigated, Prosecutor Says', BBC News, 7 July 2022, www.bbc.co.uk/news/world-europe-62073669 (accessed 24 February 2025).

3 'Prazdnovanie 80–letiya pobedy v Kurskoi bitve', website of the Presidential Administration (hereafter WPA), 23 August 2023, http://kremlin.ru/events/president/news/72094; 'Plenarnoe zasedanie Peterburgskovo mezhdunarodnovo ekonomicheskovo foruma', WPA, 17 June 2022, http://kremlin.ru/events/president/news/68669; 'Obrashchenie Prezidenta Rossiiskoi Federatsii', WPA, 24 February 2022, http://kremlin.ru/events/president/news/67843 (all accessed 24 February 2025).

4 'Chief of the General Staff Speech'.

5 Ibid.

6 'Ukraine War: Russia Must be Defeated But Not Crushed, Macron Says', BBC News, 19 February 2023, www.bbc.co.uk/news/uk-64693691 (accessed 24 February 2025); 'Video Address to the Participants and Guests of the 11th Moscow Conference on International Security', WPA, 15 August 2023, http://www.en.kremlin.ru/events/president/transcripts/speeches/72040/photos (accessed 24 February 2025); S. Karaganov, 'An Age of Wars?', *Russia in Global Affairs*, 1 January 2024, https://eng.globalaffairs.ru/articles/an-age-of-wars-article-one/ (accessed 24 February 2025); 'Russia Could Attack a NATO Country Within 3 to 5 Years, Denmark Warns', *Financial Times*, 9 February 2024, www.ft.com/content/b3101099-9516-4b0b-92c6-179997d7e4cf (accessed 24 February 2025).

7 General Philip Breedlove, cited in 'Russia and the Menace of Unreality', *The Atlantic*, 9 September 2014, www.theatlantic.com/international/archive/2014/09/russia-putin-revolutionizing-information-warfare/379880/ (accessed 24 February 2025).

8 R. Thornton, 'The Russian Military's "New Main Emphasis"', *RUSI Journal*, 162, no. 4, 2017, pp. 18–28; E. Braw, 'Conventional Wars have Fallen Out of Fashion. Grey-zone Aggression is the New Thing', *International Centre for Defence and Security*, 23 November 2021, https://icds.ee/en/conventional-wars-have-fallen-out-of-fashion-grey-zone-aggression-is-the-new-thing/ (accessed 24 February 2025).

9 Interviews with senior Western officers, January 2024.

Introduction

1 'Ukaz "Ob obyavlenii chastichnoi mobilizatsii v Rossiiskoi Federatsii"', WPA, 21 September 2022, http://kremlin.ru/events/president/news/

Notes

69391; 'Zasedaniye Soveta Bezopasnosti', WPA, 19 October 2022, http://kremlin.ru/events/president/news/69636 (all accessed 24 February 2025).

2   '"Shoigu, Gerasimov, gde **** boepripasy?" Prigozhin prigrozil vyvesti ChVK "Vagner" iz Bakhmuta', *TV Rain*, 5 May 2023, www.youtube.com/watch?v=5DtilNfHbh8 (accessed 24 February 2025).

3   'Itogi goda s Vladimirom Putinym', WPA, 14 December 2023, http://kremlin.ru/events/president/news/72994 (accessed 24 February 2025).

4   D. Medvedev, 'Nashi lyudi, nasha zemlya, nasha pravda', *Rossiiskaya gazeta*, 25 December 2022; 'Kirienko: Rossiya vyigraet voinu, esli ona stanet narodnoi', *Kommersant*, 22 October 2022, www.kommersant.ru/doc/5631885?from=top_main_3 (accessed 24 February 2025).

5   'Special Operation Being Turned into War Does Not Mean State of War de Jure – Kremlin', TASS, 22 March 2024, https://tass.com/politics/1763755 (accessed 24 February 2025).

6   'Plenarnoe zasedanie Peterburgskovo mezhdunarodnovo ekonomicheskovo foruma', WPA, 17 June 2022, http://kremlin.ru/events/president/news/68669 (accessed 24 February 2025).

7   'Zasedanie kollegii Ministerstva oborony', WPA, 21 December 2022, http://kremlin.ru/events/president/transcripts/70159; 'Parad Pobedy na Krasnoi ploshchadi', WPA, 9 May 2022, http://kremlin.ru/events/president/news/71104 (all accessed 24 February 2025).

8   'Zasedanie kollegii', 21 December 2022.

9   'Ukaz Prezidenta Rossiiskoi Federatsii ot 26.02.2024 No. 141 "O voenno-administrativnom delenii Rossiiskoi Federatsii"', website of the Russian Government, 26 February 2024, http://publication.pravo.gov.ru/document/0001202402260031 (accessed 24 February 2025).

10 J. Keegan, *A History of Warfare*, London: Pimlico, 1994, pp. 387–8; P. Porter, *Military Orientalism: Eastern War Through Western Eyes*, London: Hurst, 2009; 'Episode 3: Baron Richards of Herstmonceux', RUSI Western Way in Warfare podcast series, 18 June 2020, https://rusi.org/podcasts/western-way-of-war/episode-3-baron-richards-herstmonceux (accessed 24 February 2025).

11 D. Kilcullen, *The Dragons and the Snakes: How the Rest Learned to Fight the West*, London: Hurst, 2020; M. Cancian, *Inflicting Surprise: Gaining Competitive Advantage in Great Power Conflicts*, Center for Strategic and International Studies, January 2021, pp. 34–5.

12 L. Freedman, 'Kyiv and Moscow are Fighting Two Different Wars', *Foreign Affairs*, 17 February 2023, www.foreignaffairs.com/ukraine/

Notes

kyiv-and-moscow-are-fighting-two-different-wars (accessed 24 February 2025).

13 O. Scholz, 'The Global Zeitenwende', *Foreign Affairs*, 5 December 2022, www.foreignaffairs.com/germany/olaf-scholz-global-zeitenwende-how-avoid-new-cold-war (accessed 24 February 2025).

14 J. Snyder, *The Soviet Strategic Culture: Implications for Limited Nuclear Operations*, R-2154-AF, September 1977, www.rand.org/content/dam/rand/pubs/reports/2005/R2154.pdf (accessed 24 February 2025); C. Roberts, 'The Challenges of Decoding Russian Coercion', in M. Kofman (ed.), 'Book Review Roundtable: Russian Ways of Thinking about Deterrence', *Texas National Security Review*, 10 September 2024, https://tnsr.org/roundtable/book-review-roundtable-russian-ways-of-thinking-about-deterrence/#essay3 (accessed 24 February 2025).

15 'X' (George F. Kennan), 'The Sources of Soviet Conduct', *Foreign Affairs*, 1 July 1947, www.foreignaffairs.com/russian-federation/george-kennan-sources-soviet-conduct (accessed 24 February 2025); F. Roberts, *Dealing with Dictators*, London: Weidenfeld and Nicolson, 1991; G. Niemeyer, *An Inquiry into Soviet Mentality*, New York: Frederick A. Praeger, 1956.

16 P. Vigor, *The Soviet View of War, Peace and Neutrality*, London: Routledge and Kegan Paul, 1975.

17 N. Leites, *Soviet Style in War*, New York: Crane Russak, 1982, pp. 43–6, 205–8; P. Vigor, *Soviet Blitzkrieg Theory*, New York: St Martin's Press, 1983.

18 R. Hingley, *The Russian Mind*, New York: Charles Scribner's Sons, 1977, pp. 40–1.

19 I. Goncharov, *Oblomov*, London: Penguin, 2005; A. Kennaway, 'The Mental and Psychological Inheritance of Contemporary Russia', in A. Kennaway, *Collected Writings, 1990–2000*, Camberley: Conflict Studies Research Centre, 2000, pp. 13–14; M. Saltykov-Shchedrin, *Istoriya odnovo goroda*, Moscow: Eksmo, 2023.

20 M. Bulgakov, *Heart of a Dog*, trans. M. Glenny, London: Vintage, 2009.

21 C. Gray, 'Strategic Culture as Context: The First Generation of Theory Strikes Back', *Review of International Studies*, 25, no. 1, 1999, pp. 49–69; I. Johnstone, *Cultural Realism: Strategic Culture and Grand Strategy in Chinese History*, Princeton, NJ: Princeton University Press, 1995; H. Strachan, *The Direction of War: Contemporary Strategy in Historical Perspective*, Cambridge: Cambridge University Press, 2013, esp. ch. 7.

22 Alongside this, though usually separate, are examinations of Russian political culture. For two different approaches, see M. Urban, *Cultures of Power in Post-Communist Russia: An Analysis of Elite Political Discourse*, Cambridge: Cambridge University Press, 2010; A. Ledeneva, *How Russia Really Works: The Informal Practices that Shaped Post-Soviet Politics and Business*, Ithaca, NY: Cornell University Press, 2006.

23 O. Alekseeva-Karnevali, *Kak voennye vidyat 'sobytie'? Evolyutsiya voiny i granitsy vozmozhnovo i mirovoi politike XXI veka*, Moscow: URSS, 2021; A. Vershinin and A. Krivopalov, 'Rossiiskaya strategicheskaya kultura: opyt istoricheskoi perspektivy', *Russia in Global Affairs*, 6, November/December 2023, https://globalaffairs.ru/articles/strategicheskaya-kultura-ru/ (accessed 24 February 2025); D. Adamsky, *The Russian Way of Deterrence: Strategic Culture, Coercion and War*, Stanford, CA: Stanford University Press, 2023; D. Adamsky, *The Culture of Military Innovation: The Impact of Cultural Factors on the Revolution in Military Affairs in Russia, the US and Israel*, Stanford, CA: Stanford University Press, 2010, pp. 20–2.

24 This includes almost all the work on Russian 'hybrid warfare' and much war gaming. D. Shlapak and M. W. Johnson, *Reinforcing Deterrence on NATO's Eastern Flank: Wargaming the Defense of the Baltics*, RAND RR1253, 2016, www.rand.org/content/dam/rand/pubs/research_reports/RR1200/RR1253/RAND_RR1253.pdf (accessed 24 February 2025); R. Hooker, 'Major Theatre War: Russia Attacks the Baltic States', *RUSI Journal*, 165, no. 7, 2021, https://rusi.org/explore-our-research/publications/rusi-journal/major-theatre-war-russia-attacks-baltic-states (accessed 24 February 2025).

25 P. H. Wilson, *Iron and Blood: A Military History of the German-Speaking Peoples Since 1500*, London: Penguin, 2022; R. Weighley, *The American Way of War: A History of United States Military Strategy and Policy*, Bloomington: Indiana University Press, 1960; R. Harrison, *The Russian Way of War: Operational Art, 1904–1940*, Lawrence: University Press of Kansas, 2001.

26 B. Liddell Hart, 'Economic Pressure or Continental Victories', *RUSI Journal*, 76, no. 503, 1931; B. Liddell Hart, *The British Way in War*, London: Faber and Faber, 1932; B. Liddell Hart, *The Strategy of Indirect Approach*, London: Faber and Faber, 1941.

27 B. Holden Reid, 'The British Way in War', *RUSI Journal*, 156, no. 6, 2011; Strachan, *Direction of War*, pp. 136–9; A. Lambert, *The British*

Notes

War of War: Julian Corbett and the Battle for a National Strategy, New Haven, CT: Yale University Press, 2021.

28 A. Danchev, 'Liddell Hart's Big Idea', *Review of International Studies*, 25, no. 1, 1999, pp. 29–48.

29 M. Howard, *The Continental Commitment: The Dilemma of British Defence Policy in the Era of Two World Wars*, London: Penguin, 1974.

30 'Osoboe mnenie', *Ekho moskvy*, 13 November 2017; I. Vorobyov and V. Kiselev, 'Strategiya nepryamykh deistvii v novom oblike', *Voennaya mysl*, 9 September 2006, pp. 2–10.

31 A. Kersnovsky, *Istoria Russkoi armii*, Moscow: Golos, 1999, vol. 1, p. 7.

32 A. Beevor, 'Russia's New Winter War: Could Putin go the Way of Napoleon and Hitler?', *Foreign Affairs*, 29 December 2022, www. foreignaffairs.com/russian-federation/russias-new-winter-war (accessed 24 February 2025); B. Connable, 'Russians Do Break: Historical and Cultural Context for a Prospective Ukrainian Victory', *War on the Rocks*, 25 September 2024, https://warontherocks.com/2024/09/russians-do-break-historical-and-cultural-context-for-a-prospective-ukrainian-victory/ (accessed 24 February 2025).

33 F. Hill and A. Stent, 'The World Putin Wants: How Distortions About the Past Feed Delusions About the Future', *Foreign Affairs*, September/October 2022, www.foreignaffairs.com/russian-federation/world-putin-wants-fiona-hill-angela-stent (accessed 24 February 2025).

34 J. Plumb, *The Death of the Past*, London: Palgrave Macmillan, 1969.

35 J. Boff, 'Merrie England: 21st Century Military History', lecture, 5 April 2024, www.youtube.com/watch?v=PQz8QcGzK7A (accessed 24 February 2025); J. Black, *Rethinking Military History*, London: Routledge, 2004.

36 J. Guldi and D. Armitage, *The History Manifesto*, Cambridge: Cambridge University Press, 2014; M. Howard, *The Lessons of History*, New Haven, CT: Yale University Press, 1992; E. H. Carr, *What is History?*, London: Penguin, 2018.

37 V. Medinsky and A. Torkunov, *Istoria Rossii, 1945 god – nachalo XXI veka*, Moscow, 2023; A. Krivopalov, *V teni teorii glubokoi operatsii: podgotovka krasnoi armii k voine na zapadnoi granitse v 1926–1941gg*, Moscow: Rossiiskoe voenno-istoricheskoe obshchestvo, 2022; V. Tikhonov, *Poleznoe proshloe. Istoriya v Stalinskom SSSR*, Moscow: Novoe Literaturnoe Obozrenie, 2024; L. P. Muromtseva and V. B. Perkhavko, *Voenno-politicheskaya*

istoria Rossii, Moscow: Rospen, 2022; B. Akunin, *Istoria Rossiiskovo gosudarstva: Razrushenie i voskreshenie imperii, 1917–1953*, BABook, 2024.

38 P. Zhilin, *O Voine i voennoi istorii*, Moscow: Voenizdat, 1984; A. Svechin, *Strategiya*, Moscow: Rodina, 2023; M. Gareev, *Srazheniya na voenno-istoricheskom fronte*, Moscow: Insan, 2010.

39 V. Gerasimov, 'Sila Velikoi Pobedy', *Voenno-promyshlenny kurier* (hereafter *VPK*), 11 March 2015; V. Gerasimov, 'Komandnye kadry sovremennoi Rossiiskoi armii i flota dolzhny znat uroki minuvshei voiny', *VPK*, 15 May 2015.

40 V. Zolotarev, *Istoria voennoi strategii Rossii*, Moscow: Kuchkovo pole, 2000; P. Zhilin, *Problemy veonnoi istorii*, Moscow: Voenizdat, 1975.

41 Zhilin, *Problemy*, p. 373.

42 V. Zamulin, *Demolishing the Myth. The Tank Battle at Prokhorovka, Kursk, July 1943: An Operational Narrative*, trans. and ed. S. Britton, Solihull: Helion, 2011; Gareev, *Srazheniya*, pp. 8–148.

43 S. Main, '"You Cannot Generate Ideas by Orders": The Continuing Importance of Studying Soviet Military History – G. S. Isserson and Russia's Current Geo-Political Stance', *The Journal of Slavic Military Studies*, 29, no. 1, 2016, pp. 48–72.

44 'Prizrak Tukhachevskovo brodit po Rossii', *Topwar.ru*, 13 August 2020, https://topwar.ru/174054-prizrak-tukhachevskogo-brodit-po-rossii. html; 'Doktrina Ogarkova v proshlom i nastoyashchem', *Topwar.ru*, 20 December 2019, https://topwar.ru/165683-doktrina-ogarkova-v-proshlom-i-nastojaschem.html?utm_source=warfiles.ru; 'Operedivshii vremya', *Krasnaya Zvezda*, 31 October 2017, http://archive.redstar.ru/ index.php/newspaper/item/34952-operedivshij-vremya (all accessed 24 February 2025).

45 L. Freedman, 'Introduction', in L. Freedman (ed.), *Strategic Coercion: Concepts and Cases*, Oxford: Oxford University Press, 1998, pp. 15–36.

46 Porter, *Military Orientalism*; Adamsky, *The Culture of Military Innovation*.

47 Among some fine English-language military histories of Russia, a good one-volume overview is D. Stone, *A Military History of Russia From Ivan the Terrible to the War in Chechnya*, London: Praeger International, 2006. Many Russian military history books offer both broader sweep and examination of specific questions: Muromtseva and Perkhavko, *Voenno-politicheskaya istoria Rossii*; Krivopalov, *V teni teorii glubokoi operatsii*.

48 The author is grateful to one reviewer of the MS who pointed this out.

49 *NATO 2022 – Strategic Concept,* NATO website, 29 June 2022, www.nato.int/strategic-concept/ (accessed 24 February 2025); V. Gerasimov, 'V period do 2030 goda uroven potentsialnoi voennoi opasnosti znachitenlo povysitsya', *VPK,* 18 February 2013, https://vpk.name/news/84463_v_period_do_2030_goda_uroven_potencialnoi_voennoi_opasnosti_znachitelno_povysitsya_valerii_gerasimov.html (accessed 24 February 2025).

1 What is 'war' to the Russians, anyway?

1 G. Carleton, *Russia: The Story of War,* Cambridge, MA: Harvard University Press, 2017.

2 'Russia's Unprovoked and Unjustified Full-Scale Invasion and War in Ukraine One Year Later', website of the European External Action Service, 23 February 2023, www.eeas.europa.eu/delegations/trinidad-and-tobago/february-24-2023-russias-unprovoked-and-unjustified-full-scale-invasion-and-war-ukraine-one-year_en?s=156 (accessed 24 February 2025).

3 'Parad Pobedy na Krasnoi ploshchadi', WPA, 9 May 2023, http://kremlin.ru/events/president/news/71104 (accessed 24 February 2025).

4 'Could Putin Launch New "Short, Victorious War"? Yes, But…', Warsaw Institute, 22 March 2021, https://warsawinstitute.org/putin-launch-new-short-victorious-war-yes/ (accessed 24 February 2025). Since 2014 some have argued that NATO enlargement provoked Russia's attack on Ukraine, a view rejected by others, who deny that Moscow disapproved of NATO enlargement and assert that this is merely a pretext for imperialist invasion. Moscow has long objected not just to NATO enlargement but to its very *existence.* That there are obvious, explicit disagreements over the European security architecture does not dilute the point that Moscow ordered the assaults on Ukraine. J. Mearsheimer, 'Why the Ukraine Crisis is the West's Fault', *Foreign Affairs,* September–October 2014, www.foreignaffairs.com/articles/russia-fsu/2014-08-18/why-ukraine-crisis-west-s-fault; 'Alex Stubb on Why Mearsheimer is Wrong About the War in Ukraine', EUI, 8 July 2022, www.eui.eu/news-hub?id=alex-stubb-on-why-mearsheimer-is-wrong-about-the-war-in-ukraine; 'Vystuplenie i diskussiya na Myunkhenskoi konferentsii po voprosam politiki bezopasnosti', WPA, 10 February 2007, http://kremlin.

Notes

ru/events/president/transcripts/24034 (all accessed 24 February 2025).

5 C. von Clausewitz, *On War*, ed. and trans. M. Howard and P. Paret, Princeton, NJ: Princeton University Press, 1976, pp. 88–9.

6 V. Gerasimov, 'Razvitie voennoi strategii v sovremennykh usloviyakh. Zadachi voennoi nauki', *Vestnik akademii voennykh nauk* (hereafter *VAVN*), 2, 2019; 'Parad Pobedy na Krasnoi ploshchadi', WPA, 9 May 2022, http://kremlin.ru/events/president/news/68366 (accessed 24 February 2025). The use of this phrase 'pre-emptive' is essential – both in how it distinguishes official Russian views from Western ones about the causes of Moscow's invasion, and in terms of Russian thinking about war.

7 'UK PM Hits Back at Putin's "Clearly Ridiculous" NATO Expansion Claims', *The Guardian*, 9 February 2024, www.theguardian.com/world/live/2024/feb/09/vladimir-putin-interview-tucker-carlson-russia-ukraine-zelenskiy-europe-latest-news (accessed 24 February 2025).

8 'Press-Konferentsia po itogam rossiisko-germanskikh peregovorov', WPA, 15 February 2022, http://kremlin.ru/events/president/transcripts/67774/photos (accessed 24 February 2025).

9 M. Howard, 'What's in a Name?', *Foreign Affairs*, January–February 2002, www.foreignaffairs.com/united-states/whats-name-how-fight-terrorism (accessed 24 February 2025).

10 This is when Frank Hoffman developed his thinking on 'hybrid wars', which subsequently became so influential in analysis of Russia nearly a decade later. F. Hoffman, *Conflict in the 21st Century: The Rise of Hybrid Wars*, Potomac Institute for Policy Studies, December 2007, www.potomacinstitute.org/images/stories/publications/potomac_hybrid-war_0108.pdf (accessed 24 February 2025).

11 H. Strachan, *The Direction of War: Contemporary Strategy in Historical Perspective*, Cambridge: Cambridge University Press, 2013; M. Dudziak, *War Time. An Idea: Its History, Its Consequences*, Oxford: Oxford University Press, pp. 133–5.

12 H. Strachan, 'Introduction', in M. Strohn (ed.), *Winning Wars: The Enduring Nature and Changing Character of Victory from Antiquity to the 21st Century*, Oxford: Casemate, 2020, p. 8.

13 *The Report of the Iraq Inquiry*, website of the UK Government, 6 July 2016, www.gov.uk/government/publications/the-report-of-the-iraq-inquiry (accessed 24 February 2025).

Notes

14 H. Strachan and S. Scheipers, 'Introduction: The Changing Character of War', in H. Strachan and S. Scheipers (eds), *The Changing Character of War*, Oxford: Oxford University Press, 2011, pp. 6–7.

15 D. B. G. Heuser, *War: A Genealogy of Western Ideas and Practices*, Oxford: Oxford University Press, 2022, ch. 1.

16 A. Karp, R. Karp and T. Terriff, *Global Insurgency and the Future of Armed Conflict: Debating Fourth Generation Warfare*, Abingdon: Routledge, 2007.

17 A. Gavrilov, I. Grudinin and D. Maiburov, 'Nekotorye prikladnye aspekty sovremennoi transformatsii kategorii "voina"', *VAVN*, 78, no. 1, 2022.

18 V. Gerasimov, 'Tsennost nauki v predvidenii', *VPK*, 27 February 2013.

19 'Voina', Encyclopedia, undated, website of the Russian Ministry of Defence (emphasis added), https://encyclopedia.mil.ru/encyclopedia/dictionary/details.htm?id=12849@morfDictionary (accessed 24 February 2025); Section 8, d, *Voennaya Doktrina Rossiskoi Federatsii*, no. 2976, approved 25 December 2014, website of the National Security Council, http://scrf.gov.ru/security/military/document129/ (accessed 24 February 2025).

20 *Voennaya Doktrina*.

21 S. Alexievich, *Boys in Zinc*, trans. A. Bromfield, London: Penguin, 2017, pp. 17, 25, 46.

22 'Pobeda v voine', Encyclopedia, website of the Russian Ministry of Defence, undated, https://encyclopedia.mil.ru/encyclopedia/dictionary/details.htm?id=8964@morfDictionary (accessed 24 February 2025).

23 'Porazhenie' and 'porazhenie obyekta [tseli]', Encyclopedia, website of the Russian Ministry of Defence, undated, https://encyclopedia.mil.ru/encyclopedia/dictionary/details.htm?id=9202@morfDictionary and https://encyclopedia.mil.ru/encyclopedia/dictionary/details.htm?id=14640@morfDictionary (accessed 24 February 2025).

24 I. Popov and M. Khamzatov, *Voina budushchevo. Kontseptualnye osnovy i prakticheskie vyvody*, Moscow: Kuchkovo pole, 2016, p. 446.

25 'Voennoe iskusstvo', Encyclopedia, website of the Russian Ministry of Defence, undated, https://encyclopedia.mil.ru/encyclopedia/dictionary/details.htm?id=12817@morfDictionary (accessed 24 February 2025); N. Tyutyunnikov, *Voennaya mysl v terminakh i opredeleniyakh. V tryokh tomakh*, vol. 1, Moscow: Pero, 2018. pp. 156–7; D. Rogozin (ed.), *Voina i mir v terminakh i opredeleniyakh. Voenno-politicheski slovar*, Moscow: Veche, 2017, pp. 111–12.

Notes

26 'Voennaya nauka', Encyclopedia, website of the Russian Ministry of Defence, undated, https://encyclopedia.mil.ru/encyclopedia/diction-ary/details.htm?id=4339@morfDictionary (accessed 24 February 2025).

27 Rogozin (ed.), *Voina i mir*, p. 76.

28 D. B. G. Heuser, *The Evolution of Strategy: Thinking War From Antiquity to the Present*, Cambridge: Cambridge University Press, 2010; Strachan, *The Direction of War*; C. Gray, 'Why Strategy is Difficult', *Joint Forces Quarterly*, summer 1999, pp. 6–12, https://ndupress.ndu.edu/portals/68/Documents/jfq/jfq-22.pdf (accessed 24 February 2025).

29 O. Fridman (ed.), *Strategiya: The Foundations of the Russian Art of Strategy*, London: Hurst, 2021.

30 'Mobilizatsiya', Encyclopedia, website of the Russian Ministry of Defence, undated, https://encyclopedia.mil.ru/encyclopedia/diction-ary/details.htm?id=8206@morfDictionary (accessed 24 February 2025).

31 N. Ogarkov, 'Strategiya voennaya', *Sovietskaya voennaya entsiklopedia*, vol. 7, Moscow: Voenizdat, 1979, pp. 555–7.

32 'Strategiya voennaya', Encyclopedia, website of the Russian Ministry of Defence, undated, https://encyclopedia.mil.ru/encyclopedia/dictionary/details.htm?id=14383@morfDictionary (accessed 24 February 2025).

33 Ibid.

34 Gerasimov, 'Tsennost nauki'.

35 V. Zolotarev, *Istoria voennoi strategii Rossii*, Moscow: Kuchkovo pole, 2000, p. 551.

36 N. Ogarkov, 'Strategiya voennaya', *Sovietskaya voennaya entsiklopedia*, vol. 7, Moscow: Voenizdat, 1979, pp. 557–60.

37 V. Gerasimov, 'Razvitie voennoi strategii v sovremennykh usloviyakh. Zadachi voennoi nauki', *VAVN*, 2, 2019.

38 M. Gareev and V. Slipchenko, *Budushchaya voina*, Moscow: Polit.ru, 2005; C. Bartles, 'Sixth Generation War and Russia's Global Theatres of Military Activity', in A. Monaghan (ed.), *Russian Grand Strategy in the Era of Global Power Competition*, Manchester: Manchester University Press, 2022, pp. 71–97.

39 Gerasimov, 'Razvitie voennoi strategii'.

40 Exemplifying an extensive bibliography: J. P. Harris, 'The Myth of Blitzkrieg', *War in History*, 2, no. 3, 1995, pp. 335–52; A. Searle, *Armoured Warfare: A Military, Political and Global History*, London: Bloosmbury Academic, 2017, ch. 3; K-H. Freiser, *The Blitzkrieg Legend: The 1940 Campaign in the West*, Annapolis, MD: Naval Institute Press, 2005.

41 'Molnienosnaya voina'/'Blitzkrieg', Encyclopedia, website of the Russian Ministry of Defence, undated, https://encyclopedia.mil.ru/encyclopedia/dictionary/details.htm?id=8231@morfDictionary (accessed 24 February 2025).

42 'Strategiya izmora', Encyclopedia, website of the Russian Ministry of Defence, undated, https://encyclopedia.mil.ru/encyclopedia/dictionary/details.htm?id=10394@morfDictionary (accessed 24 February 2025).

2 Winning revolutionary war

1 'Otkrytie pamyatnika geroyam Pervoi mirovoi voiny', WPA, 1 August 2014, http://kremlin.ru/events/president/news/46385; 'Vstrecha s molodymi uchonymi i prepodavatelyami istorii', WPA, 5 November 2014, http://kremlin.ru/events/president/news/46951 (all accessed 24 February 2025).

2 V. Medinsky, M. Myagkov and Yu. Nikiforov, *Voennaya istoria Rossii*, Moscow: Russian Military Historical Society, 2018, pp. 306, 310.

3 'Voenniy kommunizm', *Bolshaya sovetskaya entsiklopedia*, vol. 12, Moscow: AOSE, 1928, pp. 368–83.

4 This episode gives just a flavour of the brutality of a struggle of escalating reprisals. Uritski was assassinated by Leonid Kanegisser, a graduate of the Mikhailovsky artillery academy, in revenge for the execution by the Bolsheviks of 21 officers from the academy. For discussion of the ChK in general, and the Red Terror in particular, see G. Leggett, *The CHEKA: Lenin's Political Police*, Oxford: Clarendon Press, 1981, esp. pp. 104–20.

5 E. Mawdsley, *The Russian Civil War*, London: Allen and Unwin, 1987.

6 M. Frunze, 'Sodoklad Tov. Frunze', Diskussiya na temu o edinoi voennoi doktrine, Stenograficheskii otchet 2–go dnya soveshchaniya voennykh delegatov XI-go Sezd R. K. P., Moscow: Vysshii voennyi redaktsionni sovet, 1 April 1922, http://rkka.ru/analys/doktrin/main.htm#s3 (accessed 24 February 2025).

7 R. Garthoff, *How Russia Makes War*, London: George Allen and Unwin, 1954, p. 45; R. Harrison, *The Russian Way of War: Operational Art, 1904–1940*, Lawrence: University Press of Kansas, 2001, pp. 80–4.

8 'Voina: voina kak sotsialnoe yavlenie', *Bolshaya sovetskaya entsiklopedia*, vol. 12, Moscow: AOSE, 1928, pp. 552–3.

Notes

9 For a concise elaboration of Marxist-Leninist views of war, see P. Vigor, *The Soviet View of War, Peace and Neutrality*, London: Routledge and Kegan Paul, 1975, pp. 1–25.

10 L. Trotsky, 'Doklad Tov. Trotskovo', 'Diskussiya na temu o edinoi voennoi doctrine', http://rkka.ru/analys/doktrin/main.htm#s2 (accessed 24 February 2025).

11 'Voina', p. 553; V. Lenin, 'War and Revolution', in H. F. Scott and W. F. Scott (eds), *The Soviet Art of War: Doctrine, Strategy and Tactics*, Boulder, CO: Westview Press, 1982, pp. 24–5; Frunze, 'Sodoklad'.

12 'Voina: voina kak problema vooruzhonnoi borby', *Bolshaya sovetskaya entsiklopedia*, pp. 577–9.

13 'Voennoe iskusstvo', *Bolshaya sovetskaya entsiklopedia*, pp. 218–29.

14 'Voennaya doktrina', *Bolshaya sovetskaya entsiklopedia*, pp. 163–5.

15 Ibid., p. 165.

16 'Frunze, M. V.', Encyclopedia, undated, website of the Russian Ministry of Defence, https://encyclopedia.mil.ru/encyclopedia/history_department/more.htm?id=11588154@SD_Employee (accessed 24 February 2025); M. Gareev, *M. V. Frunze – voenniy teoretik*, Moscow: Voenizdat, 1985.

17 M. Frunze, 'Edinaya voenaya doktrina i Krasnaya armiya' (1921), in M. Frunze, *Izbrannie proizvedeniya*, vol. 2, Moscow: Voenizdat, 1957, pp. 4–21.

18 'Rech Tov. Muralova', 'Rech Tov. Tukhachevskovo' and 'Rech Tov. Mikhalenka (8 Str. div.), all in 'Diskussiya na temu o edinoi voennoi doctrine'.

19 Trotsky, 'Doklad Tov. Trotskovo'.

20 Cited in A. Kokoshin, *Soviet Strategic Thought, 1917–91*, Cambridge, MA: MIT Press, 1998, p. 18.

21 M. Tukhachevsky, 'Voina kak problema vooruzhonnoi borby', in M. Tukhachevsky, *Izbrannie proizvedenie*, vol. 2, Moscow: Voenizdat, 1964, https://militera.lib.ru/science/tuhachevsky/23.html# (accessed 24 February 2025).

22 Cited in Kokoshin, *Soviet Strategic Thought*, p. 38.

23 A. Svechin, *Strategiya (Glavnyi trud russkovo Klauzewitza)*, Moscow: Yauza-Press, 2023.

24 Ibid., pp. 82–4.

25 Ibid., pp. 50–4.

26 B. Shaposhnikov, *Mozg armii*, Moscow: OSLN, 2016, esp. vol. 3, chs 6–9.

27 M. Tukhachevsky, 'Voprosy sovremennoi strategii', in Tukhachevsky, *Izbrannie proizvedeniya*, vol. 1, https://militera.lib.ru/science/tuhachevsky/16.html (accessed 24 February 2025); M. Frunze, 'Front i tyl v voine budushchevo' (1924), in Frunze, *Izbrannie proizvedeniya*, p. 133.

28 P. Whitewood, 'The International Situation: Fear of Invasion and Growing Authoritarianism', in L. Douds, J. Harris and P. Whitewood (eds), *The Fate of the Bolshevik Revolution: Illiberal Liberation, 1917–41*, London: Bloomsbury, 2020, pp. 173–86.

29 J. Sontag, 'The Soviet War Scare of 1926–27', *The Russian Review*, 34, no. 1, 1975, pp. 66–77; N. Simonov, 'The "War Scare" of 1927 and the Birth of the Defence-Industry Complex', in J. Barber and M. Harrison (eds), *The Soviet Defence-Industry Complex from Stalin to Khrushchev*, Basingstoke: Palgrave Macmillan, 2000, pp. 33–46.

30 Tukhachevsky, 'Voprosy sovremennoi strategii'.

31 'Budushchaya voina', May 1928. For detailed discussion, see L. Samuelson, *Plans for Stalin's War Machine: Tukhachevsky and Military-Economic Planning, 1925–1941*, London: Macmillan, 2000, pp. 21–8.

32 The note was republished in I. Danilenko, 'Duel umov pod grifom "sekretno"', *Nezavisimoe voennoe obozrenie*, no. 27, 24 July 1998.

33 M. Tukhachevsky, 'Voennye plany nyneshnei Germanii', in Tukhachevsky, *Izbrannie proizvedeniya*, vol. 2, https://militera.lib.ru/science/tuhachevsky/09.html (accessed 24 February 2025).

34 The film is available at www.youtube.com/watch?v=NidxI8xyaPk (accessed 24 February 2025).

35 Svechin, *Strategiya*, *passim*; A. Svechin, *Klauzewitz*, Moscow: ZhGO, 1935; Shaposhnikov, *Mozg armii*, vol. 3, chs 6 and 7.

36 Frunze, 'Front i tyl v voine budushchevo', p. 133; M. Tukhachevsky, 'Pokhod za Vislu', in Tukhachevsky, *Izbrannie proizvedeniya*, vol. 1, https://militera.lib.ru/science/tuhachevsky/09.html (accessed 24 February 2025).

37 For a good recent examination, see I. Ona Johnson, *Faustian Bargain: The Soviet–German Partnership and the Origins of the Second World War*, Oxford: Oxford University Press, 2021.

38 V. Triandafillov, *The Nature of the Operations of Modern Armies*, ed. J. Kipp, trans. W. Burhans, London: Routledge, 1994, p. 27.

39 M. Tukhachevsky, 'Predislovie k knige Dzh. Fullera 'Reformatsiya voiny' (30 November 1930), in M. Tukhachevsky, *Izbrannie proizvedeniya*, vol. 2, Moscow: Voenizdat, 1964, https://militera.lib.ru/science/tuhachevsky/32.html (accessed 24 February 2025).

40 Svechin, *Strategiya*, pp. 70–80; Danilenko, 'Duel umov pod grifom "sekretno"'.

41 M. Tukhachevsky, 'Presidlovie k knige G. Delbryuka 'Istoriya voennovo iskusstva v ramkakh politicheskoi istorii', in Tukhachevsky, *Izbrannie proizvedeniya*, vol. 2, https://militera.lib.ru/science/tuhachevsky/31.html (accessed 24 February 2025).

42 Svechin, *Strategiya*, pp. 270–7; Shaposhnikov, *Mozg armii*, vol. 3, ch. 8.

43 G. Isserson, *Novye formy borby*, Moscow: Voengiz, 1940.

44 M. Tukhachevsky, 'O novom polevom ustave RKKA', in Tukhachevsky, *Izbrannie proizvedeniya*, vol. 2, https://militera.lib.ru/science/tuhachevsky/43.html (accessed 24 February 2025).

45 M. Tukhachevsky, 'O novom polevom ustave RKKA', cited in J. Erickson, *The Road to Stalingrad*, London: Phoenix, 1998, p. 5.

46 V. Shlykov, 'Foreword', in Samuelson, *Plans for Stalin's War Machine*, pp. xii–xxiii.

47 I. Babel, *Collected Stories*, ed. E. Sicher, trans. D. McDuff, London, Penguin, 1994.

48 L. Graham, *The Ghost of the Executed Engineer: Technology and the Fall of the Soviet Union*, Cambridge, MA: Harvard University Press, 1993; P. Josephson, *Totalitarian Science and Technology*, Atlantic Highlands, NJ: Humanities Press, 1996.

49 Svechin, *Strategiya*, pp. 39–40.

50 N. Achkasov (ed.), *Voennaya istoria. Uchebnik dlya voennykh vuzov*, St Petersburg: Piter, 2020, pp. 210–13.

51 'Pavlov, D. G.', Encyclopedia, undated, website of the Russian Ministry of Defence, https://xn–d1abichglj9dyd8a.xn–90anlfbebar6i.xn–p1ai/encyclopedia/dictionary/details_rvsn.htm?id=8479@morfDictionary (accessed 24 February 2025).

52 Achkasov (ed.), *Voennaya istoria*, pp. 213–15; Medinsky, Myagkov and Nikiforov, *Voennaya istoria Rossii*, pp. 326–31.

53 Achkasov (ed.), *Voennaya istoria*, pp. 215–18; Harrison, *The Russian Way of War*, pp. 237–42.

54 Medinsky, Myagkov and Nikiforov, *Voennaya istoria Rossii*, pp. 330–1.

55 Harrison, *The Russian Way of War*, p. 242.

56 Achkasov (ed.), *Voennaya istoria*, pp. 218–21; A. Hill, 'Voroshilov's Lightning War – The Soviet Invasion of Poland, September 1939', *Journal of Slavic Military Studies*, 27, no. 3, 2014, pp. 404–19.

57 For detailed examination, see C. van Dyke, *The Soviet Invasion of Finland, 1939–40*, London: Routledge, 1997; Medinsky, Myagkov and Nikiforov, *Voennaya istoria Rossii*, pp. 331, 334–5; Achkasov (ed.), *Voennaya istoria*, pp. 221–6.

58 P. Vigor, *Soviet Blitzkrieg Theory*, New York: St Martin's Press, 1983, p. 53.

59 A. Lieven and A. Little, 'Ukraine Should Take a Page Out of Finland's Fight with Stalin', *Responsible Statecraft*, 21 December 2023, https:// responsiblestatecraft.org/ukraine-neutrality/ (accessed 24 February 2025); 'Russia's Military Struggles in Ukraine are Starting to Look Like a Bloody Soviet Attack on a Smaller Neighbor During World War II', *Business Insider*, 20 March 2022, www.businessinsider.com/ russian-war-in-ukraine-draws-comparison-to-winter-war-finland-2022-3 (accessed 24 February 2025).

60 'Vstrecha s uchastnikami uchreditelnovo sezda Rossiiskovo voenno-istoricheskovo obshchestva', WPA, 14 March 2013, http://kremlin. ru/events/president/news/17677 (accessed 24 February 2025).

61 A. Korolchenko, *Vybityi generalitet. Istoricheskoe povestvovanie*, Rostov-na-Donu: Feniks, 2000.

62 Kokoshin, *Soviet Strategic Thought*, p. 8.

63 B. Sokolov, *Marshal Malinovskii: Hero of the Soviet Union, Architect of the Modern Soviet Army*, trans. R. Harrison, Solihull: Helion, 2017, p. 332; V. Anfilov, 'Semyon Mikhailovich Budenny', in H. Shukman (ed.), *Stalin's Generals*, London: Phoenix, 2001, pp. 64–5.

64 T. Butson, *The Tsar's Lieutenant, the Soviet Marshal*, New York: Praeger Scientific, 1984, p. 170.

65 D. Volkogonov, *Stalin: Triumph and Tragedy*, London: Prima Lifestyles, 1996, pp. 249, 322, 355–6; D. Volkogonov, 'Kliment Yefremovich Voroshilov', in Shukman (ed.), *Stalin's Generals*, pp. 313–24.

66 M. Gareev, 'Krovnoe delo komandira – chast I', *VPK*, 3 October 2017; V. Gerasimov, 'Tsennost nauki v predvidennie', *VPK*, 26 February 2013.

67 H. Shukman, 'Introduction', in Shukman (ed.), *Stalin's Generals*, pp. 2–4; A. Hill, *The Red Army and the Second World War*, Cambridge: Cambridge University Press, 2017, p. 51.

68 Approved by Stalin, the film was a fictionalised biographical depiction of some of the civil war action in which Chapayev fought. Popular during the Soviet era, Putin has suggested that it is one of

his favourite films. 'Primaya liniya s Vladimirom Putinym', WPA, 17 April 2014, http://kremlin.ru/events/president/news/20796 (accessed 24 February 2025). The film can be viewed at www.youtube.com/watch?v=aePu4MtzKjY (accessed 24 February 2025).

69 'Mentalnost protiv taktiki', 30 June 2015, https://birserg-1977.livejournal.com/360440.html (accessed 24 February 2025); A. Smirnov, *Boevaya vyuchka Krasnoi armii nakanune repressii 1937–1938 gg*, vol. 2. Moscow: Rodina-media, 2013.

70 'Mentalnost protiv taktiki'.

71 Having lunched together, Wavell said of Tukhachevsky that he was 'undoubtedly able, ambitious and energetic', though he was also 'rather a nasty piece of work' to whom Wavell took an 'instant dislike': 'if there was a plot, he would certainly have been in it'. *Wavell in Russia*, ADH Printing, 2017, pp. 70–2; G. Martell, *The Russian Outlook*, London: Michael Joseph, 1947, ch. 1.

72 See, for instance, the 1938 (propaganda) film *Esli zavtra voina*, www.youtube.com/watch?v=NidxI8xyaPk (accessed 24 February 2025).

73 Shukman, 'Introduction', pp. 2–4; Volkogonov, *Stalin*; Hill, *The Red Army*, pp. 67–9.

74 Harrison, *The Russian Way of War*, pp. 246, 300; Medinsky, Myagkov and Nikiforov, *Voennaya istoria Rossii*, p. 335.

3 Operation Barbarossa and the Great Victory

1 G. K. Zhukov, *Vospominaniya i razmyshleniya*, Moscow: Izdatelsvto Agenstva Pechati Novosti, 1969; N. Ogarkov, 'Podvig, ravnovo kotoromu ne znala istoriya', *Zarubezhnoe voennoe obozrenie*, no. 4, 1989; A. Kokoshin and B. Larionov, 'Kurskaya bitva v svete sovremennoi oboronitelnoi doktriny', *Mezhdunarodnaya ekonomika i mezhdunarodnie otnosheniya*, no. 8, 1987; V. Zolotarev (ed.), *Voennaya istoriya gosudarstva Rossiiskovo*, Moscow: Kuchkovo pole, 2015, pp. 520–8. There are many fine English-language publications (and translations from Russian) that deal with the war as a whole, and with specific episodes and battles. For overviews, see D. Glantz, *The Soviet–German War, 1941–45: Myths and Realities. A Survey Essay*, 20th Anniversary Distinguished Lecture, Clemson University, 11 October 2001, www.scribd.com/document/22531803/Soviet-German-War-1941–45 (accessed 24 February 2025); C. Dick, *From Defeat to Victory: The Eastern Front, Summer 1944*,

Notes

Lawrence: University Press of Kansas, 2016. Prit Buttar and Richard Harrison have produced excellent examinations of specific offensives and campaigns including the Soviet experience: P. Buttar, *Retribution: The Soviet Reconquest of Central Ukraine, 1943*, Oxford: Osprey, 2019; R. Harrison (ed.), *The Battle of the Dnepr: The Red Army's Forcing of the East Wall, September–December 1943*, Solihull: Helion, 2018.

2 M. Harrison, *Accounting For War: Soviet Production, Employment and the Defence Burden, 1940–1945*, Cambridge: Cambridge University Press, 1996.

3 Zhukov, *Vospominaniya i razmyshleniya*, pp. 238–44; S. Kotkin, 'When Stalin Faced Hitler', *Foreign Affairs*, 19 September 2017, www.foreignaffairs.com/russia-fsu/when-stalin-faced-hitler?check_logged_in=1 (accessed 24 February 2025).

4 Zhukov, *Vospominaniya i razmyshleniya*, pp. 291–5. Partly, this was the result of ongoing repressions: in 1941 senior officers were being held in Lubyanka. Those who had borne the brunt of Operation Barbarossa were also punished: Pavlov was shot, as were his chief of staff and the commander of the 4th Army. The outbreak of war also provided an occasion for an increase in police power and activity, with grudges paid off against those who had escaped the 1936–38 repression. R. Conquest, *The Great Terror: A Reassessment*, London: Pimlico, 2008, pp. 454–5.

5 S. Talbott (ed. and trans.), *Khrushchev Remembers*, London: André Deutsch, 1971, pp. 182–9, 592–4.

6 Zhukov, *Vospominaniya i razmyshleniya*, pp. 425–7.

7 V. Zamulin, 'To Defeat the Enemy was Less a Problem than the Laziness and Indolence of Our Own Commanders', *Journal of Slavic Military Studies*, 29, no. 4, 2016, pp. 707–9; P. Rotmistrov, 'Tanks Against Tanks', in J. Erickson (ed.), *Main Front: Soviet Leaders Look Back on World War II*, London: Brassey's Defence Publishers, 1987, p. 109; S. Shtemenko, 'Bagration Operation Byelorussia, 1944', in Erickson (ed.), *Main Front*, pp. 182–3.

8 G. Zhukov, 'The Fall of Berlin and Unconditional Surrender', in Erickson (ed.), *Main Front*, p. 254.

9 Cited in Zamulin, 'To Defeat the Enemy', p. 724.

10 Shtemenko, 'Bagration Operation Byelorussia, 1944', p. 187.

11 B. Sokolov, *Marshal Malinovskii: Hero of the Soviet Union, Architect of the Modern Soviet Army*, trans. R. Harrison, Solihull: Helion, 2017, p. 334.

12 Voinovich's text *Zhizn i neobychainie priklyucheniya soldata Ivana Chonkina* was initially published in parts, with the first part in samizdat form in

Notes

1969. It was made into a film in 1994, and, more recently, a television series. Available in English: V. Voinovich, *The Life and Extraordinary Adventures of Private Ivan Chonkin*, trans. R. Lourie, London: Penguin, 1978, pp. 237, 240. See also the 1969 film *Na voine, kak na voine*, directed by Viktor Tregubovich, which also features these themes. The film is available at www.youtube.com/watch?v=VJGZ143LnIU (accessed 24 February 2025).

13 V. Astafev, *Proklyaty i ubity*, Moscow: Izdatelstvo AST, 2022.

14 J. Erickson, *The Road to Berlin*, London: Phoenix Giants, 1996, pp. 571–2, 622, 625.

15 Zhukov, 'The Fall of Berlin and Unconditional Surrender', pp. 245, 262, 269.

16 D. Glantz, *The Soviet Strategic Offensive in Manchuria, 1945: 'August Storm'*, London: Routledge, 2003; P. Vigor, *Soviet Blitzkrieg Theory*, New York: St Martin's Press, 1983, ch. 9.

17 Cited in Sokolov, *Marshal Malinovskii*, p. 351.

18 Better known as Churchill's 'Iron Curtain' speech. W. S. Churchill, 'Sinews of Peace', 5 March 1946, website of America's National Churchill Museum, www.nationalchurchillmuseum.org/sinews-of-peace-iron-curtain-speech.html (accessed 24 February 2025). Stalin's interview with *Pravda* was published on 14 March 1946, https://soviethistory.msu.edu/1947-2/cold-war/cold-war-texts/stalin-on-churchills-iron-curtain-speech/ (accessed 24 February 2025).

19 Following a substantial preparatory effort in 1948, the alliance was officially established on 4 April 1949, and held its first major exercises in autumn 1951.

20 S. Khrushchev (ed.), *Memoirs of Nikita Khrushchev. Vol. 2: Reformer, 1945–64*, University Park, PA: Pennsylvania State University Press, 2006, p. 427; E. Morris, *The Russian Navy: Myth and Reality*, London: Hamish Hamilton, 1977, pp. 30–1.

21 Cited in G. Barrass, *The Great Cold War: A Journey Through the Hall of Mirrors*, Stanford, CA: Stanford University Press, 2009, p. 54.

22 Conquest, *The Great Terror*, pp. 454–63.

23 V. Shalamov, *Kolyma Tales*, London: Penguin, 1994, esp. pp. 242, 248–9, 254.

24 Sokolov, *Marshal Malinovskii*, pp. 349–51.

25 Talbott (ed. and trans.), *Khrushchev Remembers*, pp. 258, 283, 601. The 'doctors' plot' was alleged to concern a 'terrorist group' of nine Kremlin doctors who, guided by Western imperialists, sought to use

medical treatment to kill the top Soviet political and military leadership. L. Rapoport, *Stalin's War Against the Jews: The Doctors' Plot and the Soviet Solution*, Oxford: Maxwell MacMillan International, 1990.

26 Morris, *The Russian Navy*, p. 35.

27 Alexander Solzhenitsyn described the post-war experience of the sharashka in *The First Circle*, London: Harvill Press, 1996. '"Sharashki": pochemu luchshee oruzhie Krasnoi Armii sozdali "ZEKi"', *Rambler*, 19 December 2021, https://news.rambler.ru/weapon/47798217-sharashki-pochemu-luchshee-oruzhie-krasnoy-armii-sozdali-zeki/ (accessed 24 February 2025).

28 E. Ashby, 'Science and the Soviet Army', in B. Liddell Hart (ed.), *The Red Army*, New York: Harcourt, Brace, 1956, pp. 452–60.

29 In some senses, Soviet nuclear culture echoed that of the US, UK and France. P. Josephson, 'Atomic Powered Communism: Nuclear Culture in the Post-War USSR', *Slavic Review*, 55, no. 2, 1996, pp. 297–324.

30 M. Kim and A. Fadeev, 'Ob osnovnykh problemakh otechestvennoi istorii', *Voprosi istorii*, no. 2, 28 February 1961; R. Markwick, *Rewriting History in Soviet Russia: The Politics of Revisionist Historiography, 1956–1974*, London: Palgrave, 2001. The author is grateful to Geoffrey Hosking, John Gooding, Roger Markwick and Steven Main for discussions on these themes.

31 Cited in R. Garthoff, *How Russia Makes War: Soviet Military Doctrine*, London: George Allen and Unwin, 1954, p. 59.

32 A. Kokoshin, *Soviet Strategic Thought, 1917–91*, Cambridge, MA: MIT Press, 1998, pp. 44–6, 172.

33 'Za tvorcheskoe izuchenie istorii sovetskikh vooruzhonnykh sil', *Voprosi istorii*, no. 2, 28 February 1958.

34 *Bolshaya sovetskaya entsykopedia*, vol. 52, Moscow: Sovetskaya entsiklopedia, 1947, p. 942; *Bolshaya sovetskaya entsykopedia*, vol. 8, 1951, pp. 570–5.

35 J. Hines, E. Mishulovich and J. Shull, *Soviet Intentions, 1965–1985*, Soviet Post Cold War Testimonial Evidence, BDM Federal Inc., September 1995, p. 54, https://nsarchive.gwu.edu/document/17326-document-25-series-five-interviews (accessed 24 February 2025); L. B. Ely, 'A General Assessment', in Liddell Hart (ed.), *The Red Army*, pp. 197–202.

36 The film is available at www.youtube.com/watch?v=t-hZam8dXHU&t=188s (accessed 24 February 2025).

37 M. Mackintosh, *Juggernaut: A History of the Soviet Armed Forces*, London: Secker and Warburg, 1967, pp. 278, 280.

38 Zhukov, *Vospominaniya i razmyshleniya*, pp. 415–16; R. Garthoff, *The Soviet Image of Future War*, Washington, DC: Public Affairs Press, 1959, esp. pp. 82–3.

39 I. Maryganov, *Peredovoi kharakter Sovetskoi voennoi nauki*, Moscow: Voenizdat, 1953, p. 110.

40 Prikaz narodnovo komissara oborony SSSR no. 55, 23 February 1942, https://c21ch.newcastle.edu.au/stalin/t15/t15_19.htm (accessed 24 February 2025).

41 Cited in Garthoff, *Soviet Image of Future War*, pp. 31–2, 48.

42 I. Baz, 'Soviet Military Science on the Character of Contemporary War', *Voenniy vestnik*, no. 6, June 1958, translated and reprinted in Garthoff, *Soviet Image of Future War*, pp. 86–107; B. Liddell Hart, *The Revolution in Warfare*, London: Faber and Faber, 1946; B. Liddell Hart, 'Foreword', in H. Guderian, *Panzer Leader*, New York: Da Capo, 1952.

43 Kokoshin, *Soviet Strategic Thought*, pp. 111, 113; *Voennaya mysl*, nos 9 and 10, 1953.

44 Kokoshin, *Soviet Strategic Thought*, pp. 114–15.

45 Krushchev (ed.), *Memoirs of Nikita Khrushchev*, pp. 238, 425–6.

46 P. Rotmistrov, 'O roli vnezapnosti v sovremennoi voine', *Voennaya mysl*, no. 2, 1955; Garthoff, *Soviet Image of Future War*, pp. 64–6.

47 *Bolshaya sovetskaya entsykopedia*, vol. 41, 1956, pp. 65–6.

48 Baz 'Soviet Military Science'.

49 I. Korotkov, 'On Fundamental Factors Which Determine the Course and Outcome of Wars', *Sovetskaya aviatsia*, translated and reprinted in Garthoff, *Soviet Image of Future War*, pp. 108–17; P. Sidorov, 'The Creative Character of Soviet Military Science', *Sovetskii Flot*, 11 December 1958, translated and reprinted in Garthoff, *Soviet Image of Future War*, pp. 118–28.

50 Danilevich in Hines, Mishulovich and Shull, *Soviet Intentions*, p. 67.

51 P. H. Vigor and C. Donnelly, 'The Manchurian Campaign and its Relevance to Modern Strategy', *Comparative Strategy*, 2, no. 2, 1980, pp. 159–78.

52 'Vnezapnost', Encyclopedia, website of the Russian Ministry of Defence, undated, https://encyclopedia.mil.ru/encyclopedia/dictionary/details.htm?id=4272@morfDictionary (accessed 24 February 2025).

53 Zhukov, *Vospominaniya i razmyshleniya*, p. 446.

54 Ibid., pp. 451–583.

Notes

55 Dick, *From Defeat to Victory*, p. 241; D. Glantz, *Soviet Military Deception in the Second World War*, London: Frank Cass, 1989.

56 'Maskirovka', Encyclopedia, website of the Russian Ministry of Defence, undated, https://encyclopedia.mil.ru/encyclopedia/diction-ary/details.htm?id=13494@morfDictionary (accessed 24 February 2025).

57 Ibid.

58 'Khitrost voennaya', Encyclopedia, website of the Russian Ministry of Defence, undated, https://encyclopedia.mil.ru/encyclopedia/dictionary/details.htm?id=11498@morfDictionary (accessed 24 February 2025).

59 Ibid.

60 V. Zolotarev, *Istoria voennoi strategii Rossii*, Moscow: Kuchkovo pole, 2000, p. 14; M. Matveevsky, 'Voennaya khitrost v boevykh primerakh', *Armeiski sbornik*, no. 5, 2017.

61 N. S. Khruschev, 'Memorandum on Military Reform, 8 December 1959', in Khrushchev (ed.), *Memoirs of Nikita Khrushchev*, pp. 654–61.

62 'Novoe predlozhenie o sokraschenii vooruzhennykh sil sovetskovo soyuza', Zasedaniya Verkhovnovo Soveta SSSR 5–vo sozyva chet-vyortaya sessia (14–15 yanvarya 1960 g.): stenographicheskii otchet, pp. 33–9, http://elib.shpl.ru/ru/nodes/32457-zasedaniya-verhovnogo-soveta-sssr-5-go-sozyva-chetvertaya-sessiya-14-15-yanvarya-#mode/inspect/page/37/zoom/4 (accessed 24 February 2025).

4 Winning a war in the nuclear age

1 I. Bagramian, *Istoria voin i voennovo iskusstva*, Moscow: Voenizdat, 1970, pp. 466–9.

2 N. S. Khruschev, 'Memorandum on Military Reform, 8 December 1959', in S. Khrushchev (ed), *Memoirs of Nikita Khrushchev. Vol. 2: Reformer, 1945–64*, University Park, PA: Pennsylvania University Press, 2006; S. Talbott (ed. and trans.), *Khrushchev Remembers*, London: André Deutsch, 1971, p. 516.

3 B. Sokolov, *Marshal Malinovskii: Hero of the Soviet Union, Architect of the Modern Soviet Army*, trans. R. Harrison, Solihull: Helion, 2017, p. 389.

4 Ibid., p. 374.

5 N. Polmar, T. Brooks and G. Fedoroff, *Admiral Gorshkov: The Man Who Challenged the U.S. Navy*, Annapolis, MD: Naval Institute Press, 2019,

Notes

pp. 126–8; M. Mackintosh, *Juggernaut: A History of the Soviet Armed Forces*, London: Secker and Warburg, 1967, p. 298.

6 Khrushchev (ed.), *Memoirs*, p. 655; Sokolov, *Marshal Malinovskii*, p. x

7 Danilevich in J. Hines, E. Mishulovich and J. Shull, *Soviet Intentions, 1965–1985*, Soviet Post Cold War Testimonial Evidence, BDM Federal Inc., September 1995, p. 31.

8 Zakharov was reinstated as CGS in late 1964, when his replacement, Sergey Biryuzov, was killed in a crash.

9 Moscow deployed the army and security services to crush unarmed protests, killing 26 and wounding many more. Matvey Shaposhnikov, Hero of the Soviet Union and 1st Deputy Commander of the North Caucasus Military District, refused to comply with the order to attack the protesters with tanks. He was demoted and expelled from the CPSU. The protests remained an official secret until 1992. Sokolov, *Marshal Malinovskii*, pp. 383, 390.

10 Hines, Mishulovich and Shull, *Soviet Intentions*, p. 23; Sokolov, *Marshal Malinovskii*, p. 390.

11 V. Sokolovsky, *Voennaya strategiya*, Moscow: Voenizdat, 1968, pp. 24, 192–3, 212–14.

12 A. Kokoshin, *Soviet Strategic Thought, 1917–91*, Cambridge, MA: MIT Press, 1998, p. 49. Not everyone agreed: Malinovskii's biographer suggested that although he was 'close' to Zhukov, he was 'never viewed as an influential and independent figure in the military hierarchy'. Sokolov, *Marshal Malinovskii*, p. 360.

13 Sokolovsky, *Voennaya strategiya*, pp. 14, 16, 27–9, 55.

14 Ibid., pp. 37–55.

15 Ibid., pp. 27–47.

16 Ibid., p. 458.

17 Ibid., pp. 154, 166, 185–6, 458.

18 Ibid., pp. 20, 243. When discussing the impact of scientific change on strategy, Sokolovsky repeatedly uses variations of the term *korennoi*, indicating change at the roots.

19 Ibid., pp. 19–22, 243–7.

20 Ibid., pp. 255, 460.

21 Ibid., pp. 20, 21, 244, 255, 460. Emphasis added.

22 Danilevich in Hines, Mishulovich and Shull, *Soviet Intentions*, p. 55.

23 *Marxism-Leninism o voine i armii*, Moscow, 1968, pp. 299–303, 346–59; D. Volkogonov and S. Tyushkevich, 'Voina', *Bolshaya sovetskaya entsykolpedia*, vol. 2, Moscow: Voenizdat, 1976, pp. 305–10.

Notes

24 P. Kurochkin, 'Critique of Soviet Military Strategy', *Krasnaya Zvezda* (hereafter *KZ*), 22 September 1962, translated and republished in V. Sokolovsky, *(Soviet) Military Strategy*, trans. H. Dinerstein, L. Goure and T. Wolfe, Santa Monica, CA: RAND, 1963, pp. 525, 527. Critical reviews were also published in *Voenny vestnik* and *Voenno-istoricheskii zhurnal* respectively in January and May 1963.

25 Kurochkin, 'Critique', p. 526.

26 Bagramian, *Istoria voin*, p. 490; Kokoshin, *Soviet Strategic Thought*, p. 124.

27 Khrushchev (ed.), *Memoirs*, p. 242.

28 Danilevich in Hines, Mishulovich and Shull, *Soviet Intentions*, pp. 23–5.

29 Ibid., pp. 40, 55; N. Ogarkov, *Istoria uchit bditelnosti*, Moscow: Voenizdat, 1985, pp. 51, 88. This was reflected in a speech by Brezhnev in Tula on 18 January 1977. An English-language transcript is available at www.cia.gov/readingroom/docs/CIA-RDP05S00365R000100020001-2.pdf (accessed 24 February 2025). This was when Western observers began to study Soviet strategic culture. J. Snyder, *The Soviet Strategic Culture: Implications for Limited Nuclear Operations*, R-2154-AF, September 1977, www.rand.org/content/dam/rand/pubs/reports/2005/R2154.pdf (accessed 24 February 2025).

30 N. Ogarkov, 'Strategiya voennaya', *Sovetskaya voennaya entsiklopedia*, vol. 7, Moscow: Voenizdat, 1979, pp. 555–65; A. Grechko, *Vooruzhonnye sily sovetskovo gosudarstva*, Moscow: Voenizdat, 1974.

31 Ogarkov, 'Strategiya voennaya', p. 559.

32 Ibid., p. 563; Grechko, *Vooruzhonnye sily*.

33 Ogarkov, 'Strategiya voennaya', p. 563.

34 Sokolovsky, *Voennaya strategiya*, p. 460.

35 S. Ivanov, *Nachalnyi period voiny*, Moscow: Voenizdat, 1974, pp. 5–7.

36 Ibid., pp. 5–7.

37 Ibid., pp. 7, 49, 64–5.

38 Ibid., pp. 49, 64–5.

39 Ibid., pp. 299–301.

40 Sokolovsky, *Voennaya strategiya*, pp. 246–7; S. Gorshkov, 'Voenno-morskie floty v voinakh i v mirnoe vremya', *Morskoi sbornik*, no. 2, February 1972, pp. 20–9.

41 Ivanov, *Nachalniy period*, pp. 62–6; S. Gorshkov, *Morskaya moshch gosudarstva*, Moscow: Voenizdat, 1976, ch. 3.

42 Cited in Kokoshin, *Soviet Strategic Thought*, p. 130.

Notes

43 S. Gorshkov, 'Korabelnyi ustav – osnova sluzhby voennovo moryaka', *Morskoi sbornik*, no. 5, 1978, pp. 3–7.

44 Kokoshin, *Soviet Strategic Thought*, p. 131; Polmar, Brooks and Fedoroff, *Admiral Gorshkov*, pp. 190–1.

45 Gorshkov, *Morskaya moshch*, introduction, ch. 3, ch. 4, conclusion.

46 Ogarkov, *Istoria uchit*, pp. 48–9.

47 Born in 1921, Danilevich joined the Red Army in 1940, serving with distinction in the Great Fatherland War, including in the battles of Moscow and Kursk. In 1964 he became head of the General Staff's department of war art development, and subsequently an aide to the Chief of General Staff on operational questions. He became a leading authority on military affairs, publishing books on war strategy (1966), strategic operations (1967) and contributing to the history of World War II in 12 volumes (1973–82). He advised Ogarkov, Akhromeev and then Moiseev, before retiring in 1989. In retirement, he continued to contribute actively to military affairs in the 1990s, becoming a professor at the Academy of War Sciences until his death in 1995.

48 Ogarkov, *Istoria uchit*, p. 58.

49 Ogarkov, 'Strategiya voennaya', p. 563.

50 Danilevich in Hines, Mishulovich and Shull, *Soviet Intentions*, p. 67; M. Monakov, *Glavkom. Zhizn i deyatelnost Admirala flota Sovetskovo Soyuza S. G. Gorshkova*, Moscow: Kuchkovo pole, 2008, pp. 626–7; M. Gareev, '23 yanvarya 1994 goda ushyol iz zhizni vydayushchisya sovetskii voenachalnik Marshal Sovetskovo Soyuza Ogaarkov Nikolai Vasilievich', *Arsenal Otechestva*, 23 January 2019, https://arsenal-otechestva.ru/new/1196-23-yanvarya-1994-goda-ushjol-iz-zhizni-vydayushchijsya-sovetskij-voenachalnik-marshal-sovetskogo-soyuza-ogarkov-nikolaj-vasilevich (accessed 24 February 2025).

51 Tukhachevsky was one of the most prominent of those rehabilitated. A. Todorsky, *Marshal Tukhachevsky*, Moscow: Izdatelslvo politicheskoi literatury, 1964; M. Zotov, *Marshal Tukhachevsky: vospominaniya druzei i soratnikov*, Moscow: Voenizdat, 1965.

52 Sokolovsky, *Voennaya strategiya*, p. 248.

53 A full English translation of the book, with discussion, critique and praise, was published in V. Petrov, *'June 22, 1941' Soviet Historians and the German Invasion*, Columbia: University of South Carolina Press, 1968.

54 In the early-to-mid 1960s, Georgi Isserson, himself a victim of the repression and subsequently rehabilitated, had published articles in *Voenno-istoricheskii zhurnal*. This may have indicated that Tukhachevsky

was no longer officially taboo, but it took longer for his work to be officially countenanced.

55 N. Ogarkov, 'Glubokaya operatsiya', *Sovetskaya voennaya entsiklopedia*, vol. 2, Moscow: Voenizdat, 1976, pp. 574–745; Ogarkov, 'Strategiya voennaya', p. 561. Ogarkov also noted the work of Shaposhnikov, Triandafillov, Egorov, Uborevich and Yakir.

56 Cited in R. Davies, *Soviet History in the Gorbachev Revolution*, London: Macmillan, 1989, pp. 101–7.

57 'Materialy k zasedaniyam Sekretariata TsK KPSS besposhchadno razoblachayut sovetskuyu deistvitelnost', *Nezavisimaya Gazeta*, 27 August 2023, www.ng.ru/editorial/2023-08-27/2_8810_editorial.html (accessed 24 February 2025).

58 A. Nove, *An Economic History of the USSR, 1917–91*, London: Penguin, 1993, p. 381.

59 Danilevich in Hines, Mishulovich and Shull, *Soviet Intentions*, p. 67. For discussion of scientific and technological development, see B. Parrott, *Politics and Technology in the USSR*, Cambridge, MA: MIT Press, 1983.

60 Danilevich in Hines, Mishulovich and Shull, *Soviet Intentions*, p. 31; Gareev, '23 yanvarya 1994'.

61 Ogarkov, *Istoria uchit*, pp. 50–1.

62 M. Gorbachev, *Perestroika: New Thinking for Our Country and the World*, London: HarperCollins, 1987, pp. 17–22.

63 Ibid., p. 139.

64 The armed forces were to be cut by some 500,000 and defence spending by 14.2 per cent. M. Moiseev, 'Sovetskaya voennaya doktrina: realizatsiya eyo oboronitelnoi napravlennosti', *Pravda*, 13 March 1989. For discussion of the military industrial complex and *konversiya*, see J. Cooper, *The Soviet Defence Industry*, London: Continuum, 1991, p. 35.

65 M. Gareev, 'The Revised Soviet Military Doctrine', *Bulletin of Atomic Scientists*, December 1988, pp. 30–2; Moiseev, 'Sovetskaya voennaya doktrina'; A. Kokoshin, and V. Larionov, 'Kurskaya bitva v svete sovremennoi oboronitelnoi doktriny', *Mezhdunarodnaya ekonomika i mezhdunarodniye otnosheniya*, no. 8, 1987, p. 33.

66 Kokoshin, *Soviet Strategic Thought*, p. 58.

67 Cited in W. Odom, 'Soviet Military Doctrine', *Foreign Affairs*, 1 December 1988, www.foreignaffairs.com/articles/russia-fsu/1988-12-01/soviet-military-doctrine (accessed 24 February 2025); M. Gareev, *M. V. Frunze – voenniy teoretik*, Moscow: Voenizdat, 1985.

68 Moiseev, 'Sovetskaya voennaya doktrina'.

69 Cooper, *Soviet Defence Industry*, p. 35.

70 Kokoshin and Larionov, 'Kurskaya bitva', p. 33.

71 V. Makhrebsky, 'Blitzkrig v epokhu nauchno-tekhnicheskoi revolutsii', *Voennaya Znania*, no. 9, 1986.

72 V. Ivanov, *Marshal M. N. Tukhachevsky*, Moscow: Voenizdat, 1985; Gareev, *Frunze*; Kokoshin and Larionov, 'Kurskaya bitva'; N. Ogarkov, 'Podvig, ravnovo kotoromu ne znala istoriya', *Zarubezhnoe voennoe obozrenie*, no. 4, 1989, p. 3.

73 Gareev, *Frunze*; Kokoshin and Larionov, 'Kurskaya bitva', pp. 37–8; A. Khorkov, 'Nekotoriye voprosi strategicheskovo razvyortivaniya Sovetskikh Vooruzhennykh Sil v nachale Velikoi Otechestvennoi voini', *Voenno-istoricheski zhurnal* (hereafter *VIZh*), no. 1, 1986, p. 12.

74 K. Rokossovsky, 'Soldatskii dolg', *VIZh*, no. 5, 1989, pp. 59–62; Ogarkov, 'Podvig', p. 3.

75 Ogarkov, 'Podvig', p. 3; A. Maryshev, 'Nekotorie voprosy strategicheskovo oborony v Velikoi Otechesstvennoi voine', *VIZh*, no. 6, 1986, pp. 13, 16; N. Glazunov, 'Proval fashistskovo plana Barbarossa', *VIZh*, no. 5, 1986, p. 70; V. Lobov, 'Voennaya khitrost', *VIZh*, no. 3, 1987, pp. 11–18; P. Simchenkov, 'Dostizhenie skrytnosti', *VIZh*, no. 6, 1986, pp. 17–24.

76 Kokoshin and Larionov, 'Kurskaya bitva', pp. 32, 38–9; Maryshev, 'Nekotorie voprosy strategicheskovo', p. 16; S. Postnikov, 'Razvitie sovetskovo voennovo iskusstva v Kurskoi bitve', *VIZh*, no. 7, 1988, pp. 10–18.

77 F. Gaivoronsky, 'Prevoskhodstvo sovetskoi voennoi nauki i voennovo iskusstva v Velikoi Otechestvennoi Voine', *VIZh*, no. 4, 1986, pp. 13–15, 21; Glazunov, 'Proval fashistskovo plana Barbarossa', p. 70.

78 Danilevich in Hines, Mishulovich and Shull, *Soviet Intentions*, pp. 43–4, 68.

79 The Soviets finally completed their withdrawal from Afghanistan in February 1989.

5 War in the information age

1 J. Tritten, 'The Changing Role of Naval Forces: The Russian View of the 1991 Persian Gulf War', *Journal of Soviet Military Studies*, 5, no. 4, 1992, p. 576.

2 The campaign has since been extensively analysed in both West and East. D. Betz, 'The More You Know, the Less You Understand. The Problem with Information Warfare', *Journal of Strategic Studies*, 29, no. 3, 2006; L. Freedman, *The Future of War: A History*, London: Allen Lane, 2017.

3 D. Glantz, *The Soviet Strategic Offensive in Manchuria, 1945, 'August Storm'*, London: Frank Cass, 2003, pp. xix–xx.

4 'Pervye uroki voiny', *Voennaya mysl* (hereafter *VM*), May 1991, pp. 60–71; M. Gareev, 'O voennoi reforme', *VM*, August 1991, pp. 39–45.

5 'Kolesnikov, Mikhail Petrovich', Encyclopedia, undated, website of the Russian Ministry of Defence, https://encyclopedia.mil.ru/encyclopedia/history/more.htm?id=12131829@cmsArticle (accessed 24 February 2025).

6 G. Troshev, *Chechensky izlom*, Moscow: Veche, 2018, p. 58.

7 'Istoriya sozdaniya Rossiiskoi armii', *Nezavisimoe voennoe obozrenie* (hereafter *NVO*), 6 September 2019, https://nvo.ng.ru/nvo/2019-09-06/1_1060_army.html (accessed 24 February 2025).

8 'Osnovy voennoi doktriny', *VM*, Special Edition, no. 5, May 1992. pp. 3–9.

9 B. Yeltsin, *Midnight Diaries*, trans. C. Fitzpatrick, New York: Public Affairs, 2000, p. 59.

10 An English-language text of the doctrine can be found on the website of the Federation of American Scientists at https://nuke.fas.org/guide/russia/doctrine/russia-mil-doc.html (accessed 24 February 2025). C. Dick, 'The Military Doctrine of the Russian Federation', *Journal of Slavic Military Studies*, 7, no. 3, 1994, pp. 481–506.

11 'Strategiya dlya Rossii' [19 August 1992], in S. Karaganov (ed.), *Strategiya dlya Rossii: 10 let SVOP*, Moscow: Vagrius, 2000, pp. 8–23.

12 'Kontseptsiya vneshnei politiki Rossiiskoi Federatsii', *Diplomaticheskii vestnik*, January 1993, pp. 3–5.

13 'Doktrina voennaya', *Russian Military Encyclopaedia*, vol. 3, Moscow: Voenizdat, 1995, p. 102.

14 'Voina', *Russian Military Encyclopaedia*, vol. 2, Moscow: Voenizdat, 1994, pp. 233–5; 'Doktrina voennaya', pp. 102–6.

15 M. Gareev, 'On Military Doctrine and Military Reform in Russia', *Journal of Slavic Military Studies*, 5, no. 4, 1992, pp. 539–51. Proposals to continue to work at the wider CIS level faced sustained objections from the newly independent states. For Russian peacekeeping, see D.

Notes

Lynch, *Russian Peacekeeping Strategies in the CIS: The Cases of Moldova, Georgia and Tajikistan*, Basingstoke: Palgrave Macmillan, 2000.

16 A. Goltz, *Armiya Rossii: 11 poteryannykh let*, Moscow: Zakharov, 2004, pp. 5–6.

17 V. Shlykov, 'The Crisis in the Russian Economy', 30 June 1997, pp. 3, 8. Paper in author's collection.

18 Yeltsin, *Midnight Diaries*, p. 59.

19 J. Cooper, *The Soviet Defence Industry: Conversion and Reform*, London: Pinter Publishers, 1991; J. Cooper, 'From USSR to Russia: The Fate of the Military Economy', in P. Hare and G. Turley (eds), *Handbook of Economics and the Political Economy of Transition*, Abingdon: Routledge, 2013, pp. 98–107.

20 V. Shlykov, 'Economic Readjustment Within the Russian Defense-Industrial Complex', *Security Dialogue*, 26, no. 19, 1995, p. 23.

21 Shlykov, 'The Crisis', p. 15.

22 Discussion between Vitaly Shlykov and Sergei Kurginyan in S. Kurginyan, N. Svanidze and L. Mlechin, *Sud vremeni. Vypusk No. 35–46*, 29 November 2013, www.litlife.club/books/182547; Shlykov, 'Economic Readjustment', p. 28.

23 Shlykov, 'Economic Readjustment', pp. 28–30.

24 Goltz, *Armiya Rossii*, pp. 6–9.

25 A. Babchenko, *One Soldier's War in Chechnya*, trans. N. Allen, London: Portobello Books, 2007, pp. 81–3; C. Dick, 'A Bear Without Claws: The Russian Army in the 1990s', *Journal of Slavic Military Studies*, 10, no. 1, 1997, p. 5.

26 Babchenko, *One Soldier's War*, p. 83.

27 'Evolyutsiya voennovo suitsida', *NVO*, 8 August 2003, https://nvo.ng.ru/forces/2003-08-08/3_suidcide.html (accessed 24 February 2025).

28 Dick, 'A Bear Without Claws', p. 6.

29 'Viktor Murakhovsky: "23 Fevralya prevratili v Den malchikov. Eto uzhas!"', *Business-gazeta*, 23 February 2021, www.business-gazeta.ru/article/500205 (accessed 24 February 2025).

30 Cited in Dick, 'A Bear Without Claws', p. 9.

31 'Advokaty namereny razvalit dela o korruptsii voennykh', *Kommersant*, 10 November 1994, www.kommersant.ru/doc/94685?query=%D0%B3%D1%80%D0%B0%D1%87%D0%B5%D0%B2 (accessed 24 February 2025).

32 '… i luchshe vydumat ne mog', *Kommersant*, www.kommersant.ru/doc/19347 (accessed 24 February 2025).

33 For discussion and citation, see S. Simonson, 'Russia's Northern Fleet in Heavy Seas', *Journal of Slavic Military Studies*, 9, no. 4, 1996, pp. 713–31.

34 V. Lobov, 'Karl Klauzevitz. Zhizn. Idei. Sovremennoe znachenie', in C. Clausewitz, *O voine*, Moscow: Logos, 1997, pp. 8–22.

35 Goltz, *Armiya Rossii*, pp. 164–5.

36 Yeltsin, *Midnight Diaries*, p. 59.

37 Ibid., pp. 53, 55; Troshev, *Chechensky izlom*, ch. 2.

38 Yeltsin, *Midnight Diaries*, p. 59.

39 Goltz, *Armiya Rossii*, p. 164.

40 Yeltsin, *Midnight Diaries*, p. 59.

41 The film described Russian conscripts as a 'gift to Dudaev from the Russian military commissariat and Grachev'. Directed by Alexander Nevzorov, *Chistilishche* was released in March 1998. Nevzorov had reported from the Yugoslav and Transnistria wars, and became a member of the Russian parliament in 1993. He initially supported the war in Chechnya. In April 2022 the Russian state named him as a 'foreign agent'. The film can be seen at www.youtube.com/watch?v=jVUjDv_M7Co (accessed 24 February 2025).

42 A. Gayday, 'Reform of the Russian Army', in M. Barabanov (ed.), *Russia's New Army*, Moscow: Centre for Analyses of Strategies and Technologies, 2011, p. 13; A. Kulikov, 'The First Battle of Grozny', in R. Glenn (ed.), *Capital Preservation: Preparing for Urban Operations in the Twenty First Century*, Santa Monica, CA: RAND, 2000, pp. 13–58; General Troshev also published his views of the beginning of the campaign, with observations about commanders, including Kulikov. Troshev, *Chechensky izlom*, chs 3 and 4.

43 P. Baev, *The Russian Army in a Time of Troubles*, London: SAGE Publications, 1996, pp. 143–9; O. Oliker, *Russia's Chechen Wars, 1994–2000: Lessons from Urban Combat*, Santa Monica, CA: RAND, 2001.

44 Yeltsin, *Midnight Diaries*, pp. 61–5.

45 Ibid., pp. 66–7. Lebed became governor of Krasnoyarsk krai and died in a helicopter crash in 2002.

46 C. Bluth, 'Russia's Military Forces: Ambitions, Capabilities and Constraints', in R. Allison and C. Bluth (eds), *Security Dilemmas in Russia and Eurasia*, London: RIIA, 1998, p. 80.

47 Yeltsin, *Midnight Diaries*, pp. 63, 35–6.

48 N. Gevorkyan, A. Kolesnikov and N. Timakova, *Ot Pervovo litsa. Razgovory s Vladimirom Putinym*, Moscow: Vagrius, 2000, pp. 134–5, 155.

49 Yeltsin, *Midnight Diaries*, pp. 338–40; Gevorkyan, Kolesnikov and Timakova, *Ot pervovo litsa*, pp. 135–6, 153.

50 'Poslanie Federalnomy Sobraniyu Rossiiskoi Federatsii', WPA, 10 May 2006, http://kremlin.ru/events/president/transcripts/23577 (accessed 24 February 2025).

51 I. Traynor, 'No Way Back', *The Guardian*, 11 March 2000, www.theguardian.com/world/2000/mar/11/chechnya.iantraynor (accessed 24 February 2025).

52 A. Arbatov, *The Transformation of Russian Military Doctrine: Lessons Learned from Kosovo and Chechnya*, Marshall Centre, July 2000, https://www.marshallcenter.org/en/publications/marshall-center-papers/transformation-russian-military-doctrine-lessons-learned-kosovo-and-chechnya/transformation-russian-military#:~:text=Arbatov's%20paper%20provides%20an%20authoritative,between%20Russia%20and%20the%20West (accessed 24 February 2025).

53 A. Skvortsov, 'Gorizonty voennoi nauki', *VM*, no. 3, 1999.

54 S. Karaganov (ed.), *Strategiya dlya Rossii: 10 Let SVOP*, Moscow: Vagrius, 2002.

55 S. Bogdanov, 'Uroki buri v pustine', *KZ*, 17 May 1991; 'Tendentsii razvitiya voennovo iskusstva', *NVO*, 4 October 2019, https://nvo.ng.ru/realty/2019-10-04/1_1064_tendenzii.html (accessed 24 February 2025).

56 V. Pirumov, 'Methodological Aspects in the Research of Russia's National Security Problems Under Contemporary Conditions', *Journal of Slavic Military Studies*, 7, no. 3, 1994. p. 371.

57 M. Gareev, *If War Comes Tomorrow? The Contours of Future Armed Conflict*, trans. Y. Fomenko, ed. J. Kipp, London: Routledge, 1998, pp. 25–7, 38, 76, 94, 108, 179.

58 V. Lobov, 'The Significance of Svechin's Military-Theoretical Legacy Today', in A. Svechin, *Strategy*, ed. K. Lee, Minneapolis, MN: East View Information Services, 1992, p. 15; A. Savinkin, 'Klassik, zvuchshchii po sovremennomu', *NVO*, no. 9, 12 March 1999.

59 A. Kokoshin, 'Edinaya voennaya doktrina', *NVO*, no. 42, 14 November 1997; M. Gareev, 'Uroki A. A. Svechina dlya nashykh dnei', *VM*, no. 4, 1998.

60 Gareev frequently returned to these themes. A. Kvashnin and M. Gareev, 'Pervoi srazhalas mysl', *KZ*, 4 May 2000.

61 Gareev, *If War Comes Tomorrow?*; M. Gareev, 'Sem urokov Velikoi Otechestvennoi', *NVO*, no. 15, 28 April 2000; S. Bogdanov, 'Osobennosti

nachalnovo perioda voin proshlovo i budushchevo', *VM*, no. 5, 2003, pp. 17–20.

62 V. Gulin, 'O novoi kontseptsii voini', *VM*, no. 7, 1997; A. Demidyuk and M. Khamzatov, '"Molnienosnaya voina" novovo pokoloeniya: vozmozhnii stsenarii', *VM*, no. 10, October 2004.

63 V. Slipchenko, *Voina budushchevo*, Moscow: MONF, 1999; V. Slipchenko, *Voina novovo pokoleniia: distansionnye i bezkontaktnye*, Moscow: OLMA-Press, 2004; V. Slipchenko, 'For What Kind of War Must Russia be Prepared?', in *Future War*, trans. J. Kipp, Fort Leavenworth, KS: FMSO, 2007, pp. 9–28.

64 V. Kirillov, 'Netraditsionnie voini: est li u nykh budushchee?', *VM*, no. 6, 1998; O. Bulatov, G. Moiseev and S. Ivanov, 'Blizhni boi ili distantsionnyi ognevoi razgrom?', *VM*, no. 5, 2000.

65 M. Gareev, M. 'Ugrozy i voiny XXI veka', *KZ*, 14 February 2003, http://old.redstar.ru/2003/02/14_02/1_01.html (accessed 24 February 2025).

66 R. Connolly, *The Russian Economy: A Very Short Introduction*, Oxford: Oxford University Press, 2020, pp. 57–60, 62–8.

67 V. Putin, 'Russia at the Turn of the Millenium', 31 December 1999, reprinted in V. Putin, *First Person: An Astonishingly Frank Self Portrait by Russia's President*, trans. Catherine Fitzpatrick, London: Hutchinson, 2000, pp. 209–19; 'Poslanie Federalnomu Sobraniyu Rossiiskoi Federatsii', WPA, 3 April 2001, http://kremlin.ru/events/president/transcripts/21216 (accessed 24 February 2025); 'Poslanie Federalnomu Sobraniyu Rossiiskoi Federatsii', WPA, 18 April 2002, http://kremlin.ru/events/president/transcripts/21567 (accessed 24 February 2025).

68 Ukaz Prezidenta no. 24, *O Kontseptsii natsionalnoi bezpoasnosti Rossiiskoi Federatsii*, 10 April 2000, website of the Presidential Library, www.prlib.ru/en/node/352298 (accessed 24 February 2025).

69 *Voennaya doktrina Rossiskoi Federatsii*, 21 April 2000. Author's collection. An abridged, English-language version can be found in Arbatov, *Transformation of Russian Military Doctrine*.

70 'Poslanie', 18 April 2002; 'Poslanie Federalnomu Sobraniyu Rossiiskoi Federatsii', WPA, 16 May 2003, http://kremlin.ru/events/president/transcripts/21998 (accessed 24 February 2025).

71 S. Ivanov, 'Russia's Geopolitical Priorities and Armed Forces', *Russia in Global Affairs*, no. 1, January-February 2004, https://eng.globalaffairs.ru/articles/russias-geopolitical-priorities-and-armed-forces/ (accessed 24 February 2025). Emphasis added.

72 'Poslanie', 18 April 2002.

73 Ivanov, 'Russia's Geopolitical Priorities'. Emphasis added.

74 'Naznachenie i otstavki', *KZ*, 20 July 2004, http://old.redstar. ru/2004/07/20_07/1_02.html (accessed 24 February 2025); 'Rossiya pokazala svoi kharakter', *Vesti DOSAAF*, 30 March 2019, http:// vestidosaaf.ru/2019/03/30/10984/ (accessed 24 February 2025).

75 Y. Baluyevsky, *Military Security of the Russian Federation in the 21st Century*, Moscow: Centre for Military Strategic Studies, 2004.

76 'Poslanie Federalnomu Sobraniyu Rossiiskoi Federatsii', WPA, 10 May 2006, http://kremlin.ru/events/president/transcripts/23577 (accessed 24 February 2025).

77 Correspondence with Julian Cooper.

78 Gayday, 'Reform of the Russian Army', p. 17.

79 'V Ekaterinburge polkovnik zastrelilsya na ucheniyakh na glazakh u komandovaniya, ne vyderzhav kritiki', *Newsru*, 22 April 2004, www. newsru.com/arch/russia/22apr2004/colonel.html (accessed 24 February 2025); 'Russia: Can Sergei Ivanov End Hazing?', RFE/RL, 14 February 2006, www.rferl.org/a/1065769.html (accessed 24 February 2025).

80 V. Orlyansky, 'Operativnaya maskirovka ili obman protivnika', *VM*, no. 7, 2003; V. Orlyansky, 'Voennaya khitrost termin ne dlya professionalov', *VM*, no. 7, 2005.

81 A. Malyshev, 'Voennaya strategiya Rossiiskoi Federatsii v nachale XXI Veka', *VM*, no. 11, 2007, pp. 18–22.

82 M. Gareev, 'Struktura i osnovnoe soderzhanie novoi voennoi doktriny Rossii', *VM*, no. 3, 2007, p. 9.

6 A twenty-first-century blitzkrieg

1 'Putin's Speech: Back to Cold War?', BBC, 10 February 2007, http:// news.bbc.co.uk/2/hi/europe/6350847.stm (accessed 24 February 2025).

2 'Vystuplenie i diskussiya na Myunkhenskoi konferenstii po voprosam politiki bezopasnosti', WPA, 10 February 2007, http://kremlin.ru/ events/president/transcripts/24034 (accessed 24 February 2025).

3 A. Monaghan, *Power in Modern Russia: Strategy and Mobilisation*, Manchester: Manchester University Press, 2017.

4 A. Kokoshin, *O strategicheskom planirovanii v politike*, Moscow: URSS, 2007, pp. 8–10.

Notes

5 '"Rossiya, vperyod!" Statya Dmitriya Medvedeva', WPA, 10 September 2009, http://kremlin.ru/events/president/news/5413 (accessed 24 February 2025).

6 'O novoi voennoi doctrine', *Zashchita bezopasnosti*, no. 4, December 2009, p. 4.

7 A *taburetka* is the most basic form of stool or bench, often humorously or critically used to indicate a lack of sophistication in an individual. V. Bolshakov, *Serdyukov i zhenskii batalyon*, Moscow: Algorithm, 2013, p. 258.

8 'Serdyukov Cleans Up the Arbat', *Moscow Defense Brief*, no. 2, 12, 2008, https://web.archive.org/web/20080818210933/http://mdb.cast.ru/mdb/1-2008/item2/article1/ (accessed 24 February 2025).

9 Cited in ibid.

10 'Generalski afront', *NVO*, 28 March 2008, https://nvo.ng.ru/forces/2008-03-28/1_afront.html (accessed 24 February 2025).

11 V. Shlykov, 'Taini blitzkriga Serdyukova', *Rossiya v globalnoi politike*, no. 6, November/December 2009, https://globalaffairs.ru/articles/tajny-bliczkriga-serdyukova/ (accessed 24 February 2025); A. Gayday, 'Reform of the Russian Army', in M. Barabanov (ed.), *Russia's New Army*, Moscow: Centre for Analyses of Strategies and Technologies, 2011, p. 9.

12 V. Shlykov, 'Voina s neizvestnoi tselyu', *Rossiya v globalnoi politike*, no. 5, September/October 2008, https://globalaffairs.ru/articles/vojna-s-neizvestnoj-czelyu/ (accessed 24 February 2025).

13 'Kondoleeza Rice mne govorila: on krasnuyu chertu ne pereidet', *Kommersant*, 8 August 2018, www.kommersant.ru/doc/3707566 (accessed 24 February 2025); Gayday, 'Reform of the Russian Army', p. 20.

14 'Kondoleeza Rice'; documentary film 'Poteryanny den', 8 August 2012, www.youtube.com/watch?v=yDBy1MrcEcA (accessed 24 February 2025).

15 'Poteryanny den'.

16 Cited in Shlykov, 'Voina s neizvestnoi tselyu'; P. Litovkin, 'Tbilisskii blitzkrieg. Generaly podvodyat pervye itogo', *Nezavisimaya gazeta*, 11 August 2008, http://old.memo.ru/hr/hotpoints/caucas1/msg/2008/08/m149122.htm (accessed 24 February 2025).

17 'Ravnais! SMI... Otstavit!', *Moskovsky Komsomolets*, 10 September 2008, www.mk.ru/editions/daily/article/2008/09/10/23881-ravnyays-smi-otstavit.html (accessed 24 February 2025).

Notes

18 Ibid.; A. Lavrov, 'Poteri rossiiskoi aviatsii v Pyatidnevnoi voine s Gruziei v avguste 2008 goda', in M. Barabanov, A. Lavrov and B. Tsuleiko, *Tanki Avgusta. Sbornik statei*, Moscow: Tsentr analyza strategii i tekhnologii, 2009, pp. 109–18.

19 'Kondoleeza Rice'.

20 Cited in Shlykov, 'Voina s neizvestnoi tselyu'.

21 'Russian Soldiers in South Ossetia Living in "Horrendous" Conditions', RFE/RL, 23 December 2008, www.rferl.org/a/Russian_Soldiers_in_South_Ossetia_Living_In_Horrendous_Conditions/1362912.html (accessed 24 February 2025).

22 'Ravnais!'

23 N. Makarov, 'Tezisy vystupleniya nachalnika Generalnovo Shtaba Vooruzhonnykh Sil Rossiiskoi Federatsii – pervovo zamestitelya Ministra oborony Rossiiskoi Federatsii generala armii N. E. Makarov', *VAVN*, no. 1, 2009, pp. 19, 20–2; 'Genshtab informiruet zagranitsu', *NVO*, no. 46, 26 December 2008.

24 'Dmitry Medvedev: konflikt pokazal nashi vozmozhnosti i slabye mesta', TASS, 28 August 2023, https://tass.ru/interviews/18604069 (accessed 24 February 2025).

25 Shlykov, 'Taini blitzkriga'; 'Minoborony vybralo voennuyu ugrozu', *Kommersant*, 4 August 2008; A. Khramchikin, 'Minoborony napisalo ocherednuyu kontseptsiyu', *NVO*, no. 27, 8 August 2008.

26 Makarov, 'Tezisy vystupleniya nachalnika', pp. 22–3; Shlykov, 'Taini blitzkriga'.

27 Bolshakov, *Serdyukov i zhenskii batalyon*, pp. 234, 282–3.

28 Shlykov, 'Taini blitzkriga'.

29 A. Karnaukhov and V. Tsuleiko, 'Russian Military Doctrine and the State of its Armed Forces: Theory and Reality', in M. Barabanov (ed.), *Russia's New Army*, Moscow: Centre for Analyses of Strategies and Technologies, 2011, pp. 104, 114–15; 'Pribrezhnaya neletayushchaya staraya sverkhderzhava', *Gazeta*, 1 August 2008, www.gazeta.ru/politics/2008/08/01_a_2798901.shtml?updated (accessed 24 February 2025).

30 Gayday, 'Reform of the Russian Army', pp. 22–7.

31 'Russia's Medvedev Sacks Navy Officers for Base Fire', Reuters, 4 August 2010, www.reuters.com/article/idUKLDE6731EI/ (accessed 24 February 2025).

32 'Masshtab korruptsii v rossiiskoi armii potryasaet dazhe glavnovo prokurora', *Newsru*, 11 January 2011, www.newsru.com/russia/11jan2011/armycorruption.html; 'Oruzhie dayot "otkaty"', *Rossiiskaya Gazeta*,

24 May 2011, https://rg.ru/2011/05/24/fridinskij.html; 'Former Russian Defence Ministry Official Charged with Fraud', Reuters, 23 November 2012, www.reuters.com/article/us-russia-embezzlement-idUSBRE8AM0MY20121123/ (all accessed 24 February 2025).

33 'Gerasimov, Valeriy Vasilievich', undated, website of the Russian Ministry of Defence, https://structure.mil.ru/management/deputy/more.htm?id=11113936@SD_Employee (accessed 24 February 2025).

34 'Rasshirennoe zasedanie kollegii Ministerstva oborony', WPA, 27 February 2013, http://kremlin.ru/events/president/news/17588 (accessed 24 February 2025).

35 Ibid.

36 For a concise overview, see R. Connolly, *The Russian Economy: A Very Short Introduction*, Oxford: Oxford University Press, 2020.

37 'Zasedanie Mezhdunarodnovo diskussionnovo kluba "Valdai"', WPA, 24 October 2014, http://kremlin.ru/events/president/news/46860 (accessed 24 February 2025).

38 V. Pelevin, *S.N.U.F.F. Utopia*, Moscow: Eksmo, 2012.

39 A. Prokhanov et al., *Kholodnaya voina 2.0. Strategiya russkoi pobedy*, Moscow: Knizhnyi mir, 2015; M. Delyagin, S. Glazev and A. Fursov, *Strategiya 'bolshovo ryvka'*, Moscow: Algoritm, 2013; V. Karyakin, *Geopolitika tretei volny: transformatsiya mira v epokhu Postmoderna*, Moscow: Granitsa, 2013.

40 V. Gerasimov, 'V period do 2030 goda uroven potentsialnoi voennoi opasnosti znachitelno povysitsya – Valerii Gerasimov', *VPK*, 18 February 2012, https://vpk.name/news/84463_v_period_do_2030_goda_uroven_potencialnoi_voennoi_opasnosti_znachitelno_povysit-sya_valerii_gerasimov.html (accessed 24 February 2025); V. Gerasimov, 'Tsennost nauki v predvidenii', *VPK*, 26 February 2013.

41 Gerasimov, 'Tsennost nauki'; S. Shoigu, 'Vystuplenie ministra oborony Rossiiskoi Federatsii generala S. K. Shoigu', *VAVN*, no. 1, 2013, p. 7.

42 M. Gareev, 'Voina mirov po novym pravilam', *VPK*, 26 March 2019; V. Gerasimov, 'My poluchili obektivnuyu kartinu sostoyaniya armii i flota', *VPK*, 15 December 2014; V. Gerasimov, 'Sila Velikoi Pobedy', *VPK*, 11 May 2015.

43 See Admiral Nikolai Yevmenov's vivid criticism of conditions in the navy in 2014, 'Anti-alkogolniy instruktazh v VMF Rossii', YouTube, 12 December 2014, www.youtube.com/watch?v=JsMTz-D9Yww (accessed 24 February 2025). Yevmenov went on to command the Russian navy from 2019 to 2024; 'Rasshirennoe zasedanie', 27 February 2013; 'Pochti 120 samoubiistv sovershili rossiiskie ofitsery i soldaty v etom gody',

Interfax, 13 October 2011, www.interfax.ru/russia/211952 (accessed 24 February 2025).

44 R. Connolly, 'Russia as a Maritime Power: Economic Interests and Capabilities', in A. Monaghan and R. Connolly (eds), *The Sea in Russian Strategy*, Manchester: Manchester University Press, 2023, pp. 129–38.

45 'Soveshchanie po voprosam razvitiya Vooruzennykh Sil', WPA, 11 November 2015, http://kremlin.ru/events/president/transcripts/deliberations/50668; 'Soveshchanie po voprosam razvitiya oboronnoi promyshlennosti', WPA, 13 May 2016, http://kremlin.ru/events/president/news/51911; 'Soveshchanie po voprosam mobilizatsionnoi gotovnosti OPK', WPA, 17 November 2016, http://kremlin.ru/events/president/news/53263 (all accessed 24 February 2025).

46 'Tankovy manyovr', *Versia*, 18 June 2018, https://versia.ru/rossijskaya-armiya-vozvrashhaet-v-stroj-6-tysyach-ustarevshix-boevyx-mashin (accessed 24 February 2025).

47 'Rasshirennoe zasedanie', 27 February 2013.

48 V. Gerasimov, 'Generalny shtab i oborona strany', *VPK*, 3 February 2014; Gerasimov, 'Sila Velikoi Pobedy'.

49 'Mgnovennaya gotovnost', *Lenta.ru*, 29 December 2014, http://lenta.ru/articles/2014/11/29/ntsuo (accessed 24 February 2025).

50 'Shtab oborony v regionakh predpolagaetsa sozdavat v voennoe vremya', RIA.ru, 1 December 2016; 'Putin utverdil vvedenie otvetstvennosti ministrov i gubernatorov za mobilizatsiyu grazhdan', *Nezavisimaya Gazeta*, 22 February 2017.

51 A. Lavrov, 'Russian Again: The Military Operation for Crimea', in R. Pukhov and C. Howard (eds), *Brothers Armed: Military Aspects of the Crisis in Ukraine*, Minneapolis, MN: East View Press, 2014, pp. 157–86.

52 A. Dvornikov, 'Shtaby dlya novykh voin', *VPK*, 23 July 2018; 'Rasshirennoe zasedanie kollegii Ministerstva oborony', WPA, 11 December 2015, http://kremlin.ru/events/president/news/50913 (accessed 24 February 2025); V. Gerasimov, 'Mir na granyakh voiny', *VPK*, 13 March 2017.

53 Gerasimov, 'Mir na granyakh'; A. Dvornikov, 'Aktualniye napravleniya sovershenstvovaniya boevoi podgotovki voisk s uchetom opyta, poluchennovo v Syrii', *VM*, no. 7, 2021, pp. 100–10; V. Gerasimov, 'Sovremennie voiny i aktualnye voprosy oborony strany', *VAVN*, no. 1, March 2017, pp. 9–13.

54 'General strategicheskovo naznacheniya: u Valeriya Gerasimova – yubilei', *Moskovsky komsomolets*, 9 July 2020, www.mk.ru/politics/2020/09/07/general-strategicheskogo-naznacheniya-u-valeriya-gerasimova-yubiley.html (accessed 24 February 2025).

55 'Kondoleeza Rice'; Y. Baluyevsky, 'Voina ne konchaetsya, ona – zamiraet', *NVO*, 26 May 2017, https://nvo.ng.ru/realty/2017-05-26/1_949_rosgvardia.html (accessed 24 February 2025); Gerasimov, 'Sovremennie voiny'. This remains the case: 'Dmitry Medvedev: Konflikt pokazal nash vozmozhnosti i slabie mesta', TASS, 28 August 2023, https://tass.ru/interviews/18604069 (accessed 24 February 2025).

56 Gerasimov, 'Sovremennie voiny'.

57 Gerasimov, 'Mir na granyakh'; Section 8, d. *Military Doctrine of the Russian Federation*, no. 2976, approved on 25 December 2014, website of the Russian National Security Council, http://scrf.gov.ru/security/military/document129/ (accessed 24 February 2025).

58 V. Gerasimov, 'Po opytu Syrii', *VPK*, 7 March 2016.

59 Gerasimov, 'Tsennost nauki'. See also P. Krugman, 'The American Way of Economic War', *Foreign Affairs*, January/February 2024, www.foreignaffairs.com/reviews/american-way-economic-war-paul-krugman (accessed 24 February 2025).

60 Connolly, *The Russian Economy*, pp. 84–8; C. Gaddy and B. Ickes, *Russia's Virtual Economy*, Washington, DC: Brookings Institution Press, 1999.

61 Morskaya doktrina Rossiiskoi Federatsii, website of the Russian Security Council, undated, http://scrf.gov.ru/security/military/document34/; Strategiya natsionalnoi bezopasnosti Rossiiskoi Federatsii, website of the Russian Security Council, undated, http://scrf.gov.ru/security/docs/document133/ (all accessed 24 February 2025).

62 Connolly, 'Russia as a Maritime Power', pp. 138–43.

63 V. Gerasimov, 'Zasedaniye Kollegii Ministerstva Oborony RF po voprosu 'O khode vypolneniya ukazov Prezidenta Rossiiskoi Federatsii ot 7 maya 2012 g, i razvitii Vooruzhonnykh Sil Rossiiskoi Federatsii', website of the Russian Ministry of Defence, 7 November 2017, https://function.mil.ru/news_page/country/more.htm?id=12149743@egNews (accessed 24 February 2025).

64 Gerasimov, 'Po opytu Syrii'.

65 V. Gerasimov, 'Genshtab planiruyet udary', *VPK*, 11 March 2019.

66 'Teoriya vooruzhennovo protivoborstva nuzhdaetsa v modernizatsii', *KZ*, 19 June 2019, http://redstar.ru/teoriya-vooruzhyonnogoprotivo-borstva-nuzhdaetsya-v-modernizatsii/ (accessed 24 February 2025); contributions in *Vestnik akademii voennykh nauk*, 2, 2019.

67 Kh. Saifetdinov, 'Aleksander Andreevich Svechin – vydayushchiisya myslitel nachala XX veka', *VM*, no. 8, August 2018, pp. 101–9; Gerasimov, 'Sovremenniye voini'.

68 'Strategiya izmora', Encyclopedia, website of the Russian Ministry of Defence, undated, https://encyclopedia.mil.ru/encyclopedia/diction-ary/details.htm?id=10394@morfDictionary (accessed 24 February 2025).

69 V. Gerasimov, 'Razvitie voennoi strategii v sovremennykh usloviyakh. Zadachi voennoi nauki', *VAVN*, no. 2, 2019, pp. 6–11.

70 Gerasimov, 'Zasedaniye'; Dvornikov, 'Shtaby dlya'; M. Gareev, 'Krovnoe delo komandira – chast II', *VPK*, 9 October 2017, https://vpk-news.ru/articles/39283 (accessed 24 February 2025).

71 Gerasimov, 'Zasedaniye'; 'Poslanie Prezidenta Federalnomu Sobraniyu', WPA, 1 March 2018, http://kremlin.ru/events/president/transcripts/messages/56957 (accessed 24 February 2025).

72 'Viktor Murakhovsky: 23 Fevralya'.

73 'Generalskaya smena: shto zhdyot novovo VKC', *Gazeta*, 22 September 2017, www.gazeta.ru/army/2017/09/22/10902470.shtml?updated (accessed 24 February 2025).

74 'Shoigu otstranil ot ispolneniya obyazannostei komanduyushchevo Balt-flotom', *RIA Novosti*, 29 June 2016, https://ria.ru/20160629/1454325486.html (accessed 24 February 2025).

75 'Shoigy raskritikoval moskovskii voenkomat vo vremya proverki', *Izvestia*, 8 June 2021, https://iz.ru/1175765/2021-06-08/shoigu-otchital-sotrudnikov-voenkomata-v-moskve'; 'Borotsa s uklonistami pomozhet tsifrovizatsiya voenkomatov', *Nezavisimaya Gazeta*, 22 August 2021, www.ng.ru/armies/2021-08-22/2_8231_internet.html (all accessed 24 February 2025).

76 'Viktor Murakhovsky: 23 Fevralya'; 'Generalskaya smena: shto zhdet novovo VKC'.

77 A. Kokoshin, *Voprosy prikladnoi teorii voiny*, Moscow: HSE, 2018, pp. 219–20.

78 'Viktor Murakhovsky: 23 Fevralya'.

79 Gareev, 'Krovnoe delo komandira – chast II'. Emphasis added.

80 V. Gerasimov, 'Generalny shtab i oborona strany', *VPK*, 3 February 2014; Gerasimov, 'Po opytu Syrii'.

Notes

81 V. Gerasimov, 'Uvazhaemaya sila', *VPK*, 14 November 2017.

82 'Materialy k zasedaniyam Sekretariata TsK KPSS besposhchadno razoblachayut sovetskuyu deistvitelnost', *Nezavisimaya gazeta*, 27 August 2023, www.ng.ru/editorial/2023-08-27/2_8810_editorial.html (accessed 24 February 2025).

83 'Tyazholoe rasstavanie s mifom', *Radio Svoboda*, 20 July 2015, www. svoboda.org/a/27138620.html; 'Spravko-doklad glavnovo voennovo prokurora N. Afanasieva "O 28 panfilovtsakh"', website of the State Archive, undated, https://statearchive.ru/607; 'Medinsky prizval rukovodstvo Gosarkhiva ne davit sobstvennykh otsenok arkhivnym dokumentam', TASS, 30 July 2015, https://tass.ru/kultura/2154088 (all accessed 24 February 2025).

84 Garbuzov's articles are essential reading. 'Direktor Instituta SSHA i Kanady Valerii Garbuzov ob utrachennykh illyuziyakh ukhodyashchei epokhi', *Nezavisimaya gazeta*, 29 August 2023, www.ng.ru/ideas/2023-08-29/7_8812_illusions.html; 'Valerii Garbuzov, Prodolzhenie. Vnezapnyi shtorm na pustom meste', *Nezavisimaya gazeta*, 5 September 2023, www.ng.ru/ideas/2023-09-05/100_2309051230.html; 'V RAN nashli zamenu Garbuzovu na postu direktora Instituta SSHA i Kanady', *Vedomosti*, 4 September 2023, www.vedomosti.ru/politics/articles/2023/09/04/993248-v-ran-nashli-zamenu-garbuzovu (all accessed 24 February 2025).

85 A. Golubev and P. Kovalenko, 'Obektivnaya otsenka isstoricheskikh sobytii i eyo znachenie v vospitanii voennosluzhashchikh', *VM*, no. 9, September 2019, pp. 151–6.

86 M. Khodaryonok, 'Azbuka strategii', *VPK*, 9 June 2015; M. Khodaryonok, 'Voenno-istorichestkoe bespamyatstvo', *VPK*, 2 February 2015. These articles are essential reading on Russian war history and the development of war strategy.

87 *Osvobozhdenie* is a five-part epic film, released between 1970 and 1971, tracing the Great Fatherland War from Kursk to Berlin, www. youtube.com/watch?v=GZlzMhfx2hQ (accessed 24 February 2025). Released in 2010, *Brestskaya krepost* depicts the opening of Operation Barbarossa and the defence of Brest Fortress, www.youtube.com/watch?v=lw3mDJoqdpo (accessed 24 February 2025).

88 M. Gareev, 'Iyun 41-go: stereotipy i faktory', *VPK*, 20 July 2015, https://vpk-news.ru/articles/26195; M. Gareev, 'Krovnoe delo komandira – chast I', *VPK*, 3 October 2017, https://vpk-news.ru/articles/39283; V. Dorokhov et al., 'Ofitser na tri s minusum', *VPK*, 11 March 2015,

https://vpk-news.ru/articles/24194 (all accessed 24 February 2025); I. Danilenko, V. Kopytko and S. Chvarkov, 'Peredovaya "fabrika" voennoi mysli Rossii: proshloe, hastoyashchee, budushchee', *VM*, no. 12, December 2017, pp. 30–44.

89 R. Connolly, *Russia's Response to Sanctions: How Western Economic Statecraft is Reshaping Political Economy in Russia*, Cambridge: Cambridge University Press, 2018.

90 I. Dezhina, 'Nauchnaya politka v Rossii v 2018–2022 gg: protivorechiyie signaly', *Sotsiologicheskii zhurnal*, 29, no. 2, 2023, pp. 132–49. The author is grateful to Julian Cooper for exchanges on this theme.

91 'Kollegi arestovannovo fizika Maslova napisali Otkrytoe pismo v Administratsiyu prezidenta', *Moskovsky komsomolets*, 4 August 2022, www.mk.ru/science/2022/08/04/kollegi-arestovannogo-fizika-maslova-napisali-otkrytoe-pismo-v-administraciyu-prezidenta.html (accessed 24 February 2025); P. Josephson, 'Russia's Century of Scientific Autarky', *Engelsberg Ideas*, 21 June 2024, https://engelsbergideas.com/essays/russias-century-of-scientific-autarky/ (accessed 24 February 2025).

92 'Tankovy manyovr'.

93 'Statya Sekretarya Soveta Bezopasnosti Rossiiskoi Federatsii v "Rossiiskoi gazete"', website of the Russian Security Council, 12 November 2019, http://www.scrf.gov.ru/news/allnews/2677/; 'Zasedanie diskussionnovo kluba "Valdai"', WPA, 22 October, 2020, http://kremlin.ru/events/president/news/64261 (all accessed 24 February 2025).

94 'Prognozy krovozhadnykh politologov', *Nezavisimaya gazeta*, 3 February 2022, https://nvo.ng.ru/realty/2022-02-03/3_1175_donbass.html (accessed 24 February 2025); M. Golovlev, *SVO: Klauzevitz i pustota*, Moscow: Knizhniy mir, 2023, ch. 1.

95 'Obrashchenie Prezidenta Rossiiskoi Federatsii', WPA, 24 February 2022, http://kremlin.ru/events/president/news/67843 (accessed 24 February 2025).

96 Golovlev, *SVO*, pp. 14–15, ch. 4.

97 Golovlev, *SVO*; R. Pukhov, 'Ot "spetsialnoi" k "voennoi": uroki dvukh let operatsii v Ukraine', *Rossiya v globanoi politike*, no. 2, 2024, https://globalaffairs.ru/articles/ot-speczialnoj-k-voennoj/ (accessed 24 February 2025). Pukhov suggests that if Kyiv had been more dynamic as the first phase culminated, Moscow might have been presented with a 'Warsaw 1920' situation.

98 'SVO i revolyutsiya voennovo dela', *Armeiski standart*, 31 January 2024, https://armystandard.ru/news/2024129114-TnO1s.html (accessed 24 February 2025).

99 V. Litvinenko, 'Sushnost kategorii "voina" i 'spetsalnaya voennaya operatsiya', *Armeisky sbornik*, no. 7, 31 July 2022, pp. 13–22; R. Pukhov, 'Novaya normalnost voiny. Direktor TsAST Ruslan Pukhov na Grushinskoi konferentsii', *BMPD Livejournal*, 11 April 2024, https://bmpd.livejournal.com/4815781.html (accessed 24 February 2025).

100 A. Kokoshin, Y. Baluyevsky, V. Esin and A. Shlyakhturov, *Voprosy eskalatsii i deeskalatsii krizisnikh situatsii vooruzhennykh konfliktov i voin*, Moscow: URSS, 2021. For the escalation ladder, see pp. 60–5.

Conclusion

1 'Poslanie Prezidenta Federalnomu Sobraniyu', WPA, 29 February 2024, http://kremlin.ru/events/president/news/73585 (accessed 24 February 2025).

2 V. Zolotarev, *Istoria voennoi strategii Rossii*, Moscow: Kuchkovo pole, 2000, pp. 6–7.

3 M. Strohn (ed.), *Winning Wars: The Enduring Nature and Changing Character of Victory From Antiquity to the 21st Century*, Oxford: Casemate, 2020; E. Luttwak, 'On the Meaning of Victory', *Washington Quarterly*, 5, no. 4, 1982, pp. 17–24.

4 A. Frolov, 'Vitok istoricheskoi spirali', *Rossiya v globalnoi politike*, no. 1, 2024, https://globalaffairs.ru/articles/vitok-istoricheskoj-spirali/; V. Kashin, 'Pervyi god bolshoi voiny', *Rossiya v globalnoi politike*, no. 3, 2023, https://globalaffairs.ru/articles/pervyj-god-bolshoj-vojny/ (all accessed 24 February 2025).

5 S. Shoigu, presentation at the Moscow Conference on International Security, 15 August 2022, https://eng.mil.ru/en/mcis/2022.htm (accessed 24 February 2025); 'Bolshaya voina: iz proshlovo v nastoyashchee', *Rossiya v Globalnoi Politike*, no. 6, November/December 2023. www.globalaffairs.ru/articles/bolshaya-vojna/ (accessed 24 February 2025).

6 'Parad Pobedy na Krasnoi ploshchadi', WPA, 9 May 2024, http://kremlin.ru/events/president/news/73995 (accessed 24 February 2025).

Notes

7 'Intervyu Takeru Karlsonu', WPA, 9 February 2024, http://kremlin.
   ru/events/president/news/73411/videos (accessed 24 February 2025);
   'Foreign Minister Sergey Lavrov's Address to the Readers of the
   Monograph History of Ukraine', website of the Russian Foreign
   Ministry, 17 April 2023, www.mid.ru/tv/?id=1863777&lang=en (accessed
   24 February 2025); S. Talbott (ed. and trans.), *Khrushchev Remembers*,
   London: André Deutsch, 1971, pp. 150, 155.

8 Talbott (ed.), *Khrushchev Remembers*, pp. 140, 507; A. Kokoshin, *Soviet
   Strategic Thought, 1917–91*, Cambridge, MA: MIT Press, 1998, p. 111.

9 J. Erickson, 'Shoot First', *The Scotsman*, 16 June 1989; J. Erickson,
   Soviet Military Power, London: RUSI, 1971.

10 Frolov, 'Vitok istoricheskoi spirali'.

11 Other familiar problems include corruption and embezzlement,
   in-fighting and fratricide. 'Moscow Court Arrests Deputy Defense
   Minister Over Bribery Case', TASS, 24 April 2024, https://tass.com/
   society/1779745; 'Krymskoe delo rossiiskovo ofitsera Sungurova: ot
   "Z-geroya" do SIZO', *Krym realii*, 8 February 2024, https://ru.krymr.
   com/a/krym-rossiyskiy-ofitser-aleksandr-sungurov-ugolovnoye-delo-
   z-geroy-sizo/32811085.html; 'Prigozhinskie zeki vzyali v plen pod-
   polkovnika – kombata rossiiskoi 72 brigady vpechatlyaet', *24 Kanal*, 5
   June 2023, https://24tv.ua/ru/prigozhinskie-zjeki-vzjali-plen-kombata-
   rossijskoj-72-brigady_n2327912 (all accessed 24 February 2025).

12 'Vmyat shturmom: zachem v sukhoputnykh voiskakh vossozdayut
   desantnye brigady', *Izvestiya*, 9 April 2024, https://iz.ru/1678690/
   aleksei-mikhailov-roman-kretcul-vladimir-matveev/vmiat-shturmom-
   zachem-v-sukhoputnykh-voiskakh-vossozdaiut-desantnye-brigady
   (accessed 24 February 2025).

13 See the Sudoplatov Project's Telegram site: https://t.me/s/sudopla-
   tov_official (accessed 24 February 2025); 'The Flight of the "Ghoul":
   Russian Military Startups of the SVO Period on the Example of
   the Ural FPV Drone', *VPK*, 27 February 2024, https://vpk.name/
   en/831012_the-flight-of-the-ghoul-russian-military-startups-of-the-
   svo-period-on-the-example-of-the-ural-fpv-drone.html (accessed 24
   February 2025).

14 'Poslanie Prezidenta Federalnomu Sobraniyu', WPA, 29 February
   2024, http://kremlin.ru/events/president/news/73585 (accessed 24
   February 2025).

15 'Shoigu rasskazal o poyavlenii v Rossii 'narodnoko VPK', *RIA Novosti*,
   20 February 2024, https://ria.ru/20240220/pomosch-1928585320.

html (accessed 24 February 2025); 'Putin zayavil shto "narodnyi VPK" rabotaet vovsyu', *RBK*, 25 April 2024, www.rbc.ru/rbcfreenews/662 a67dd9a794712dd1625c8 (accessed 24 February 2025).

16 'Vstrecha s Ministrom oborony Sergeem Shoigu', WPA, 25 December 2023, http://kremlin.ru/events/president/news/73126 (accessed 24 February 2025).

17 'Zasedanie diskussionnovo kluba "Vadai"', WPA, 5 October 2023, http://kremlin.ru/events/president/news/72444 (accessed 24 February 2025).

18 Available in English: *The Concept of the Foreign Policy of the Russian Federation*, Decree no. 229, 31 March 2023, website of the Russian Foreign Ministry, https://mid.ru/en/foreign_policy/fundamental_documents/1860586/ (accessed 24 February 2025).

19 'Poslanie Prezidenta Federalnomu Sobraniyu', WPA, 29 February 2024, http://kremlin.ru/events/president/news/73585; 'Vstrecha s Ministrom oborony Sergeem Shoigu', WPA, 25 December 2023, http://kremlin.ru/events/president/news/73126 (all accessed 24 February 2025).

20 'Nachalnik Generalnovo shtaba VS RF general armii Valerii Gerasimov provel brifing dlya voennykh attashe inostrannykh gosudarstv', website of the Russian Defence Ministry, 22 December 2022, https://function.mil.ru/news_page/country/more.htm?id=12449283@egNews (accessed 24 February 2025).

21 'V Rossii poyavitsa novaya Morskaya kollegia', *Flot*, 30 July 2024, https://flot.com/2024/%D0%92%D0%BC%D1%8425/ (accessed 24 February 2025).

22 'Murakhovsky rasskazal chem mozhet udivit novaya rossiiskaya voennaya doktrina', *Moskovsky komsomolets*, 3 April 2021, www.mk.ru/politics/2021/04/03/murakhovskiy-rasskazal-chem-mozhet-udivit-novaya-rossiyskaya-voennaya-doktrina.html (accessed 24 February 2025).

23 A. Lavrov and R. Pukhov (eds), *Voina sredi sten*, Moscow: CAST, 2023, pp. 144–82.

24 *Global Trends 2035: Paradox of Progress*, Washington, DC: NIC, January 2017, p. 56, www.dni.gov/files/documents/nic/GT-Full-Report. pdf (accessed 24 February 2025); *Global Strategic Trends: Out to 2055*, London: Ministry of Defence, 2024, p. 110, https://assets.publishing. service.gov.uk/media/673602412469c5b71dbc7b6f/Global_Strategic_Trends_Out_to_2055.pdf (accessed 24 February 2025).

Index

Index

Berlin
  battle for (1945) 92, 96
  Soviet blockade (1948–49) 98
black market 171
Black Sea Fleet 219, 269
blitzkrieg
  defined 46–8
  economic 3
  'twenty-first-century' 226,
    239–40, 271
  type assault 1, 110, 112, 114,
    140
  see also lightning wars
Blitzkrieg (German) 46, 90–1, 110,
  159–60
Blyukher, Vasily 75, 76, 81–2
Bolsheviks 49–58, 81
Brezhnev, Leonid 126–7, 134, 142,
  151–2
bribery 176
British Empire 109, 112
Budyonny, Semyon 81–2, 83,
  84–5, 88, 95
buffer territory 91, 256
Burdzhalov, Eduard 105–6

carrier strike forces 103, 141
casualties 77, 92, 186, 221
Central Committee 115, 126, 150,
  151
Centre for War Strategic Research
  189
chain of command 94–5, 108,
  231–2, 264–6
change, and continuity in war
  strategy 7, 18, 30, 144, 252–5,
  273
Chechen war (1994–2009) 34, 35,
  178–88, 258

China 75, 134
Churchill, Winston 98
civilian support 262–4
Clausewitz, C. von 6, 248
'coercion to peace' 34, 206
Cold War 98, 160
'colour revolutions' 199, 213–14
command and control
  chain of command 94–5, 108,
    231–2, 264–6
  'integral commander' 61–2
  problems with 92–5, 131, 207–8,
    232–3, 264–6
Communist Party 55, 73, 105,
  106–7, 164
conscription 167, 175, 200
conservatism 150–1
'contact' war 194–5
continuity
  and change in war strategy 7,
    18, 30, 144, 252–5, 273
  in the early Russian Federation
    166, 170–1, 189
  in the Soviet Union 54, 91,
    115–16
conventional war 30, 133–7, 144–7,
  244
corruption 176
Council for Foreign and Defence
  Policy 188
counter-insurgency 28, 33–4,
  187–8
counter-offensives 80, 147, 158–60
counter-terrorism 185–6
Crimea, annexation of 4–5,
  219–22
'Crimean Affair' 101–2
Cuban missile crisis 126
Czechoslovakia 134, 258

Index

Index

Index

Index

Index

Index

EU authorised representative for GPSR:
Easy Access System Europe, Mustamäe tee 50,
10621 Tallinn, Estonia
gpsr.requests@easproject.com